VINCENT PRICE
Unmasked

by *James Robert Parish and Steven Whitney*

DRAKE PUBLISHERS INC   *NEW YORK*

Published in 1974 by
Drake Publishers Inc.
381 Park Avenue South
New York, New York 10016

Library of Congress Cataloging in Publication Data
Parish, James Robert.
    Vincent Price unmasked.
    1. Price, Vincent, 1911-   I. Whitney, Steven,
joint author.   II. Title.
PN2287.P72P3   791'.092'4 (B)   74-6151
ISBN 0-87749-667-6

Printed in the United States of America

Editor: T. Allan Taylor
Research Associates: John Robert Cocchi, Michael R. Pitts, Florence Solomon

Contents

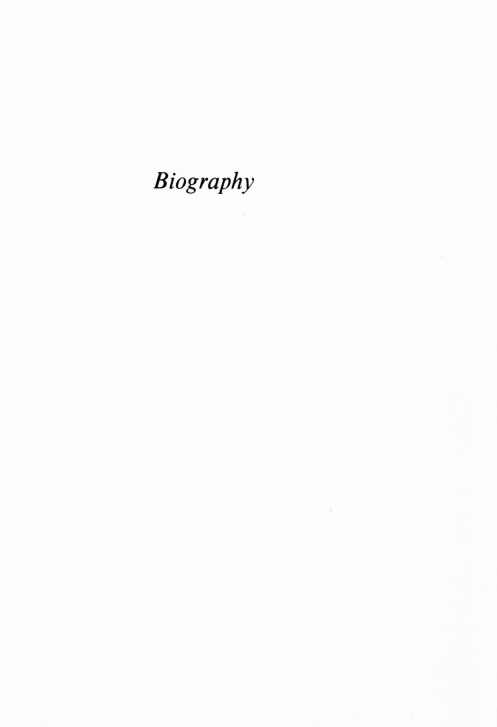

Biography

Chapter One

"He was born with a gift of laughter and a sense that
the world was mad."
                        Rafael Sabatini
                        Scaramouche

The name Vincent Price was famous in St. Louis long before the world recognized it as an icon of art appreciation and mastery of the horrific arts. In the middle of the nineteenth century, almost every American knew that Vincent Price was the owner and founder of the Price Baking Powder Company, a prosperous and growing Chicago business that was sold to Royal Gelatin Corporation in 1890.

At the start of the twentieth century, Vincent Price was noted in St. Louis as the president of the National Candy Company, an outfit famed for its jawbreakers and jellybeans. Indeed, during the 1904 Louisiana Purchase Exposition, the National Candy Company made a small fortune selling sweets to the flock of visitors.

For the record, the noted owner of the baking-powder company was the actor's grandfather, and the esteemed candy maker was the father of our subject. The man of today, Vincent Leonard Price, was born on May 27,* 1911, to Vincent Leonard Price and Marguerite Cobb (Wilcox) Price. There were already three other Price children: Harriet, age seventeen; Mortimer, age fourteen; and Lauralouise, age 10. On that day Vincent's father was presented with a commemorative plaque by his office associates honoring the newborn son as "the Candy Kid."

Price's "rivals" at the top of the horror-film circle, Christopher Lee and Peter Cushing, also have May 27 birthdays.

VINCENT PRICE UNMASKED

The Price family—in addition to their renown in the St. Louis area—claimed illustrious ancestors, being directly descended from Peregrine White, the first child born on the *Mayflower* as it approached Plymouth Rock. The Wilcox family was related to Pierre Desnoyers, a famous Detroit silversmith whose family were leaders in the political life of Michigan during their era.

When young Vincent was born, the family, though successful and affluent, could not be described as wealthy. They were, as Price himself indicates, "well-to-do." Price often quotes an old American axiom to describe his family's status: "They were not rich enough to cause envy but successful enough to deserve respect."

In many respects, the Price family was extremely normal. As Vincent's father became more and more successful, the family moved from one abode to another, each farther away from the center of town than the last. Finally, the Prices established their permanent home near the very outskirts of St. Louis. The family selected a lot across from Washington University and hired architects to build a home that met their exacting wishes and specifications. Within a year the house was completed, a stylish New England-style dwelling, complete with hanging ivy. Inside the house were many bedrooms, a grand staircase in the entranceway, a paneled dining room, a Chinese Modern sunroom, and assorted studies and "private" rooms. The furniture Marguerite Price chose or brought with her to this new house was antique American, with each of the few American periods well represented. Under almost every piece, she had glued a plain white card on which was written the name of the beneficiary who was to inherit it. One can imagine how much each of these possessions meant to her that she made so certain they would not fall into the wrong hands after her death.*

Marguerite Price was one of those women who saved almost everything that ever had any meaning to her. Everywhere throughout the new house could be observed odds and ends from various trips or periods in her life. Her son, Vincent, inherited this trait from her, and it would play an important part later in his life.

Vincent's father, who allegedly came to loathe his endeavors at the candy factory, dabbled in the stock market and with various investments. A member of the St. Louis County Club, the elder Price often played golf and indulged in other "men's" activities there. At one point in his financial explorations, he formed an investment group and attempted to convince the members to buy

Vincent inherited a pair of Biedermeier vases from this tagged lot. He has kept them throughout his life.

stock in a new soft drink, Coca-Cola. In a town where beer was almost sacred, this suggestion was speedily rejected.

Price the elder was a man with a subtle, yet undeniable wit. His most valued possession was an ornately decorated ceramic vase that bore the following legend:

I

FYO

UCAN

TKEE

PITD

OWN

THR

OWI

TUP

Aside from this one variable on Newton's theory of gravity, the elder Price showed little inclination toward the scientific.

The parents were important influences on young Vincent. With the extra time that was available to most upper-middle-class families of the period, they devoted long hours to each of their children, endeavoring to instill in them an appreciation for the finer things in life.

When Washington University initiated a building project for the School of Architecture, the officials selected a design distinctive only for its lack of any discernible beauty. Influenced by a pseudo-Roman Gothic style, the construction workers forged ahead each day under the watchful and disapproving eye of Marguerite Price. Daily she complained to the administration about the structure, and daily her protests went in vain. The School of Architecture was built as planned, and it remained an eyesore to her for the rest of her life.

If the one building displeased the Price family, there was another that delighted them. The school's administration center, which was directly opposite the entranceway to the Price dwelling, was the very best copy of the Tudor style in St. Louis. The family always referred to this edifice as "Windsor Castle."

Except for this family's rather normal interest in and appreciation of beauty, young Vincent did not receive any special indoctrination into the arts at an early age. Like most every other school-attending youth, he was gently coerced into appearing in the annual Christmas Nativity drama. His debut was as an angel when he was five years old. However, far from fulfilling any of the talent his later life would prove, he forgot all his lines.

He would often be taken to the movies by either his mother or by one of his sisters, but no more or less than any other neighborhood child. One of the first films he saw was a silent horror picture called *Der Golem*. He was terrified, but enjoyed every minute of it. In retrospect, the future king of horror said of this movie, "I wet my pants."

St. Louis was then a major stop for theatrical shows touring America, and whenever anyone of note would pass through the city, Vincent's parents would take him and his brother and two sisters to the presentation. He therefore had the opportunity to witness some of the great performers of the day—Sothern and Marlowe, Fritz Leiber, Robert Mantell, and Walter Hampden, to name just a few.

But theater and the cinema were mild diversions for the family. Of major importance was the fine cooking that Marguerite Price accomplished in the kitchen. Day after day, the Price family sampled the finest recipes from all over the world in their own dining room. Marguerite Price had traveled frequently with her husband before the children were born, and in each place she visited she made a point of obtaining a special recipe. To dine in the Price household was to sample an international cuisine very rare in the American Middle West of that period.

If the family indulged one of the arts more than any other, though, it was music. Many evenings the whole family would gather around the grand piano in the living room to join in song. Vincent's sister Harriet became an accomplished pianist. His brother Mortimer specialized in modern jazz, while his sister Lauralouise warbled in a slightly off-key soprano. Lauralouise's favorite tunes were "A Bowl of Rice," which she performed moderately well, and the "Kashmiri Song," which might have proven an embarrassment had she sung it outside the family circle. Young Vincent, although not musically inclined in his adolescence, could be persuaded to entertain the family each Christmas with an imitation of Madame Schumann-Heink singing "Silent Night."

The family songfests scarcely approached a professional standard, but they were accomplished against a background of the tolerant love that abounded in the Price family, the one undeniable feature in the formative years of Vincent Price. This love and a spirit of adventure surrounded his family's every activity. Love to the contrary, though, Vincent once told a reporter, "Music might have been the food of love, but it came close to giving my father an ulcer."

Marguerite Price had married at a very young age, so never established herself in a profession. While her children were growing up, though, she took to teaching on a non-paying, but hardly unprofessional level. Dissatisfied with the St. Louis public-school system, she and other mothers in the neighborhood started the St. Louis Community School. The school was much more progressive than the public equivalent, for the students were encouraged to read anything they wished, listen to music, and pursue whatever interests naturally developed.

Included in the unofficial curriculum of the progressive school were frequent trips to the St. Louis City Art Museum. The building that housed the St. Louis collection had been left over from the 1904 exposition, and when a few culturally-minded citizens endowed enough money to the propmsed art center, the city museum became a reality. When Vincent was attending school, the museum was still in the lengthy process of increasing its permanent collection, but its piecemeal buying over a few years had given it some community status. Although the original works housed in the museum were anything but spectacular, it did possess good copies of great works. Like many "educational" museums, the St. Louis City Art Museum aimed to provide the visitor with a brief look at the various historical periods and styles.

Marguerite Price often led the class excursions to the museums. Although not visually oriented herself, she did recognize the up-lifting quality of art and was more than conscientious in striving to have all the students' questions answered by the proper authorities. Many times, when Vincent was still quite young, she would take him to the museum by himself when he so requested.

There was a magnificent library in the Price home, one that befitted a Yale man like Vincent's father. Most of the books were histories, eternal volumes that related man's plight through the ages. Young Vincent displayed little interest in any of these, but there was one book that did lure him—*Apollo,* an illustrated history of art. Time and again, the youth would page through this volume, scanning the postage-stamp-sized reproductions of the great works. It was by means of *Apollo* that he first became familiar with the artistic masterpieces of Rembrandt, Goya, Monet, and van Gogh.

Luckily for Vincent, the city was not totally bereft of its own artists. Within his own neighborhood there were three or four artistic families. Vincent was drawn to their homes, and once inside would accept any morsels of knowledge about the art world they might offer. Aside from their artistic leanings, the boy appreciated

5

another admirable quality in these artistic families. "Here were people who were taking some kind of a chance with life," he was to say much later in life. In the middle of suburban America, it must have been very enticing and refreshing to know such people.

The art reproduction that most caught young Vincent's fancy was owned by his minister. The work was Andrea del Sarto's *Madonna of the Harpies*. After a period of viewing that one reproduction over and over, Vincent's life changed. Art became an absorption of abiding interest. For the first time, Vincent became really involved in art. He began to haunt the shop of the one art dealer in St. Louis, run by a patient soul who allowed Vincent to browse through his stock whenever he wished. In the gallery, Vincent saw many prints by Icart, but few original works of true art. It was, after all, a city where art collecting was an avocation in which relatively few indulged. The dealer, however, did stock a certain number of original etchings and engravings by Whistler, Joseph Pennell, Anders Zorn, Rembrandt, Dürer, and van Leyden. The etchings opened another world to Vincent, a world of greatness in black and white, a world wherein he could dream of possession.

Finally, these dreams of acquiring something of his very own penetrated the surface of reality. In the 1920's, the drawings and etchings of even famous artists did not demand that great a price tag. Young Vincent made a decision. He would buy a drawing!

Concomitant to this decision was a search to raise the necessary money. He began to sell magazines and newspapers, sometimes even old junk. He scraped the first five dollars together and journeyed to the print shop, where he selected his favorite: Rembrandt's etching entitled *Two Academical Nudes, One Standing*. In accordance with the deal he had made with the proprietor, Vincent made a down payment of $5.00 and was to pay the balance of $32.50 over the following six months. Although the arrangements were made specially for the twelve-year-old that Vincent then was, buying art on this sort of installment plan was to figure prominently in Price's future. But for the moment, he was the happiest kid in St. Louis, and, undoubtedly, the only one with a Rembrandt print, one he still owns.

This was a carefree period in Vincent's life. Days spent in schools. Idyllic afternoons paging through *Apollo* or going through the art shop's newest array of prints. Occasionally one of the neighborhood artists would allow Vincent to watch while he filled the canvas with blazing contrasts of color. On other free afternoons, the boy could be found listening to the readings of "The Poetess," another neighborhood artist.

6

At age twelve, Vincent graduated from the progressive school he had attended for the previous seven years. His father wanted him to attend a nearby boy's prep school to ready him academically for Yale College. As good as the progressive schooling had been, the elder Price reasoned it was important that Vincent receive a more formal education so he could properly cope with the structured curriculum of tradition-bound Yale. As to the choice of universities Vincent would attend, there was never any doubt. His father had matriculated at Yale like his father before him. His brother was a Yale man, as was his brother-in-law. Even the New England look of the Price house reflected the architecture of most of the residences near the New Haven campus.

Before enrolling at the prep school, young Vincent was permitted a true fling. He had been badgering his parents to accompany him out West for a holiday. Having seen much of the Indian art in and about St. Louis, Vincent was fascinated by the mysteries of the Old West. His parents deemed the best way to indulge this wish was to send him to summer camp on a dude ranch. They were somewhat apprehensive about sending him off alone at age twelve, but that concern evaporated when another family in the neighborhood decided to send their young son, a boy named Freddie, to the same vacation ranch. There was doubtlessly a good deal of collusion between Vincent and Freddie, since they were already best friends, but the parents smilingly fell in line with their children's plot.

The dude ranch was located in southern Colorado, and Vincent and Freddie reached it by train, spending a good part of the trip looking out the windows at the countryside. Once disembarking at the ranch, they joined the other youngsters in the planned activities: horseback riding, hiking, swimming, learning survival skills, and the rest. On their free periods, though, Vincent and Freddie would explore the foothills and plains of the surrounding terrain. It was on one of these expeditions that Vincent, after considerable digging, discovered some old Indian ruins. For days Vincent returned to the spot, fascinated by each new article he uncovered. When it became apparent the boy was on to something important, the ranch authorities called in the experts. Vincent led them to his claim, and the group spent an entire day unearthing the assorted relics. As it developed, Vincent had located a burial ground, one that could be traced back to the last period of the Mesa Verde civilization. Perhaps it was not the most significant archeological discovery of the twentieth century, but it did warrant modest coverage in the St. Louis newspaper.

At the end of the summer, the young archeologist reluctantly returned home. By this time, his quest and interest in art could not be denied. Even Vincent's father seemed to become resigned to the possibility that his younger son was not destined to be a businessman.

It was also at the end of this crucial summer that Vincent first began dreaming about one day journeying to Europe to discover even more art treasures. His paternal grandmother, the wife of the baking company owner, had traveled extensively throughout Europe with her husband, and she would spend long hours recounting her explorations to an attentive Vincent. Almost subconsciously, Vincent made the decision to go to Europe as soon as he received permission from his parents. He began to accumulate whatever money he could, but he suspected the trip would be a long time in coming.

In the fall of 1923, Vincent enrolled in the St. Louis Country Day School, a preparatory school for boys his father had chosen. Vincent continued his advanced schooling in the same spirit of normality that graced his entire formal education. Although extremely intelligent, Vincent was never first in his academic class or regarded as a boy genius. His scholastic grades were generally very good yet remained one level away from excellence. His best subjects were English and history, both somewhat related to the all-important arts.

At the prep school, as elsewhere, Vincent adapted very well to the classroom ambiance. He was popular and friendly, often amusing his contemporaries with samples of his rapacious wit. Along with his passionate curiosity about the world of art, he was a well-adjusted, happy youngster.

The school play presented Vincent with still another occasion to test his dramatic wings when he won the part of Sir Galahad. In an episode reminiscent of a Norman Rockwell illustration, Sir Galahad spent more time shooting "craps" backstage than he did onstage seeking the Holy Grail.

Vincent's father found himself in a quandary at one stage in the boy's educational career. The elder Price believed that a trip to Europe would serve to broaden his son's outlook, but at the same time he was fully aware of the rigorous reading schedule that Yale suggested before new students entered its halls of ivy. Wanting his son to devote the summer immediately preceding his entrance to Yale to that required reading list, the elder Price searched for another time for the Continental trip. He understood that his son was more than willing to go, but did not know when he and Mrs.

Price could abandon St. Louis for the requisite period. Finally, at the conclusion of Vincent's junior year in prep school, it was determined that Vincent, at age seventeen, was old enough to tour the Continent alone.

That momentous decision reflected many of the positive forces that had been working on Vincent since his birth. Not many families from the Missouri Valley states would have nurtured the notion of allowing their scions to roam around foreign lands at the tender age of seventeen, but the Prices not only permitted it, they felt secure in their decision. It had long been their plan to raise children who were totally self-sufficient. They respected their off-springs as individuals capable of making decisions and people mature enough to weather the normal storms of life even in their teen-age years. This belief did much to both bolster the security of the Price children and keep them steeped in reality.

Vincent's family owned a vacation house in Canada that they had used every summer since his birth. With the children grown, Mr. Price sold the vacation home and gave each of his four children a portion of the sale proceeds. Vincent's share naturally went toward his European trip.

For months before his scheduled departure, Vincent prepared for his journey by studying brochures and folders on the different countries he hoped to visit. His grandmother had told him most specifically about Spain, Greece, and Italy, and these illustrated guides opened up to him the other countries. Finally, he had to decide which of the many potentially wonderful tours he would take. For Vincent, it was akin to running free in an art shop.

Finally, though, he chose Tour #22, one that seemed almost specially tailored to his artistic bent. After the long train ride to New York with his father, he embarked for Europe in the middle of June, 1928. The ship was one of the Cunard Line, and the exquisite cabins were shared by the single people aboard. Vincent's trans-Atlantic roommate was a boy of his own approximate age, Pat Frank. Frank would later become a popular American novelist, the author of *Alas, Babylon* and other best sellers.

There were two official guides assigned to Tour #22, the professional tourmaster who organized the itinerary and watched after the technical portions of the tour, and "Mademoiselle," a guide used only on this particular tour to help the clients in their search for art. "Mademoiselle" was a French lady very knowledgeable in the world of fine creative offerings.

The tour listed seven capitals of Europe, most of them major art centers, and stops at other cities on the periphery of the art world.

The first stop on the trip was England. The ship docked at Southampton, and the passengers traveled by bus to the heart of London.

All the wonders of his first foreign city unfolded before Vincent's awe-struck eyes. He went to the West End theaters and the London Zoo. But what really appealed to Vincent was the British Museum. Inside its cluttered, dusty rooms, Vincent saw and touched wonders of the world he had never before imagined. The famous Rosetta Stone held Vincent's fascination, as did most of the collection, particularly the Elgin marbles. Vincent could have easily devoted the entire summer to the museum, but he moved on to the next destination with the group, promising himself to return there as soon as it was humanly and financially possible.

The group experienced a pleasant Channel crossing to France and headed to Paris, then the undisputed capital of the art world. It was the one city Vincent had been anxious to see, and his expectations were high as he rode into the massive metropolis. Not only did he look forward to viewing Parisian art, but he was eager to sample the best of French cuisine.

Unfortunately, Vincent was disappointed with Paris. Despite his six-foot-one height, he looked too young to make the rounds of the notoriously naughty night clubs, and the portions of food served him at the best restaurants were relatively small. He was favorably inclined toward the Louvre, but he preferred the clutter of the British Museum. He resented the lack of historical lines that had made the art of England so much easier to comprehend. He did leave Paris with his first hangover, a reminder of the French champagne that was so difficult to locate in St. Louis.

The group next boarded a bus that took them through Reims to Belgium. In the old French city they browsed about the famous cathedral that was still in great need of repairs following its near-destruction in World War I. Vincent loved the town, finding it very casual and leisurely, just the antidote to remedy a case of Paris blues.

After a fleeting round of Brussels, the tour proceeded to Amsterdam whose canals and quaint houses were a delightful surprise to Vincent. The Rijksmuseum was the biggest bonanza of all. In America, the most renowned European museums were the Prado, the Louvre, and the British Museum. But the Rijksmuseum, with the largest Rembrandt collection in thb world, was the equal to any of the three. Vincent ambled along the corridors looking at such famous Rembrandts as *The Night Watch, The Anatomy Lesson of*

Dr. Tulp and *The Syndics*. He had seen them all before, but, of course, only in reproductions. Here, he could view them in their full majesty. He was amazed at their overly large size, and the feeling of motion they conveyed in contrast to the stilted quality that had been projected in the reproductions. Another favorite artist with whom he became familiar in his later visits to the Rijksmuseum was Vermeer, still an underrated Flemish artist. Hugo van der Goes' *Christ* was another masterly canvas that struck the young Price's fancy.

After exploring the refined art worlds of Europe, Vincent decided it was high time to explore another, more basic leisure pastime. On the same tour there was a young blonde girl approximately the same age as Vincent. After a few conversations and exchanged smiles, Vincent decided to pursue her with the same diligence he had heretofore reserved for art. On the last night's stay in Amsterdam, he began his quest, one that would take him through many countries.

When Vincent's bus stopped by the North Sea one summer night, he attempted an experiment he knew would interest his mother when he returned home. Marguerite Price had recently taken a sharp interest in the possibilities of thought transference and extrasensory perception, commonly called ESP. As Price stood on the shoreline, he attempted to send his thoughts to his family in St. Louis. He was to learn later that his specific brain patterns did not cross the ocean to any member of his family, but perhaps he was sending nontransferable images. His mother had warned him about the dangers of girls before his trip, and it is more than likely that young Vincent was indulging in fantasies concerning his young blonde acquaintance.

The next stopover was in Germany, where the focus was on dining. Of course, the German brand of cuisine was well-known in St. Louis, but Vincent found the authentic blending of ingredients totally irresistible.

With the disruptive political situation in Germany, Berlin itself was out of bounds. But Vincent did find the Cologne Cathedral magnificent and treasured his visit to Nuremberg. It was here that he saw his first authentic Dürer, *The Praying Hands,* and he was swept up in its feeling. He found the adopted city of Luther and Cranach very charming, and in his later life constantly bemoaned its destruction in World War II.

From Nuremberg, the culture-weary party proceeded to Switzerland. Here again, more food was consumed than art viewed, but

VINCENT PRICE UNMASKED

Vincent found the Interlaken picnics and the climbing of small Alps very conducive to his continuing pursuit of his equally buoyant lady friend. In the game of summer romances, Vincent seemed to be winning at Switzerland, after having suffered emotional setbacks in Nuremberg and Cologne. Still, he was much too young, even at seventeen, to know he was slowly approaching his goal.

The arduous train ride to Austria through the Alps provided him with an excellent occasion to woo his hopeful conquest. At every unscheduled stop along the way, he and the girl climbed down from the train and stood hand in hand taking in the spectacular views. The aphrodisiac qualities of the Alps overwhelmed the young Price, and perhaps his love of beauty, both natural and man-made, was deepened.

In Vienna, the group sampled some of the world's most delicious pastries and desserts. The Kunsthistorisches Museum was one more of the many delightful surprices that Vincent experienced on this trip. The Kunsthistorisches possesses the largest collection of the works of Pieter Brueghel the Elder. The splendor of Brueghel fascinated Vincent, as it would most youthful art connoisseurs. The tragic depth that Brueghel plumbed in his search for the cosmic cycle of death and rebirth, his uncanny perception into the realms of human folly, and the revolutionary style with which he attacked the canvas, made him one of the few artistic geniuses of sixteenth-century Europe. Other artists that Vincent became familiar with at the Kunsthistorisches were Tintoretto and Correggio.

During his last dinner in Vienna, Vincent discovered a culinary treat, a delicacy called the Salzburger Knockerln. On each succeeding trip to Vienna, he would search high and low for the best available recipe for this most *wunderbar* pastry.

As the train passed out of Vienna, through the Dolmites and by lakes and towns, Vincent dreamed of his next destination, the place where he hoped at last to consummate his first romance — Venice, a city long known as the place of lovers. In his elaborate fantasies, he and his girl friend walked arm in arm over the Bridge of Sighs, through St. Mark's Square and the Palace of the Doges, and then glided through the Grand Canal as the gondolier sang of eternal bliss.

But like Paris, Venice proved an extreme disappointment to the impressionable youth. To begin with, the tour was lodged at the Hotel du Gare, literally by the railroad station, and it was a rare night that the guests were not awakened many times by the passing trains. He also thought the city was extremely dirty, with the acrid smells of the sewers wafting through every crowded street. Although he did admire the manner in which business was transacted in this age-old city, he thought the ambiance of the Rialto was too frantic. St. Mark's Square was wonderful, but might have proved more romantic without the pesky pigeons.

Disappointed, and thinking of Venice as "Hoboken with wet pavements," Vincent asked Mademoiselle if he might leave the tour a day early and rejoin the party at their next destination. When she agreed, he boarded the night train by himself and headed toward the city that would prove to enthrall him the most.

Florence was the high point of the entire trip for Vincent. In fact, it was one of the highlights of the young man's life to that point. The hotel was on the Arno itself, one of the great scenes of beauty in the world. For Vincent, Florence was everything Venice was supposed to have been but was not. It was beautiful, it was romantic, it was magical. The landmarks of the city — the Duomo, Giotto's Tower, the homes and palaces — all overwhelmed him, removing any concerns that the culture-stuffed tour might have already jaded his tastes. The Signoria, the Loggia, and the Uffizi were additional delights, each to be treasured for its own prizes.

With hardly any sleep whatsoever, Vincent traipsed to the Uffizi, expressly for the purpose of reacquainting himself with an old friend, for it was here that the original *Madonna of the Harpies* by Andrea del Sarto hung. Upon seeing the actual painting, Vincent burst into tears. As he later explained in one of his books, "Only three things have ever caused me to weep, for beauty's sake or for art's sake: the *Madonna* of Andrea del Sarto, the first time I saw John Gielgud play *Hamlet* in London, and Kirsten Flagstad's Isolde."

It was while he was gazing enraptured at del Sarto's magnificent work that an incident occurred that made him aware that the world of art was his forever. While he was standing in front of the *Madonna,* tears rolled down his face. At that moment, a middle-aged woman came up behind him and said to him, "Come over here. I'll show you the one that makes me cry."

Vincent was embarrassed. He was almost a grown man and there he was crying in the middle of the Uffizi. Burying his face in his handkerchief, he mumbled, "Sorry, something in my eye."

The woman astutely replied, "Yes, beauty."

With those two words, the kindly lady let the young man know there were others in the world who shared his passion, and that real maturity was in being able to allow one's inner feelings to flow freely. The woman took him to see Da Vinci's *Annunciation,* a beautiful masterwork of the famed Leonardo. And although Vincent was deeply touched by the painting, it did not move him in the same way the *Madonna* had — those reactions are the treasured moments of one's life.

Vincent saw many of the mysteriously affecting pieces of art in Florence — Michelangelo's figure of David, the most magnificent sculpture in the world, Cellini's Perseus, the portraitures of Bronzino, and as much of the beauty of the city itself as time permitted. Never before had Vincent been in the presence of such persistent visions, and he deeply wished to take a piece of Florence with him. He decided to buy his parents a low-priced work from Florence, not only because he wished to give them a work of beauty, but also so he could be reminded of the city when he returned to St. Louis. He had saved money for just such a purpose, and he chose a bronze sculpture, shipping it to the family home in Missouri. Over the years, that sculpture became quite valuable, more for the sums spent on it than for young Vincent's purchasing acumen. On arrival, Mr. Price had to pay sixty dollars for shipping costs. The family then decided that such a magnificent work deserved a lush surrounding, so $250 were spent on building a small pool with a carefully constructed stone foundation. When the sculpture still appeared to lack the proper setting, Marguerite Price sent away for special light bulbs, costing $350, to illuminate the piece in just the right shadings. All this effort for a bronze piece that originally cost Vincent only $25!

Vincent rejoined the group and traveled with them to Rome. Still dazzled by the beauty he had seen, he was able to concentrate on very little. Like every other tourist, he went to St. Peter's where he saw Bernini's altar and Michelangelo's great dome, the Sistine Chapel. With representations of the Creation of Man, the Last Judgment, and Moses leading his flock to the Promised Land swirling above him, Vincent was properly dizzied. But it was upon examining Michelangelo's *Pieta* that he felt a flush of despair. Someone had told Vincent that Michelangelo had been only twenty-one when he finished the *Pieta,* and Vincent realized how little time he had to fulfill his own talent as an artist. Supposedly, it was at this moment that Vincent vowed to work extremely hard to develop what talent he possessed. He reasoned that if it developed that he had little or no real talent, he would compensate for the lack by becoming the best audience he could.

The trip was almost over. Seven capitals of art had been devoured by the eager young man. Naples followed Florence, where Vincent devoted much time nourishing himself on the authentic pasta dishes. In Pompeii, he delighted in the lascivious frescoes, which reminded him of his second pursuit. The tour train raced through Pisa where Vincent glimpsed the leaning tower by sticking his head out the train window. Genoa warranted a ten-minute stop on the train schedule. They stopped a little longer in Monaco, but Vincent was too young to enjoy the particular gambling pleasures of this principality.

In Nice, Vincent experienced a highlight of a different sort — the culmination of his spawning relationship with the winsome blonde. Perhaps it was right that the romance reached fulfillment at the end of the journey. Like most summer affairs, it had proven alternately exciting and distracting. But Vincent was fortunate in one respect. It was not every American youth who discovered the wonders of sexual fulfillment midst the charming splendors of Nice.

From Paris, Vincent returned home late in the summer of 1928, and before he could finish telling his awed friends about his magnificent European holiday, he was back at school. More than anything, Vincent intended to keep his promise to parcel out his reservoir of artistic talent. Every spare moment, Vincent could be found sketching something, whether it was a bowl of apples — or an uncooperative sister.

He spent long afternoons in the St. Louis City Art Museum, attempting to copy some of the old masters in the hope that some of their techniques might rub off onto him. He was therefore fortunate that the museum had purchased an El Greco canvas early in 1929, for in that canvas he was able to give much study to the distinctive individual style that was El Greco's trademark. And Vincent badly needed that sense of style in his own creative, if derivative, work. He spent a lot of time on a portrait of his mother, one that she liked so well that she had it framed and hung in the Price living room for everyone to see. Unfortunately, that was more a display of maternal devotion than a tribute to the young man's artistic accomplishments. Vincent never walked into the parlor after that without cringing a bit from embarrassment. When his mother died some years later, he inherited the painting. Upon receiving it from the executor, Vincent summarily burned it.

Even his one extracurricular activity at school in his senior year was directed toward art. He was chosen by the teachers and his classmates to illustrate the senior yearbook with skytches of school life. He worked diligently throughout the year on the consuming

KETCHES?

project, and although the results were good, they hardly indicated the birth of a major new talent. It was beginning to dawn on Price that perhaps he should keep the figurative door open for another profession.

Still, he did want to impart his love of art to others. When his class was searching for the proper senior gift, Vincent suggested a set of lithographs by Joseph Pennell. His classmates not only rejected his idea, but almost laughed themselves silly at the thought of it. The class finally voted to provide the school with a cement bench. One could easily forgive Price if he were to indulge in the last laugh years later, when Joseph Pennell ranked among the top artists of the day.

But perhaps that incident made it a little easier for Vincent to leave St. Louis after he graduated from high school. When he left the city, he knew that he would come back to St. Louis only to visit. He sensed that his life would lead him elsewhere in order to filfull his desires. So, with the knowledge that his childhood was well over, and with his mother's warnings about the girls of New England, Vincent Price left St. Louis. It was the fall of 1929.

The formative years had passed. Vincent was, by this time, close to becoming the man he would be. The history of St. Louis, with its French culture, its community spirit, its Spanish touches, and its absorption of the ideas of the German Reformation, had made its permanent mark on the college-bound student. Equally, Price's family had left its mark, a mark of love that made him a person secure within himself and his beliefs. It was a love that allowed humor, and kindness, and exploration.

LEFT: In *The Shoemaker's Holiday* on Broadway in 1938. BELOW: With Basil Rathbone and Boris Karloff in *Tower of London* (Universal, 1939).

TOP LEFT: With Nan Grey, Harry Stubbs, and For-
ester Harvey in *The Invisible Man Returns* (Univer-
sal, 1940). TOP CENTER: With Paul Everton and
Cornel Wilde in *Leave Her to Heaven* (Twentieth
Century-Fox, 1944). TOP RIGHT: With Margaret
Lindsay and George Sanders in *The House of Seven
Gables* (Universal, 1940). ABOVE: With Constance
Bennett in *Service De Luxe* (Universal, 1938).
RIGHT: With Clifton Webb, Gene Tierney, and
Judith Anderson in *Laura* (Twentieth Century-Fox,
1944).

FAR LEFT: With Edith Price examining the charcoal portrait of Mme. Maria Ouspenskaya done by Ginger Rogers in 1947. LEFT: With Ava Gardner on the set of *The Bribe* (MGM, 1949). RIGHT: Publicity pose for *The Three Musketeers* (MGM, 1948). BELOW LEFT: With Gene Tierney in *Dragonwyck* (Twentieth Century-Fox, 1946). BELOW: With Maureen O'Hara in *Baghdad* (Universal, 1949).

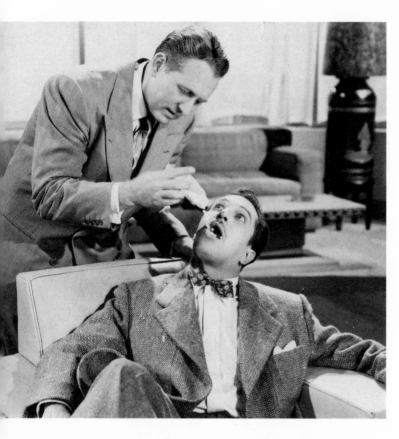

ABOVE: With Art Linkletter in *Champagne for Caesar* (United Artists, 1950). TOP LEFT: With Bob Hope in *Casanova's Big Night* (Paramount, 1954). TOP RIGHT: With Eve Arden in a publicity pose from *Curtain Call at Cactus Creek* (Universal, 1950). RIGHT: With Philip Tonge and Paul Cavanagh in *House of Wax* (Warner Bros., 1953).

RIGHT: In a publicity pose as *The Mad Magician* (Columbia, 1954). BELOW: With Gene Roth and Robert O'Neil in *The Baron of Arizona* (Lippert, 1950).

Chapter Two

"If I had it to do all over again, I'd still go to Yale,
I'd still major in art, and I'd still be an actor, because
acting opens all the other doors."
                                        Vincent Price

When Vincent traveled to Yale in the fall of 1929, he was
expecting the campus to prove itself the Athens of American life —
a combination of beauty, culture, philosophy, and an appreciation
of the physical attributes. For Vincent, a Yale man was related to
the centurions of old, a man conversant with all the elements of a
disparate world.

Vincent's first room at Yale was on the Old Campus, and his first
roommate was a young chap named Ted Thomas. Ted and Vincent
were already friends from the St. Louis Country Day School, and
during the course of their four-year Yale evolution, they would
remain good pals and roommates.

The first thing that struck Vincent about the campus was its
mixture of many styles. His dormitory section that first year was
indicative of the New England brick style, while other areas of the
campus were modern, Gothic, or compendiums of many other
trends.

Another friend Vincent made quite early in his Yale life was
Herman Liebert. Many were the afternoons that Vincent, Ted, and
Herbert would haunt the galleries and movie theaters of New
Haven together.

During his first Yale year Vincent was assigned to one creat-
ive-art class. His first assignment there was to complete a charcoal
rendition of a plaster-cast model. After working several days on the

proposed piece, Vincent realized his artistic talent was deficient, and he decided to relegate himself thereafter to appreciating the works of others.

It was at this juncture that he first thought seriously about acting as a career. Certainly, he had flirted with the notion in his youth, as most young children are wont to do, but he had always assumed he would be an artist, so gave it very little thought. As a youngster he had loved both motion pictures and the legitimate theater, and when forced to compromise on his choice of a career, he thought the theatrical profession would strike the proper balance between artist and businessman. As an actor, the world of art would accept him and, if successful, he would be able to hobnob with the best artists in the world.

Fortunately, Vincent had not committed himself to the art school yet — mainly because he thought it very dull — so he switched his major from History of Art to English. Vincent believed that academic art was counterproductive and for him the proof was that Yale produced far better writers than artists. Through some of his acquaintances he met and was befriended by James Thurber, the famous American humorist and cartoonist. He spent many days with Thurber, drawing cartoons or talking about trends in American literature. Thurber, who was more of an art buff than an art historian, introduced Vincent to some of his New York circle. After that, whenever Vincent visited Manhattan on weekends, the galeries and the art dealers opened their doors to him with the utmost hospitality.

This open-door policy was essential for Vincent's cultural growth, for the Yale Gallery was mundane at best. Although Yale produced some of the country's great collectors, at that time, they had done little to enrich their own art holdings. What they did have on exhibit consisted largely of silver pieces made in the eighteenth century, early American furniture, and the works of Trumbull and Samuel F. B. Morse. Vincent's favorite work at the Yale Gallery was Cosimo's *Lady and a Rabbit,* perhaps the most unusual work in the collection.

Shortly after Vincent's arrival at Yale, the stock-market crash torpedoed the American economy. The dropout rate at Yale, as at other schools, was enormous, Luckily, the candy business, a concern that existed on pennies and not dollars, was not as adversely affected as most other businesses. Also, Vincent's father had made some very wise investments in real estate. Vincent's friends, Ted Thomas and Herman Liebert, also managed to weather the economic storm of 1929, thereby staying in school.

VINCENT PRICE UNMASKED

In his freshman year at Yale, Vincent submitted a cartoon to the Yale humor magazine, which was accepted. No doubt his blossoming friendship with Thurber had improved his sketching style, but drawing cartoons was a lark for Vincent, a leisure-time activity, and nothing he regarded very seriously.

During the first two academic years, his favorite course was the History of Religion. This was indicative of the two major interests in his life at that time — drama and art. While religion had served for thousands of years as an inspiration for and sometimes patron of art, it had also produced an anthology of the world's most dramatic stories.

Vincent was also a member of the freshman crew, an activity to which he devoted long invigorating hours. It is again indicative that he would choose a sport in which he could combine his love of nature and the great outdoors and his desire for physical excellence.

During his sophomore year he considered joining the Drama School of Yale, but decided against it. He found the group too "precious"; perhaps his was a rebellion against any group that concentrated so much time on one goal to the exclusion of total life experiences. Indeed, although he had by now apparently made the decision to become an actor, he approached it with the same theories he maintained on art. Vincent believed then, and still does to a large extent, that there are two elements necessary to working in either the theater or in art. He believed one should experience the most in life, thereby discovering its deceits and truths along with its wonders. Further, he believed the only way to perceive and learn was by actually doing. Vincent had met too many would-be actors and artists who could fill a book with intellectual theories concerning their chosen profession, but very few who had the courage or stamina to go out and do it, to work every night for years, if necessary. Just as the apprentices of Rembrandt developed their skills by painting their own works in the presence of the master, so did Vincent feel that young actors had to perform with more experienced actors to learn "the tricks of the trade."

But Vincent did believe one could also learn by watching the craftsmen of any particular field. He began attending movies on a regular basis and caught whatever pre-Broadway shows played in New Haven, long considered the only tryout town in the theatrical game. As he said later, "I think I can honestly say I saw every movie, good and bad, made between the years 1930 and 1933. And I didn't miss many concerts, plays, or revues, either."

In his years at Yale he bowed once to the considerations of

19

academic theater, and that was a course on Shakespeare taught by scholar Carl Young. Fittingly enough, he was somewhat disappointed with the lecture contents, since Young approached the Bard's works as literature rather than theater. But the course was salvaged by Young's fiery and brilliant interpretation of *The Tempest,* the only lectures in the course that Vincent felt approached the true, zesty spirit of Shakespeare.

Carl Rollins, a painter and teacher at Yale, was another in the line of people who helped Vincent mature into an artist. Rollins was also a friend of Thurber and, together with the humorist, helped Price to enter some of the higher inner circles of the New York art world. One day, while discussing the different museums and galleries in New York with Vincent, Rollins mentioned the Morgan Museum, an out-of-the-way place that Vincent had never visited. By mail, Rollins introduced Vincent to the curator of the Morgan, and that palace of art became one of Vincent's favorite hangouts when visiting New York.

Throughout his four undergraduate years at Yale, Vincent would commute to New York as often as time and funds permitted. Once in the big city, he would attend the Broadway plays and regularly visit his favorite galleries. When he found himself flush, he would occasionally purchase a piece at some of those expensive establishments. One day he bought a self-portrait by Alphonse Legros, and the price he paid would have to be ranked as a steal of the decade. He also bought a bronze sculpture by a woman named Harriet Frishmuth called *The Vine.* Although that *objet d'art* did not grow in economical worth, it was still a bargain, mainly and rightly because Vincent liked it so much.

The pattern that he set early in his life in the matter of art is another characteristic that has followed him throughout life. Vincent Price has never gone out of his way to buy only famous works or works whose economic value he thought would escalate. Although many of the items he acquired did become valuable at a later date, he maintained only one criteria — that he like what he purchased. He bought art then, and still does, with which to live not sell.

Vincent also "heeled" the Yale *Record* in his sophomore year, adding to the literary side of his burgeoning nature. Through a friend on The Record, Vincent was convinced to try out for the Glee Club, one of the top groups of its kind in the country. With a fine baritone voice that had developed in the family sing-alongs, he won acceptance in the organization.

VINCENT PRICE UNMASKED

Vincent was hardly the most devoted member of the august Yale Glee Club. Although he had an enjoyable time, his friends good-naturedly kidded him, with a hint of accusation, about joining the men's singing group just a few months before it was scheduled to tour Europe. Indeed, the planned trip was just the sort of thing that would lure Vincent into the musical fold. During the summer of 1931, not a particularly bright one economically for most Americans, Vincent and the Glee Club toured the Continent, but this trip was far different from the one Vincent had enjoyed a few years before.

Whereas the debut trip had provided the young tyro of the art world with a fascinating look at the major works of the Continent, the tour he took with the Glee Club was devoted almost exclusively to wine, women, and song. At that the song portion of that triad came in a distant third. In fact, years later Vincent had trouble recalling any of the concerts the club had performed, but he could remember the nightly fraternal bouts with the "whiffenpoof song," sung all evening long by his slightly inebriated comrades and himself. Toward the end of the European lark, Vincent was involved in a fishing-trip travesty, along with two pals, Jack Parlin and Don Wylie. A stunning photograph of Vincent posing in pajamas and fishing line was featured in the campus newspaper.

His remaining two years at college were devoted to the normal pursuit of obtaining a bachelor's degree, and playing the part of a typical "Eli." In another bow to the theatrical muse, Vincent joined the Elizabethan Club of Alpha Sigma Phi, but this was more to satisfy his curiosity about Elizabethan history than it was to study Marlowe, Shakespeare, and other Britich dramatists of the period.

More important than any of the singular aspects of his college career, though, was the undeniable pattern that Price established during his college years. Instead of specializing in one specific area, Vincent chose to explore many cultural avenues. He became involved in a variety of experiences, all as important to him as any of the others. What stands out in this is his absolute individuality. Vincent was never swayed by the crowd, even though he was an integral part of his class. He chose to be both the ultimate Yale man and to remove himself enough to remain singular at all times.

University life, especially on an Ivy League campus, is many things to many people. For some it provides an opportunity to compete with others in a preliminary bout for their later careers. Others see it as one long playtime. Still others absorb their "majors" and learn everything that can be taught by teachers and books. Vincent seems to have approached Yale with the attitude that his college days filled a transitional period in his maturing, one in which he should endeavor to immerse himself in the atmosphere that a versatile university provides. It was apparently his resolve from the start to acquire the taste, refinement, and the spirit of learning that is requisite to the continuing growth of the individual once he steps outside the doors of academia. And it was in that outside world that Vincent suspected he would acquire his real education, especially regarding the theater.

Upon graduation, Vincent moved to New York in order to insinuate himself somehow into the theater world. The first weeks were spent in the waiting rooms of agents' offices and going to the movies and Broadway plays. One night, though, Vincent attended a party hosted by a Yale alumnus. At the gathering, Vincent was offered a job teaching school. One proviso of the offer was that Vincent had to serve as a camp counselor in the Adirondacks for two months prior to the job's start. Reflecting on his initial lack of success in the acting world, Vincent thought it might prove worthwhile to have some funds, so he accepted the job offer.

In the fall of 1933, he began teaching at the Riverdale Country Day School in Yonkers, New York. Even though his first classroom assignments were scattered through the curriculum, he did have occasion to explore the visual arts with his young charges. He taught an art-appreciation class that covered works with which he believed his students could identify without undue intellectual strain. He was also very careful not to talk down to his classes. He knew, and tried to impart, that all that was needed in art appreciation was a respect for beauty in any form.

At Riverdale, he became friendly with Marc and Cecil Baldwin. They urged him to direct some amateur productions for the school, a task that gave great satisfaction. It also enabled him to learn more about dramatic structure, how scenes flowed one into the other, how a playwright built the work, and how actors should look in their roles. He also had a great deal of fun coaching the youngsters, and he was careful not to be arbitrary with them in his stage directions. He felt then, as he does now, that young people should be encouraged to find their own solutions with whatever guidance and patience can be supplied by the supervising adult.

At the same time, he was continuing his siege on the theatrical agencies of Manhattan, but no one seemed the least bit interested in this gangly, six-foot-four young man. In acting, he had chosen perhaps the one field where his education worked against him.

VINCENT PRICE UNMASKED

One of the most appalling preconceptions of actors held by agents, producers, and even some directors, concerns the notion that actors are, by and large, a stupid breed. A part of this mistaken idea comes from the fact that acting, at its very best, is usually considered to be more a *feeling* art than a *thinking* art. However, thinking and feeling are not necessarily exclusive of one another, and most good actors have thought about their roles before they go onstage as much as they feel them while performing. Nevertheless, an actor with obvious intelligence is somewhat suspect. One can easily imagine the difficulty someone with Vincent Price's background might have undergone when forced to deal with the usual theatrical agent. His only New York credit came from an appearance as the captain in Gilbert and Sullivan's *H.M.S. Pinafore* for the Riverdale school. His height, his accent, and his well-honed sense of the ridiculous all served him well in this production, which was seen by just a few hundred people, mostly friends of the school.

Predictably, then, Vincent found no response among the casting offices on Broadway. When the end of the first term at the Riverdale school approached, Vincent had to decide whether to stay with the teaching while continuing to make the acting rounds, or to try some other occupation.

It was at this point that Price decided to use the eleven hundred dollars received as a graduation gift from his father. He decided to use the funds to obtain his master's degree. It was not only a matter of where to study, a quandary that was quickly resolved. On both his European trips, Vincent had been enchanted by London. The museums and the theaters provided him with a soul-satisfying ambiance. When the Yale Glee Club had passed through London, Vincent had discovered the existence of the University of London and its many academic branches. One of these divisions was the University of Fine Arts located in the Courtauld Institute. The Courtauld Institute had long held the reputation of being one of the finest schools of its kind in the world, the type only an excellent student from a good undergraduate institution could hope to attend.

The program that the Courtauld offered, plus the natural charms of London, lured Vincent from his New York base. He took third-class passage to England and enrolled in the school. The tuition at the time was only two hundred dollars. Vincent set his monthly budget at seventy-five dollars, not only a goodly sum in those days, but also an amount that was worth more in England because of the strength of the American dollar. Even though he was not permitted a regular job under immigration rules, the eleven

23

hundred dollars were just enough to see him through the study period if he adhered to his budget.

The Courtauld Institute was situated in a building called Home House that had been built by the Adams brothers for the countess of Home. Home House was one of the really magnificent London structures, a house whose interior was as grand and airy as one could possibly imagine. And the Courtauld endowed Home House with one of the most selective collections in the world.

The first time Vincent was seated in the Courtauld classroom, he was surrounded by paintings such as *The Cardplayers* by Cezanne, *Wheatfields at Arles* by van Gogh, *Jane Avril Leaving the Theater* by Toulouse-Lautrec, *Don Quixote* by Daumiers, and the *Ballet Rehearsal* of Degas. One can easily appreciate why Vincent was distracted in a classroom of that design. Luckily, though, Vincent's degree had little to do with classroom work.

Vincent chose as the subject for his master's degree "Dürer and the School of the Danube." It was the tradition at the Courtauld to assign to each student a "Master," someone who could assist the pupil with his topic in whatever way seemed appropriate. Campbell Dodgson, keeper of the prints at the British Museum, was assigned to guide Vincent through the maze that art history could sometimes be. Not only was Dodgson important to Vincent in providing him access to the rich files at the British Museum, he was also the world's leading authority on Dürer and perhaps of the entire German Renaissance period.

Contemporary world politics helped serve Vincent another plum on his thesis plate. The year was 1933. On the Continent, a meglomaniacal dictator named Adolf Hitler was banning from Germany almost every artist whose politics did not coincide with his own Aryan philosophy. Like the rest of the world, England benefited from Hitler's rejection of these fine minds. Many came to London, either to live or to visit, and those who did were often hounded by the over-eager Vincent, who urged them to divulge their views or insights into Dürer and the other Danube artists.

Quite naturally, Vincent was active in other areas of the varied and rich London life. He particularly thrived on attending all the Sir Jacob Epstein sculpture openings at the Leicester Galleries and haunting the various small bookshops on Charing Cross Road. Scores of British print shops were visited by Vincent more than once during his academic stay, and sometimes when an art work was priced low enough, the student would indulge himself by buying one or another of the prints. The Tate Gallery, with its fine collection of Gauguins and French Impressionists, was another favorite of Vincent's. In addition, the Tate collection contained a strong representation of English artists, such as Blake and Turner, both of whom appealed to Vincent and the public at that time.

Whenever possible, Price frequented the thriving London theater. He loved the heady traditions behind the theater, and appreciated, in a way only an American might, the low prices charged for each performance. British theater was the perfect illustration of theater for the people, with admission fees scaled so that almost anyone could afford some kind of seat. Vincent had long held that "Art was for everyone" but, during this London stay, his views on the matter became even stronger. To see firsthand that the cultural life of the British was an integral part of their national character thrilled Price and he hoped one day to help bring this same exciting concept to America.

A great deal of time was spent early in his Courtauld phase traveling to the tiny galleries and local museums tracking down works within his subject area. Campbell Dodgson was an invaluable help in this endeavor; not only did he map out all these discoveries for Vincent, but he also gave him letters of introduction so that he could peruse certain items almost at will. .

Another great aide during this fruitful period was W.G. Constable, head of the Courtauld institution. Constable, like most of the men at the heads of the different university branches, had many friends in the city who were more than pleased to open their doors to his young proteges. Constable willingly paved the way for Vincent to gain permission to examine the storehouse of drawings held in Windsor Castle. In the great edifice, Vincent spent many an afternoon pouring over some of the superb drawings collected by many generations of English royalty.

Quite aside from his educational pursuit, Vincent kept returning to the National Gallery to view Tintoretto's *Origin of the Milky Way*. Indeed, this was Price's favorite work during this historical period and has remained one of his favorites throughout his life. Another of Price's most treasured paintings also hangs in the National Gallery, van Eyck's *Arnolfini Wedding*.

Other activities that consumed his time during his stay were observing restorations at the national insitutions or examining the private stocks of a few of London's greatest collectors, all by courtesy of his Courtauld attachment.

The most important private collection that Vincent had occasion to view was that of Sir Robert Witt. With a letter of introduction from Constable, Witt's secretary permitted the American access to the works not seen by the regular public. This collection was so vast that Vincent visited Witt's library once a week for seven months before he had examined it all. During the many sessions he never once met Witt.

These first months in England were idyllic. On the other hand, Vincent had sufficient money to tide him over, and therefore did not have to be overly concerned about his next meal. In addition, he was being allowed access to art repositories he would never have seen under ordinary circumstances, places where even money could not buy entrance.

Finally, though, Vincent had to come to grips with the subject matter of his thesis. It was necessary for the completion of his project to travel to Vienna to see the collection at the Albertina, storehouse of the greatest collection of Dürers in the world. After a very rough train ride across Europe, Vincent found a room behind the Karlskirche in Vienna for a dollar a day and presented himself to the proprietess of the Albertina. Vienna was then on the periphery of the ferment raging throughout Germany under Hitler's dictatorship. Artists and liberals were fleeing the city in astonishing numbers, while fear gripped those who stayed. It seemed only a matter of time before Austria was "annexed" to Germany's Third Reich. Despite this ever-present turmoil, Vincent could not have been treated more kindly by the Albertina staff. Dr. Hilda Spitzmueller read the letter from Campbell Dodgson that Vincent presented her, and gladly opened the locks on the treasures under her care.

As Vincent later described it, he became one of the family, and every day for several weeks he could be found examining the masterpieces, from nine in the morning until closing time at five in the afternoon. Price has many times recounted this Viennese interlude as one of the high points in his artistic life. Not only did he have the chance to study firsthand the great masterpieces of Dürer, he also could visit the Tintorettos, Correggios, and Brueghels housed in the Kunsthistoriches. Nevertheless, it was at the Albertina that he made his greatest finds, the lesser-known black-and-white ink drawings, Christmas cards, preliminary design sketches for later paintings and engravings, and many other assorted priceless, Dürer memorabilia. Along with the Dürer treasures, Vincent was privileged to study some of the hidden greats of the German Renaissance all stored below the regular collection. Occasionally, Dr. Spitzmueller would refresh her young charge by showing him an obscure collection of drawings from Rembrandt or

Rubens or Fragonard. Vienna was serving a rich artistic dish to the appreciative Price, and the art gourmet consumed all of it very happily.

When, sadly, he had to leave Vienna, he went again to Nuremberg, the place of Dürer's birth. Now that he had viewed the great majority of the artist's lifework, a second look at the artist's birthplace helped to focus Vincent on the elements that had shaped not only Dürer's work but his life as well. He found Nuremberg a much-changed village, for the wave of Fascism and fear had swept through the countryside and found a home in nearly every dwelling. Little was left of the village that Dürer had once known.

From Nuremberg he went to Bamberg, and then to Frankfort to glimpse the rest of the important Dürers, about the only ones he had not yet studied. His curiosity satisfied, Price returned to London to complete his curriculum at the Courtauld. He settled down to the task of finishing his thesis, a writing job that was difficult and tedious but which still left him many hours to explore his other interests.

He found himself with more leisure time than during any other period since his arrival in England. He decided to explore the English pub life with his friends. No small part of his pub-hopping stemmed from the gourmet side of his character. As an added pleasure, the best food in England is often found in out-of-the-way pubs and taverns, and the prices were then ridiculously nominal.

Vincent was invited to join an amateur theatrical company composed of many of his fellow students, and he readily accepted. While he was involved with this group, a friend suggested he pop down to the Gate Theatre and attempt to win a part as one of the American policemen in the pending production of Maurice Watkin's *Chicago*. After inquiring of other friends, Vincent found a pal of his who knew an associate of actor John Gielgud. Gielgud was a friend of Norman Marshall, the producer of the Gate, and it was thought that Gielgud's associate could wrangle Vincent an appointment with Marshall. True to English hospitality, Vincent obtained both the appointment and the part, although even Price admits he earned the role only because he was truly American and could be used as part-time consultant on the Chicago atmosphere. *Chicago* was a well-received Gate production, winning for the small but respected theater club much praise, if little money.

During the run of *Chicago,* Vincent heard that Marshall was next planning to stage Laurence Houseman's *Victoria Regina.* Knowing a bit of English history, Price applied in person for the role of

Prince Albert, consort to the long-lived queen. He informed Marshall that he bore a strong physical resemblance to the prince, which he did, and that he could easily handle the requisite German accent, since he already spoke fluent German. Marshall might have been a bit dubious, but the next day he called for Vincent and told him he had won the role.

Vincent tackled the sizable part with his customary enthusiasm, accomplishing much research on German Prince Albert at the British Museum. Meanwhile, Roger Furse, who was later to become one of London's top set designers, was confronting the problem of creating Windsor and Buckingham Palace, and Balmoral in Scotland, on a stage that was no larger than an average living room. The budget for the entire Gate production of *Victoria Regina* was $750. As for salary, Vincent was to receive five pounds weekly once the show actually opened. That translated into about $24 a week for the young man, not a great deal, but enough on which to exist when added to the reserves of his original London funding.

When *Victoria Regina* debuted at the Gate, with Pamela Stanley in the demanding title role, Vincent managed to steal the acting honors. American producer Gilbert Miller, who owned the rights for the U.S. production of the drama, saw Vincent's performance and was immediately impressed by his display of histrionics. Miller summoned Helen Hayes, who had been engaged by Miller to play the queen on Broadway, to the Gate. (She had come to England to do research on her forthcoming role.) She attended a performance with Miller, and the two agreed that Price was perfect for the part and should be hired for the New York version. Miller delayed in asking the young actor to join the Broadway cast, however, because he was under the mistaken impression that Price was British.

At the same time, Sydney Carroll asked Vincent to appear in his Shakespearean productions at the Open-Air Theatre in Regent's Park over the summer. Vincent agreed, believing this was just the opportunity he needed to have to act in the classical field. He accepted the roles of Orsino in *Twelfth Night* and of Orlando in *As You Like It*.

When word reached British Actors' Equity that an American had been hired to round out the casting of the Bard's work, the group raised a tremendous fuss. After all, there were so many qualified and unemployed British actors available for the roles. The union took their case to the Ministry of Labour, which promptly summoned Carroll to explain his action. Carroll was prepared for just such a showdown, and arrived at a workable solution. Vincent had already told Carroll that he would act in the plays for no salary since they would so richly add to his experience. Thus Carroll told the ministry that he would not pay Price any fee, and further, he would pay a sum eqaul to what Price should be earning to the Actors' Benevolent Fund. The ministry seemed satisfied and agreed to the compromise.

The actors' committee was not as easily placated, however, and they registered further protests. Finally, to ease what had become an increasingly sticky situation, the Ministry of Labour refused to issue Vincent the necessary work permit and, without such a permit, it was illegal for him to appear in the summer productions.

Since the Gate Theatre was a private subscription club, Vincent had not needed work papers for his engagement there, so he went into the small role of Max in Schnitzler's *The Affairs of Anatole* at the Gate. In late June, *Twelfth Night* with Phyllis Neilson-Terry as Olivia, Lesley Wareing as Viola, Baliol Holloway as Malvolio, Leslie French as Feste, and Robert Atkins as Sir Toby Belch opened at the Regent's Park Theatre with great success. Undoubtedly, the rejected young Price was overcome with remorse at the lost opportunity to perform Shakespeare with such a professional company.

Fortunately for the shape of Vincent's acting career, Gilbert Miller had read a small item in the London *Times* that detailed the whole Price affair. Upon learning that Vincent was American, he rushed to the Gate and offered him the part of Prince Albert in the pending Broadway production of *Victoria Regina*. Vincent was, of course, delighted. By the time he finished his work at the Gate, he had completed his education at the esteemed Courtauld. He had also completely absorbed the British atmosphere, and, although he loved London very much indeed, he was homesick for America.

Little did the young actor realize that as the final curtain rang down on the Gate Theatre's rendition of *Victoria Regina*, Gilbert Miller was in New York publicizing his London "discovery" who would be playing Prince Albert opposite the much loved and respected First Lady of the Theater, Miss Helen Hayes.

Vincent Price was returning to America a star. He was then twenty-four years old.

Chapter Three

"Actors are freaks in America, and Hollywood is all freaksville. I think it was because I started my acting in Great Britain that I excaped all this. Right from the beginning I noticed people like Emelyn Williams and Gielgud were into 'everything' — writing, painting, and music."

EMLYN

Vincent Price

Gilbert Miller's lavish production of *Victoria Regina* was due to commence rehearsals in mid-November 1935. During the early fall of that year, Miller could be found all around Manhattan touting the forthcoming show and lauding the performances that Helen Hayes and the unknown Price would offer. Miller, always a showman, was never reluctant to boost the professional standing of performers under contract to him, but even the more jaded members of the inner Broadway circles were aware of the tremendous paternalism the producer was displaying toward this man named Price. And Miller, who had a reputation for importing veteran London performers to bolster the caliber of his Broadway offerings, was now having the last laugh on himself, and on those New York theater folk who had admonished his repeated habit of giving good stage roles to foreigners. "Imagine it," chuckled Miller, "I finally hire an American actor, and I had to go all the way to London to find him!"

All the publicity that Miller was generating for the Houseman play was occurring while his young "discovery" was still in London. Vincent was preoccupied at the time with packing all the odds and ends he had purchased during his London stay, and he was also attempting to find a proper home for a very ragged black cat who had wandered into the Gate on opening night and had been adopted by the company. When the show became a hit, the cat became the troupe's mascot. Vincent, living alone and possessing a tremendous love of animals, was designated to care for the feline creature newly dubbed "Albert." As often happens, Vincent fell for Albert and when he left for America, he found he could not part with him.

At this juncture Price was nearly broke, although he had good expectancies. He had signed a run-of-the-play contract with Miller who promised him $250 weekly. Price decided to wire Miller for an advance on his salary in order to pay for the crossing back to America. When Miller received the cable, he thought his latest employee was jesting and sent a reply suggesting that Price stop fooling and return to New York. With no other feasible options open to him, Vincent was forced to choose a steerage-class ticket when booking passage on the S.S. *Aquitania*. Price did send Miller another cable, this time alerting him of the date of his arrival in New York harbor.

Publicity-alert Miller was quick to see the potential of capitalizing on Price's return. He arranged for a press conference with his young star to take place as the boat docked in New York. He did not bother to advise Price of this decision. When the ship steamed into New York harbor and the passengers eventually began disembarking from the first class ramp, everyone wondered what the commotion was about. Gilbert Miller had stationed himself at the end of the gangway with at least two dozen newspapermen in tow.

At the other end of the vessel, Price stood for a moment on the steerage gangway before setting foot on American soil. He carried topcoats over one arm, while pairs of shoes strung together by their laces were dangling over the other. Tucked firmly against his chest was Albert, one-time Siamese mascot of the Gate Theatre. Price had wrapped a scarf around the cat's body to keep him warm, and only the small, black, furry head was visible. A porter assisted Price with the rest of his luggage, passing him through Customs with a minimum of difficulty. The porter was also instrumental in maneuvering Albert past Customs officials. Vincent then hailed a taxi and sped off to his hotel.

Meantime, Miller was growing impatient waiting for his "star" to descend the lofty first class gangway. Rushing past the seamen helping the guests off the ship, Miller hastily, almost frantically began searching the ship. When he later checked with Customs and found Price had already left, Miller was forced to make abject apologies to the restless newsmen. To his intimates, Miller accused Price of "pulling a Garbo." When the producer and young actor met at the theater later in the day, the misunderstanding was eventually rectified, but not before the irate producer had ranted at his bewildered "Prince Albert" for sometime.

Rehearsals went well under Miller's professional supervision. For Vincent, preparing for this opening was easier than for the rest of the cast, as he already knew his lines and had already done the major work in developing his characterization. While Miss Hayes and the others were busily working on their role interpretations, Price was establishing himself in a new apartment he had rented in midtown Manhattan just off Sixth Avenue.

He had played Prince Albert brilliantly in London, but working opposite Hayes, the petite dynamo of the American theater, was infinitely more intimidating than appearing with Pamela Stanley at the Gate. The added pressure created by Gilbert Miller's raves about him to the press proved no small obstacle, either.

The hard work paid off for the cast of *Victoria Regina*. When the play opened at the Broadhurst Theater on December 26, 1935, it received plaudits from the critics. As expected, Miss Hayes received her usual fine notices, but it was the unexpectedly well-defined performance of Price that surprised the unsuspecting reviewers and the public. "Mr. Price," wrote Percy Hammond of the *New York Herald-Tribune,* "being princely of appearance, and a good actor besides, adds bountifully to the appeal of *Victoria Regina,* making the role pictorial, gently dignified and romantic." Brooks Atkinson of *The New York Times* added, he "...plays it beautifully enough to evoke all the romance that lay under the surface of a singular royal marriage."

Overnight, Vincent became the man of the hour about town. The daily newspapers ran feature stories on this amazing young man who had traveled from Yale to New York to London and back to New York.

Through his association with *Victoria Regina,* Vincent found his way into the upper echelons of New York's smartest society circles. Cast parties were numerous, and at many such occasions Price was requested to perform "Drink to Me Only with Thine Eyes," the song he so touchingly sang in the play. For Vincent, the best element of such fashionable parties was that they were often held in fashionable homes containing priceless collections of art. One such was the party that Jules Bache, Gilbert Miller's father-in-law, gave in his 814 Fifth Avenue residence. The Bache collection was reputed in art circles to be one of the best private groupings in America.

Vincent was dazzled by it, and, as usual, spent much of the party inspecting the works of art instead of mingling with the chic crowd.

These were rewarding days for Vincent — a young man with a considerable salary to spend, the toast of the town, and invited into the homes of the city's most cultured people. He was also perfecting his new craft working with the very best talents in the business. Helen Hayes became a good friend and tutor, and he was very friendly with George Macready and George Zucco, who were also in the company. Many afternoons were spent wandering through the galleries of New York in the company of Miss Hayes or Macready or zany, witty Beatrice Lillie, an actress known to her friends and public alike as Bea. Although there was no opportunism involved, Vincent and Macready thrived on the entrees into the art world provided by the two female celebrities. It was not only the best, but probably the only way in which the two young actors could break through the famous shell of superiority presented by a great many of the elite art dealers.

Price loved to mock the stuffy dealers, the ones he found to be self-important little men with a marked tendency toward pomposity. When he was visiting the city during his Yale years he had first encouctered many of these pedantic parasites of the art world, and now when he was accepted in their world by virtue of his present success, he rebelled at their scoffing treatment of the ordinary citizen. Somewhere within Price a seed was being planted, an inkling that would one day blossom into his plan for overhauling the twentieth-century concepts of "presenting" art to a skeptical public.

Despite his disinclination to some of the dealers, he was very friendly with the reputable ones who displayed a sincere interest in their work. Antoinette Kraushaar and Frank Rehn, two of the most praised art dealers in Manhattan, became fast and loyal friends. The sales staff at the world-famous Knoedler Gallery were also part of Vincent's intimate circle, as was Alma Reed, dealer in primitive art.

Vincent's wealth of knowledge about art did not remain a private matter for long. Soon many Broadway stars were seeking his advice concerning potential purchases. In most instances, he declined. He held that no one should buy art "just as an investment," but rather because a particular work struck an emotional chord within. Art was very personal for Vincent and, subsequently, he made suggestions only to those he knew well, like Helen Hayes or Bea Lillie.

Although the former was a tasteful collector, the latter bought very few works of art. Vincent searched for months to find something suitable for the flamboyant star. Finally he located a comic work by Modigliani and he suggested to Miss Lillie that she buy it. Although wary at first, she did, at a very low price. Years later, when the value of the Modigliani piece soared, the comic portrait was one of the actress's most treasured items.

During the run of *Victoria Regina,* Vincent was very busy indeed spending his own salary on art, a pursuit that never tired him. One of his first acquisitions was *The Defenders* by William Gropper. He purchased a Vlaminck flower piece for four hundred dollars and a pencil sketch by Modigliani for twenty-five dollars. Perhaps the biggest bargain he located was a series of Goya etchings. A Bronzini portrait was more expensive, but he admired the work so tremendously that he hardly cared. He also purchased a very funny and sexy *Noon* done by Doris Lee. Perhaps the most offbeat addition to his burgeoning collection was a poster by Toulouse-lautrec that cost him forty-five dollars. This was long before the vogue for "poster art" came into being. At the time many of Price's acquaintances privately thought their young friend had gone off the deep end with his latest buy. To pay that much for a poster was unheard of; to happily dole out the money bordered on insanity. As the years went by, though, Lautrec achieved his rightful place in the spectrum of art history, and those same associates realized the depths of Price's intuition.

The first half of 1936 was filled with excitement for Vincent. *Victoria* continued to reign on Broadway, and Hollywood began to take an interest in the newest matinee idol of the American stage. It was standard practice at the time for plays on Broadway to break for a summer respite, for in the days before air-conditioning, a stifling New York theater held little lure for prospective ticket purchasers. When *Victoria* broke in June of 1936, *Variety* reported that Vincent had gone to the West Coast for a screen test. The rumors that filtered back to New York hinted that the Price celluloid testing had gone extremely well and that several studios were anxious to sign the performer. Unfortunately, Price seemed to be balking at the contracts. He returned to New York and refused to discuss with the press what had transpired in Hollywood. Instead, he immediately thrust himself back into Manhattan life, taking time out to appear on the "Standard Brands Radio Hour with Rudy Vallee" on NBC, enacting a scene from *There's Always Juliet* with Cornelia Otis Skinner.

34

There were still several weeks to go before *Victoria Regina* resumed its Broadway engagement, and upon the advice of Miss Hayes, who agreed that Vincent was correct in rejecting Hollywood offers at this stage in his career, he accepted any type of stage work to fill in his empty hours. Because he was now considered a Broadway star, he found it easy to select from a wide variety of roles in which to hone his craft even further. He played the earl of Essex in *Elizabeth the Queen* at the Mt. Kisco summer stock company with Mildred Natwick in the title role. In White Plains, he did *What Every Woman Knows* and *The Passing of the Third Floor Back*. In Suffern, he played in *The Firebrand,* a play dealing with Benvenuto Cellini, which had starred Joseph Schildkraut on Broadway and Fredric March on screen.

All of these modest engagements were one-week runs and Vincent learned quickly that an actor did not have leisure time to waste in stock theater, what with only a week in which to learn the lines and blocking for a believable characterization. When he returned to *Victoria Regina* on August 8, he was a vastly more confident and accomplished actor.

Victoria Regina, which was still drawing patrons, continued its popular run throughout the latter half of 1936. The excitement of starring in a Broadway play had worn off, and the work of settling into a very long run began. Vincent knew that if he could develop the habit of offering a sustained performance night after night in the same play, it would prove invaluable to his growth as a performer. During the days, he continued to haunt the city's museums and galleries, most often in the company of George Macready. At night the two went dutifully back to the Broadhurst and the nineteenth century.

For the Christmas of 1936, Miss Hayes gave Vincent a landscape by Alexander Brook. One day while going through a gallery, Vincent had openly admired this particular work, so the actress later returned to the establishment alone and purchased it. Although he did like the Brook canvas, it was not his favorite, and he subsequently traded this for Lautrec's lithograph of May Belfont. Miss Hayes was aware of the transaction and approved of Vincent's new art addition, believing like Vincent that, in essence, the Lautrec acquisition was still her gift to him.

The first three months of 1937 were almost a repeat of the previous year, with Vincent performing *Victoria Regina* eight times weekly. In April, though, Gilbert Miller decided that when the play closed in May for its summer recess, he would tour the hit show around the country instead of reopening it on Broadway. Miller asked each member of the cast if he or she wished to go on tour, and many accepted. Vincent, however, declined. He believed he had reached the point of diminishing returns with the part and decided he would learn more by going into a new play. Nothing was being offered him at the moment, but he was ever hopeful.

Word of Vincent's imminent unemployment reached Hollywood, and he was promptly besieged with screen offers. *Variety* quoted a reliable source as saying that Metro-Goldwyn-Mayer had offered Vincent a long-term contract starting at fifteen hundred dollars for the standard forty-week work year. Vincent surprised a good portion of the New York theater community by rejecting that offer. Although the money was fabulous by Broadway standards, Vincent wanted the option to be free for six months each year to work on the stage. Universal Pictures, then in strained corporate circumstances, learned of Price's demand and rightly reasoned that in exchange for the much-wanted six-month clause, Price's acting services could be obtained for a far lesser figure than MGM had offered. They were correct. Shortly after *Victoria Regina* closed, he signed a seven-year contract with Universal.

The studio was then keeping its financial head above bankruptcy largely due to the contractual presence of young Deanna Durbin, whose movie musicals were a sure guarantee of large box-office returns. Other players on the company's roster were Boris Karloff, who, in tandem with Bela Lugosi or alone, was continuing to churn out low-budget, horror-film entries. There were Buck Jones and John Wayne for Western-action films, John Boles and Louis Hayward for romantic leads, an occasional big-budget picture with Irene Dunne or Margaret Sullavan; or programmer fluff featuring Wendy Barrie, Sally Eilers, James Dunn, Jean Rogers, Jane Wyatt, Walter Pidgeon, or Cesar Romero; and cliff-hanging serials starring Johnny Mack Brown, Grant Withers, and Larry "Buster" Crabbe.

Universal's general manager authorized Vincent's first studio assignment to be *Road Movie,* a programmer to star Wendy Barrie, but the executives had a change of heart and decided a popular Broadway star should be given a more deluxe showcase for his cinema debut. The picture, retitled *Prescription for Romance* (1937), starred Kent Taylor in the anemic male lead. Price was then re-scheduled to begin *That Certain Age* (1938) with Deanna Durbin under the careful tutelage of producer Joseph Pasternak, but the bigwigs at the studio decided he was too young to play the "older" foreign correspondent who is idolized by Durbin, and debonair

VINCENT PRICE UNMASKED

Melvyn Douglas, a decade older than Price, was hired for the role. Next time around at the conference table, he was penciled in for a juicy role in the latest remake of *The Storm* (1938), a melodrama to star Charles Bickford, Barton MacLane, Nan Grey, and Andy Devine. That too, as far as Price was concerned, fell through, and Preston Foster was substituted. Price was next offered a leading role, not in Hollywood, but back on Broadway. It was a new comedy entitled *Jean,* and Price accepted the bid. However the producer could not raise the necessary capital, and the show was abandoned.

During this period of artistic disillusionment, Price agreed to perform a scene from *Victoria Regina* on radio with Helen Hayes and George Macready. He then returned to the world of summer theater, where at least he was wanted, and he could at the same time improve his acting skills.

It was while he appeared in *Eden End* at the famous Skowhegan, Maine theater that he met Willard Cummings, one of the best-known art collectors in the United States, specializing in early American art. Price knew Cumming's name from his studies and was pleased to make the elder gentleman's acquaintance. Cummings was then very enthusiastic about primitive art, and he was perhaps Vincent's first important guide through it. After examining Cummings' extensive collection, Vincent became an immediate aficionado of this creative genre. Later in his life, Price gave credit to Cummings as being his first knowledgeable tutor in the primitive arts. When Vincent returned to New York later that summer, he contacted Edith Halpert of the Downtown Gallery, and she, a friend of Cummings, continued to educate the willing, apt actor-collector.

Vincent reappeared on the New York scene with renewed enthusiasm for his profession. During the summer, in addition to *Eden End,* he had appeared in stock productions of *Parnell* and *The Wild Duck.* On a personal level, he was excited about a new relationship he had begun with a young actress named Edith Barrett who had performed in *Parnell* with him. She was an art lover, too, although perhaps less knowledgeable about the subject than Vincent. In New York they began to spend a great deal of time socializing together.

Professionally, things were picking up for the available Price. He was offered the male lead in a new Broadway show, *The Lady Has a Heart* by Ladislaus Bus-Fekete. In this tale of a butler who falls in love with the daughter of a European prime minister and romances

37

her after he becomes the deputized leader of the country's revolutionists, Price's co-star was beautiful Elissa Landi, the Italian-born stage and film personality. On-screen she was perhaps best known for her sensitive interpretation of the Christian Mercia in Cecil B. De Mille's *The Sign of the Cross* (1932).

Universal was only too happy to have Price off their hands for the time being, as they could not pigeonhole him for any appropriate screen assignment. *The Lady Has a Heart* went into rehearsal in late August of 1937, and opened for a tryout week in New Haven on September 20. The preview was fairly well received, and on September 25, the play debuted at the Longacre Theater on Broadway.

Vincent again received outstanding critical accolades. "The lad should make a grand catch for Hollywood, possessing as he does both looks and ability" said the *New York Herald-Tribune*. The *New York Times* corroborated that he "...walked off with acting honors." Unfortunately, the play itself did not fare very well. The verdict was mixed at best, most of the criticism being leveled at Rufus Phillips and Watson Barratt, co-directors and co-producers of the venture. The New York aisle sitters decided the play suffered from diffuse points of views and lacked the directional focus that one director might have provided. *The Lady Has a Heart* limped along for a few weeks, helped by a promotional appearance on the "RCA Magic Key" radio show by Price and Landi who read a scene from the play. Finally the play folded after only ninety performances. (Screen rights were sold to 20th Century-Fox, who in 1938 translated it to the screen as a vehicle for William Powell and European import Annabella. The refurbished scenario was entitled *The Baroness and the Butler.*)

During the run of the ill-fated *The Lady Has a Heart,* Vincent was invited to speak at Hunter College in New York. He chose as his topic, "Why I Don't Want to Be a Matinee Idol." This luncheon talk attracted the attention of the *New York Daily News,* whose roving reporter commented on the irony that the most exciting new matinee star of the day was delivering such a talk. Irony aside, Price's talk was a success, and he was engaged to speak at thirty-one additional luncheons during the play's run, hopefully creating enough good will to sell tickets to the faltering show.

When *The Lady Has a Heart* closed, it was mid-November and no time to be out of a job. Universal was urging him to return to California, but Price wanted to take full advantage of his six-month stage clause. At this juncture, the creative team of Orson Welles and John Houseman came to the rescue. The resourceful duo were experiencing difficulties at their Mercury Theater on West 43rd Street. After a smash opening of Welles' contemporized version of *Julius Caesar,* Welles and Houseman decided the second play of their planned repertory schedule did not fully complement the Shakespearean work. Welles and Houseman decided to drop *The Silent Woman* and substitute Thomas Dekker's *The Shoemaker's Holiday* as the next attraction to be presented by the company that season. *The Shoemaker's Holiday* seemed an ideal choice; it was colorful, happy, and democratic, although it was perhaps a bit more risque than the Broadway audience was accustomed to seeing. This play, published in 1600, also had a charming, if nonsensical, musical-comedy-type plot. The problem was that *The Shoemaker's Holiday* required a large cast, much larger than could be filled by the complement of Mercury Players. Seven recruits were needed, and Vincent Price, whose availability was known, was at the top of the list. Price was invited to join the company for the run of the Dekker play at a weekly salary of $125. Vincent accepted the offer enthusiastically. Orson Welles was being hailed as the "boy wonder" of the American theater, and a position with the Mercury could be a very valuable experience.

Rehearsals for *The Shoemaker's Holiday* were as lively and erratically brilliant as was Welles' personality. The Mercury "regulars," who included Joseph Cotten, Ruth Ford, and Hiram "Chubby" Sherman, were all familiar with the pace Welles demanded from his actors. However, Vincent spent the first three weeks in a totally exhausted state. As consolation, he was able to spend a great deal of his time with Edith Barrett, the girl he had met the previous summer. Welles had cast her in the play, and she and Vincent took up their romance where it had been interrupted by *The Lady Has a Heart.* There is a touch of irony in the fact that while Vincent was interpreting the role of philandering Master Hammond onstage, offstage he was displaying the first real mature commitment to a woman in his life.

The first public performance of *The Shoemaker's Holiday* took place at midnight on Christmas Day of 1937. The Mercury had presented a special performance of the enormously popular *Julius Caesar* that evening, and at the final curtain, Welles had stepped out in front to invite the audience to a free preview of the Dekker work. It was to be a Christmas gift from the Mercury to the public. The company required only about two hours to set up the new scenery, and in the interim the audience was requested to wait outside. Some of the patrons naturally enough spent the free time in nearby Broadway taverns, telling their friends of Welles' gesture.

By the time the theatergoers refilled the theater for the special performance, the Mercury was overflowing with people standing at the back and sitting in the aisles.

The curtain rose exactly at midnight, as scheduled, and for approximately the next ninety minutes the theater was filled with the sounds of laughter and rollicking good humor. The Mercury had restored the spirit of Christmas joy, and it reverberated through Times Square as the pleased audience left the theater.

It was much the same on opening night, January 1, 1938. The critics raved about both the direction by Welles and the performances of the cast. "...the total effect is one of poetry that derives from a vital bounce, a festival surface and a love of life...." (*The New York Daily News*) *The New York Times* called it "the most entertaining theatrical event" and the New York *Herald-Tribune* hailed it as "the funniest jig of the season." The reviewers were hesitant about singling out any particular performer for particular praise, although Hiram "Chubby" Sherman received most frequent special mention. Vincent impressed his peers with a fine flair for the ridiculous.

Life at and with the Mercury in January, 1938, was very hectic indeed. *The Shoemaker's Holiday* opened on the first of the month and on the fourth, a revival of the Federal Theater's production of Marc Blitzstein's *The Cradle Will Rock* joined *Julius Caesar* and *Shoemaker* in repertory. Blitzstein's play had launched Houseman and Welles in their project #891 under a WPA-sponsored grant a few years before. The two now brought it back under the aegis of the Mercury with substantially the same cast. Then, on January 24, the Mercury company moved from their 41st Street home to the much larger National Theater in order to meet demands for ticket orders. Both *Julius Caesar* and *The Shoemaker's Holiday* were restaged to accommodate the larger stage and audiences at the National. Midst all this success and chaos, one might have expected the Mercury to pause for a breather. But, true to their spirit, yet another fresh production was planned. Welles and Houseman had wanted to do John Webster's *The Duchess of Malfi* (c. 1614) since their early days with the Federal Theater. Now they brought the poetic drama out of the proverbial mothballs and began pre-production work on it. Pavel Tchelitchew, the enigmatic artist whose major work, *Hide and Seek,* belongs to the permanent collection of the Museum of Modern Art, was selected to design the decor. Aline MacMahon was cast in the title part, and Vincent, still involved with *The Shoemaker's Holiday,* was given one of the other plum roles.

Vincent was unsure how he should formulate his characterization for the new production. But then, one day while wandering through the corridors of the Metropolitan Museum with Edith Barrett, he came across a portrait of a Medici prince done by Bronzini. In a flash, he realized he was looking at the visualization of the role he was to soon play onstage. For the next few afternoons, Vincent came to the museum to gaze only at that one Bronzini work.

Although the Bronzini obviously helped him find the character, *The Duchess of Malfi,* as interpreted by Welles and Houseman, was destined not to open. One evening after a performance of *The Shoemaker's Holiday,* Welles assembled the potential cast on the stage of the National to read the play. The results were disastrous. Apparently only Welles captured and held the extravagant Webster language, while the rest of the cast fumbled their way through the reading. Rather than fight an uphill battle, *The Duchess of Malfi* was abandoned.

At the end of January, after the cancellation of the Webster play, *The Shoemaker's Holiday* still had another three months of performances. During this time, Price and Edith Barrett were inseparable, both on and offstage. In fact, he did only one radio show in this period and that, too, was with Edith. They read a scene from the play *Ever After* on the "Standard Brands Hour" for NBC. The couple obviously took the name of the play literally, for eight days later, on April 22, 1938, they were wed. They chose a sunny Friday morning for the ceremony at the St. Thomas Episcopal Church at Fifth Avenue and 53rd Street. Dr. Roelif R. Brooks, church rector, presided over the services that were attended by Orson Welles, Walter Hampden, Blanche Yurka, Owen Davis, Harold Gould, and Arthur Byron, among others.

Edith was a Massachusetts girl from Roxbury, the daughter of Marshall Lewis Perry Williams and Edith Barrett Williams. On the maternal side, she was the granddaughter of the late Lawrence Barrett, the famous Shakespearean actor. She had made her professional debut at the age of sixteen in a walk-on part with Walter Hampden in *Cyrano de Bergerac* at the National Theater. Through the years she was seen in several Broadway productions, the most notable being *Michael and Mary* (1929), *Mrs. Moonlight* (1930), *The Perfect Marriage* (1933), *Moor Born* (1934), and *The Shining Hour* (1936). At the time of her marriage to the twenty-six-year-old Price, she was thirty-one. The difference in their ages was discounted by their close friends, who reasoned that Vincent was far more mature than his chronological age indicated.

41

The wedding party for the couple was given on the Mercury stage that same night after the regular performance. The guests included many stars of theater and radio, plus quite a few artists and dealers. Unfortunately, the couple found it impossible to take a honeymoon. Vincent had made such a good impression in *The Shoemaker's Holiday,* that Welles and Houseman had invited him to continue with the Mercury, appearing next with Geraldine Fitzgerald in George Bernard Shaw's *Heartbreak House.* Vincent felt he could not reject such a tempting offer.

The Mercury had produced three straight hits, so there were naturally high expectations for their production of *Heartbreak House.* The week it opened, *Time* magazine featured the youthful Orson Welles on its cover, showing him made up in his small role as the geriatric Captain Shotover. *Heartbreak House* debuted on April 29, 1938, seven days after Vincent's marriage. The Mercury's stock continued to soar, for they now had their fourth straight success. Once again, Price fared well with the demanding critics. The *New York Herald-Tribune* noted that Vincent was "...humorous and distinguished, an abler actor than any of his previous performances have suggested...."

Honeymoon or not, Vincent and Edith were ecstatically happy. They were youthful, in love, and working with skilled and talented people for a living wage. Vincent had developed a good rapport with Welles and wished to remain with the New York-based troupe.

Welles was then at work on what he envisioned would be his theatrical masterpiece, a work called *The Five Kings,* a play so large in scope it would require two nights to perform it. *The Five Kings* was a combination of several Shakespearean plays joined together into one. The first evening would encompass *Richard II,* Parts One and Two of *Henry IV,* and *Henry V.* The second night would conclude the rendition with all three parts of *Henry VI,* followed by *Richard III.* The same cast was to perform both nights, with some members playing as many as eight or nine different and taxing roles. It was a staggering concept, one that, to the knowledge of the New York critics, had never before been attempted. And the epic-oriented Welles seemed to be the perfect producer-writer-director-entrepreneur to attempt this near-impossible feat.

The trouble with *The Five Kings* was it would require a great deal of work before Welles would be able to present it, and, meantime, the Mercury Company had to be kept busy. Since *The Shoemaker's Holiday* had proven so viable, it was decided to run it

in repertory with Oscar Wilde's *The Importance of Being Earnest.*
Welles selected Price, Hiram "Chubby" Sherman, and Brenda
Forbes to star in Wilde's epigrammatic comedy of epicene manners,
which Welles intended to direct. While the two plays were running,
Welles hoped to complete *The Five Kings* while Houseman
watched over the everyday management of the troupe.

Unfortunately, these ambitious plans were not realized. Without
warning or notification, Chubby Sherman signed a contract with
producer Max Gordon to star in a new topical revue. George
Kaufman was contracted to direct the Sherman effort, and Welles
was left out of the picture. While Welles realized that the chance of
earning a fitting salary had lured Sherman out of the fold, he felt
betrayed by this defection. With Sherman gone, plans for the
revival of the Wilde play were dropped. Welles and Houseman
believed a suitable replacement could not be packaged as quickly as
practicality demanded, so they decided to conclude the Mercury
season with the final curtain of *Heartbreak House,* the current
production. Then Welles and Houseman signed their now-famous
CBS radio contract, which eventually led the Mercury group to
Hollywood and separate media careers in the years to come.

Since Price had never been part of the Mercury group per se, he
was in a particularly vulnerable position, having the option of
hoping for further employment via Welles-Houseman, or seeking
future Broadway parts on his own. His dilemma was resolved by a
telegram from Universal Pictures "asking" him to report to Hollywood by the end of June for his first motion-picture assignment
under his year-old contract.

Vincent left for the West Coast almost immediately. Once there,
he discovered his debut was to be in a picture called *Service de Luxe*
(1938) starring Constance Bennett, and with dependable character
actors Charlie Ruggles, Helen Broderick, and Mischa Auer supporting her. Screwball comedies of the vintage of *My Man Godfrey*
and *Nothing Sacred* were still in vogue, and Universal hoped to
cash in on the renewed interest in Miss Bennett's sagging movie
career, resulting from her appearance opposite Cary Grant in
MGM's *Topper.* Vincent learned he was to be cast as a wom-
an-dominated young inventor from upstate New York who comes
to Manhattan where he not only merchandises his revolutionary
tractor, but also falls in love with the personable head of a luxury
service company, played by the dynamic Bennett. The plot was
frail, the character types strictly of the cliche sort, but with a little

luck this above-par production — by Universal's far from de luxe standards — might do sufficiently well on the release market.

Vincent received a bizarre Hollywood-style introduction to the world of moviemaking on his first day on the Universal soundstages. It was a case of a nervous newcomer caught up in the web of celluloid fancy. Director Rowland V. Lee had scheduled a love scene between Bennett and Price for the first day of shooting on *Service de Luxe*. Not only was Vincent unaware of the proper decorum and procedures for making on-camera love, but he was tremendously in awe of Miss Bennett, the willowly blonde star who was once the highest-priced actress in Hollywood.

When the cameras began to roll, the cinematic lovers looked at each other with great longing before Vincent, on cue, put his powerful arms around petite Miss Bennett. Suddenly an anguished cry came from the lady. Vincent, of course, assumed his romantic maneuverings were all in vain and he sat back dejectedly as any cast-off lover might do. But it was not the young, over-eager Price that concerned the practical actress, it was her expensive and fragile Irene wardrobe. Price's "rough" handling of her costume had nearly caused her custom-made garment to shred. The solution was found when a prop man brought out a pair of gloves for Vincent to wear. In addition, director Lee alerted the newcomer to the requirements of gentleness on-camera, even when emoting in pseudo-ardor. Director Lee and cameraman George Robinson arranged to shoot the scene frmm a different angle to conceal Price's gloves, and the remaining clinches were executed without a hitch.

Considering the shape of Vincent's later film career, *Service de Luxe* is a tremendous oddity in Price's movie canon. In the role of Robert Wade, Price was required to emote in the true leading man tradition, playing a romantic soul, whom even chic Bennett has to agree is "tall and handsome and has a mind of his own." Interestingly, Price proved to be most at ease in the heavy comedy scenes, whether interacting with brassy Broderick, eccentric Ruggles (here as the rich businessman who would rather be a noted chef), or with visionary Russian ex-nobleman Auer. Perhaps it was an unwitting harbinger of the future that Price even had a (mock) mad scene in *Service de Luxe*. Late in the story when Price is busy perfecting his three-way tractor, Ruggles' spoiled daughter (Joy Hughes) decides that she has a crush on Price and that he would make a lovely groom-to-be. However, Price is already smitten with bossy Bennett, and has no time for this maneuvering young dilettante. She insists upon visiting his laboratory in Ruggles' basement, and despite Price's pleas that she allow him to work in peace, she continues her romantic pursuit. In order to rid himself of this disturbing damsel, Price throws a bogus fit of insanity; he chases her around the room, insisting that insanity runs in his family, and finally settles the issue by placing the frightened miss on a shelf perch.

When *Service de Luxe* was released, it fared only adequately with the critics and public alike, but Vincent's reviews were good. When questioned years later about his movie debut, Price stated that about all he gained from it was a new wardrobe.

For his second film, Price was loaned to Warner Brothers for *The Private Lives of Elizabeth and Essex* (1939), a color epic fashioned to display the talents of Bette Davis and Errol Flynn. Price's experience in this elaborate feature was very different from that in *Service de Luxe*. As he later recalled, "This was a frightening experience. I was still very new to the movie business, a greenhorn, and I walked into an atmosphere you could cut with a knife."

Indeed, from its inception, *The Private Lives of Elizabeth and Essex* was a troublesome film. Miss Davis strongly objected to Flynn as Essex, as she had wanted Laurence Olivier for her co-lead. Warner Brothers, of course, wanted the box-office safety that popular Flynn brought to any picture at this time. Moreover, the role of Essex, a charming cavalier, could not have been more suited to Flynn's talent. Playful Flynn himself thought the role so "right" that he did not bother to learn most of his lines, a problem with which Hungarian-born director Michael Curtiz had coped before while working with the reckless actor.

Flynn's casual attitude toward his pivotal part did eventually cause Curtiz to adopt a ploy with the innocent Price as the bait. Curtiz knew full well that Price had once enacted the Essex role in summer stock. Every time the undisciplined Errol flubbed a line of dialogue, Curtiz would point to Vincent, cast in the small part of Sir Walter Raleigh, and say to Flynn in his thick Hungarian accent, "I get this boy to play the part." Thus, being used as a bait and a wedge did not endear Price to Flynn but as Price later said putting the situation into perspective, "his part called for him to despise me anyway. Raleigh was a rival suitor for the queen's favor."

Despite all the problems on the set, which extended to other cast members as well — especially Donald Crisp, who was displaying his own brand of independence with his self-decided interpretation of Francis Bacon — there were a few moments of levity on the sound stages. Price recalls, "We had a contest to see who had the shapeliest calves. Everyone was surprised when Donald Crisp won out over Errol." Vincent shot more scenes than were contained in the final-release print, but it was still a featured part. Not pleased with the effort, he did not protest too loudly when the Warner officials reduced his featured role to a near-cameo.

Universal then scheduled Vincent for another home-lot picture. Producer-director Rowland V. Lee, whom Price had worked with in *Service de Luxe,* was planning to lense *Tower of London* (1939) with Basil Rathbone in the role of the perverted and murderous King Richard the Third. Since Price had fared so well onstage in historical parts, Universal gave him the small but important part of the duke of Clarence. Price performed well in this movie, winning a judgment of "excellent" from *Variety.* This was the first film that Price made that could in any way be labeled a horror story, for certainly the deeds of Richard II as depicted in this film interpretation were terrifying. But, this time, Vincent was on the receiving end of the carnage.* It did give him the on-camera opportunity of working with Rathbone and Boris Karloff, both of whom would have a large part to play in Price's later moviemaking.

With three motion pictures completed, Price was now permitted his contractual six-months freedom by Universal. He left his temporary residence at Fifield Manor, where he had been lodged during his California stay, and returned to New York. Once in Manhattan, Price received two job offers, both of which he accepted. The first was to play George Washington in a Kosciusko pageant at the Waldorf-Astoria. The Polish-American evening was strictly a charity event, so Vincent received little or no pay, but there was a special reward instead. After the performance of the tableau play, he met painter Bernard Perlin. Some of the artist's works were being exhibited that night, and Vincent liked them very much. Vincent quickly hired Perlin to paint some murals in the bathroom of his 53rd Street apartment. Perlin, a struggling painter,

---

In the scene of his demise, Price, for a change on the wrong end of the mayhem, is made drunk and then shoved head first by Rathbone and Karloff into a huge vat of wine, after which the lid is closed. Price later recalled this all-too realistic scene. During the arduous rehearsals he had nearly fainted from nausea at quaffing the goblets of fake wine (diluted Coke). "It was dreadful. They fixed a handrail at the bottom of the barrel so that I could dive down and hang on to it. The liquid was water, but Basil and Boris had used the barrel to deposit cigarette butts and old bottles; I had to hold on to the rail for a full ten counts, which seemed endless, and then a couple of hefty lads opened this damp tomb and yanked me out by the heels. I got a round of applause from the crew, but I was disappointed to find my two co-stars, who had been very nice to me so far, not on the set. I thought the least they could do was lead the applause. But they appeared a few moments later with a beautifully wrapped gift — a carton of Cokes."

readily agreed to the commission. Years later, when Perlin became world famous by representing American "magic" realism at the Brussels World Fair, those murals might have been worth a great deal of money. Unfortunately, when Price vacated the apartment, Imogene Coca leased it, and the murals were painted over in the redecorating process.

The other job offer Price received was to play the male lead in the Broadway-bound revival of Sutton Vane's morality-fantasy, *Outward Bound,* to be directed by Otto Preminger. Once again, Vincent was slated to play opposite a legendary lady of the stage, this time Laurette Taylor. Florence Reed was the third star in this production.

Outward Bound opened at the Playhouse Theater on December 22, 1938. It marked the fourth consecutive year that Vincent was appearing in a Broadway play at Christmas time. This show was a mild success, receiving respectful reviews. With the approach of 1939, *Outward Bound* seemed destined for a substantial run.

The opening months of 1939 were quite joyful for Vincent. He and wife Edith were "back home" in New York where they had many friends. Also, Vincent could continue prowling around the local museums, famous and obscure institutions alike. In a gallery one day he saw the beautiful Orozco work *Zapata,* which he greatly admired. He was following through the impetus that Willard Cummings had instilled in him back in Skowhegan, Maine, concerning primitive art. Orozco, the great Mexican artist, was perhaps the best contemporary practitioner of this style. Dealer Alma Reed asked Vincent to bid for the work. He thought she must be joking, since he could not possibly afford the piece, so he ignored making an offer. After a few more days, she again requested him to bid for the work. This time, to play along with her "joke," he bid $750. To his astonishment, she accepted it.

Obviously, Alma Reed cared for Vincent very much, and preferred to have Orozco's beautiful *Zapata* in the possession of someone who truly loved it rather than someone who would relegate it to their storehouse of art works. Vincent scraped together the requisite $750 and had the painting shipped to his apartment, where once installed the piece took up one entire wall. Vincent spent a good deal of time lying on the floor looking up at his new acquisition. Finally, deciding that art should be seen in the best perspective (which was certainly not from the floor), he lent the piece to the Museum of Modern Art in New York. Years later, he sold *Zapata* to the Chicago Art Institute.

Another steady source of income for the Prices in those days was the NBC radio serial "Valiant Lady" in which Vincent performed for three months starting in February of 1939. He played the role of Paul Morrison, a villain making constant threats toward Joan Blaine as Joan Hargrove-Scott, the "Valiant Lady" of the title. Also featured on this popular audio soap opera were Judith Lowry as Stevie, Parker Fennelly as Mike Hogan, and Everett Sloane, another Mercury player, as Lester Brennan. On another radio show, "The Chase and Sanborn Hour" for NBC, Vincent was again teamed with Helen Hayes to read the proposal scene from *Victoria Regina*.

By this time Vincent's abiding interest in art was being well publicized, with emphasis on the fact that he was one of the few actors, much less one of the few Americans, to hold a master's degree from the heralded Courtauld Institute. Because of this, he began receiving legitimate offers from local colleges and schools to discuss art with the students. Thinking it might be fun and educational, he accepted. As he wrote years later in his visual autobiography, *I Like What I Know* (1959), "If you ever want to find out what you know on any subject, accept any offer that comes along to speak out publicly on it." These beginning lectures were to spawn a whole new career for Vincent, one that would steamroll, much later, into a vital and lucrative part of his workaday life.

On those days when he was not performing on the soap opera or lecturing, Vincent and his wife would regularly visit the Museum of the American Indian, the Hispanic Society, and the Morgan Library. Vincent's interests were more and more centering upon the rediscovered art of the American Indian. While the cultural life and mistreatment of the native Indian did not become a popular issue until the late 1960s, Vincent was one of the first white Americans to openly admire their achievements and their way of life. In the Indian culture he perceived an alluring simplicity, one that spoke from the heart of man instead of from the cold rationale of logic. As time passed, Vincent would become more involved with the Indians, recalling the day when, as a young twelve-year-old explorer, he discovered those ancient Indian burial grounds.

When the run of *Outward Bound* ended in the summer of 1939, Vincent and Edith headed back to California. He had made a one-day test in early April for an Irene Dunne picture, but learned on his arrival in Hollywood that the film had been temporarily postponed. Instead, he was to report to work on *The Invisible Man Returns* (1940). This Joe May-directed film was an obvious follow-up to the Claude Rains thriller made a few years before. Even though it was well received on the action-film market when it was released, Vincent did not think much of it. During a string of badly made films in the 1940s, Price looked back to this picture and only half jokingly said it was one of his favorite film roles because "I was invisible so much of the time." (Unlike Rains' foray into *The Invisible Man* realm, the transparent man in Price's outing was of good virtue and most certainly never committed on-screen murder or mayhem, for the studio had decided to continue the series and needed to have the character survive at the picture's finale.)

Still, it must be noted that this was Vincent's initial entry into the realm of the horror and science-fiction film genre. On a more personal level, the film served to introduce him to Sir Cedric Hardwicke, who became a close friend, and to reacquaint him with Universal contract player Nan Grey, who was a frequent co-star in the years to come.

Vincent functioned well with director Joe May, a fact that led directly to his next Universal assignment, the May version of *The House of Seven Gables*. Universal had a great deal of trouble pounding out a coherent script from the Nathaniel Hawthorne original. Finally, screenwriter Lester Cole perceived that by omitting the complex events leading up to the curse of Matthew Maule on the Pyncheon household, he might produce a tight-knit script. Thus the curse discarded, and along with it the complicated plot twists, cast members George Sanders, Margaret Lindsay, and Price set out to make some sense of the script's simplified story line. For Hawthorne purists, the resultant feature was a distinct disappointment, but for less-demanding souls who thrived on romantic thrillers set in a past century, *The House of Seven Gables* had its attractive moments. In publicizing the film, Universal proudly announced that the studio art directors had duplicated exactly the original house at 54 Turner Street in Salem, Massachusetts, reputed to be the legandary Hawthorne model.

Universal initially had great plans for *Green Hell* (1940) as an elaborately budgeted adventure yarn. However, shortly before production was to commence, the studio underwent another financial reversal, and budgets on all forthcoming ventures were slashed wherever possible. *Green Hell,* which starred Douglas Fairbanks, Jr., Joan Bennett, and George Sanders, along with Price, was to be a zestful, vicarious experience for filmgoers who cherished jungle adventure tales. The result was an economy-conscious hodgepodge that clearly revealed its construction on the sound stages and back lot of Universal. Of this filmic exercise,

Price was later to recall, "it was one of the funniest films ever shot anywhere in the world. About five of the worst pictures ever made are all in that one picture." Vincent was right about *Green Hell:* nearly everyone, except children, hated this puerile, cliche-ridden concoction.

Precisely because everyone knew it was so bad, the *Green Hell* set was relaxed and nearly trouble free. Apparently, everyone was having fun, most of all director James Whale. Whale was the first "star" director with whom Price had worked at Universal. He had been responsible for *Frankenstein* (1931), *The Invisible Man* (1933), *The Bride of Frankenstein* (1934), and *Showboat* (1936), among many others. Whether Whale was working outside his genre, or losing his creative touch, or even saddled with a basically unworkable script, he did not worry. He encouraged the cast to "have fun," and they did.

In the course of the melodramatic plot line of *Green Hell,* Vincent's David Richardson is killed by a poisoned arrow. Before dying, he has time for some last-minute speculation on life. Looking up from his sound-stage deathbed, he asks expedition leader Brandy (Fairbanks, Jr.), "Tell me, Brandy, is it possible to be in love with two women at the same time and in your heart be faithful to each and yet want to be free of both of them?" That impoverished line of dialogue brought down the house whenever it played, just as Vincent knew it would when he filmed it.

Miraculously, *Green Hell* turned a small profit, a fact that says more about the American audience than it does about this Universal claptrap.

After completing this jungle rot, Vincent was uneasy on the Universal lot. The economy wave was still hanging over the studio, and it came as no real surprise to Vincent when his contract was terminated.

But if Universal had no further use for Price's services, another Hollywood studio did, namely 20th Century-Fox. Studio mogul Darryl F. Zanuck, who ran his company like an army general, had built up a varied group of stock players to bolster his assorted productions. He decided that Vincent had just as much potential as another past Zanuck protege, George Sanders. Price signed on with Fox at substantially the same terms as his past Universal agreement, even with the identical proviso that he could have six months free each year to work on the New York stage.

For his first film with Zanuck's Fox, Price was assigned the important, if still secondary, role of Joseph Smith in *Brigham*

Young — Frontiersman (1940). Price left for Lone Pine in the middle of the Sierra mountain range where the Henry Hathaway-directed picture was being shot. The filming went well, with most of the attention focusing on the romance between Tyrone Power and Linda Darnell. (Dean Jagger in the title role, in typical Hollywood fashion, was relegated to a subordinate spot in the scenario.) The lensing went well, if expensively, and Price had the pleasure of meeting Brian Donlevy, another actor-art collector. Also on the set was John Carradine, destined to become one of Vincent's great friends.

It was hoped that *Brigham Young* would be Fox's prestigious picture of the year, but it was not. Even though it was advertised as "The Greatest Film Ever Made by Fox," it was not a huge success, due mainly to the fact that Zanuck had allocated a reputed two and a half million dollars as its budget. In his solid performance as the Mormon leader, prophet, and founder of the religion who is killed by an aroused mob, Price turned in his finest screen work to that date, and the critics were lavish in their praise.

Zanuck next ordered Price cast in another historical entry, *Hudson's Bay* (1940) with Paul Muni and Gene Tierney starred. Again Price, as the bewigged King Charles, earned good personal notices, but it was a relative newcomer, oversized Laird Cregar, who stole the picture even from scene-stealer Muni. The film itself fared less well with the general public, who generally complained of the slow, almost ponderous directorial touch of Irving Pichel.

In comparison to his Universal days, Vincent was pleased by his treatment at Fox. Even though he was not receiving "star" parts, he was winning meaty character roles, something he could enjoy. With no immediate roles in the offing, Price then won approval to travel back East. First stop was St. Louis, his hometown, where he performed *The American Way* at the St. Louis Municipal Opera House with Norma Terris. The whole affair was a great success, with the city honoring their favorite son with sold-out houses nightly.

Unfortunately, Vincent could not linger to bask in the glory for he had to rush to Skowhegan, Maine, to oversee the production of his own play, *Poet's Corner,* which he had written in the previous year. For his first theatrical writing, he had formed a pleasant, screwball comedy. The plot focused on the poetic son of a nutty mother and a hypochondriacal father. The poet cannot make up his mind between love (marriage) and a career. As envisioned, everyone in the play was to be somewhat zany, but the young poet's character was apparently too sketchily drawn to hold the play together. The reviews were modest, with some praising the novelty of the idea. The Lakewood Players, it must be said, gave Vincent some fine performances, and it was only movie actor Owen Davis, Jr., in the lead role, who let the playwright down.

Certainly, Vincent was disappointed. He had hoped that results would be better, and yet he was not discouraged. Almost everyone admitted the play showed potential talent, and the general consensus was that Vincent, if he worked at it, could be an accomplished comedy playwright.

Poet's Corner would prove to be Vincent's only play to date, though hardly his only written work. In later years, he would put his writing skills to other uses.

Vincent returned to New York with Edith to wait another Broadway vehicle and, more importantly, the couple's expected child. Professionally, nothing of real interest came his way, but for the first time in his career, he was looking for a specific type of role, that of a juicy villainous nature. He had an intuitive belief that his future lay in portraying bad guys, though not in the mold of a James Cagney, Edward G. Robinson, or George Raft. Rather, Price's villain was to be the type of man who wheedled his way to nasty prominence through a combination of polish and charm. Basil Rathbone, Karloff, and Carradine had all remarked that Price's voice made him a natural for such roles, and for the first time, he pondered the wisdom of such a career switch.

In the summer of 1941, after several weeks of doting over their new-born son, Vincent Barrett Price, the actor again appeared on stage. He received an offer to appear with Ethel Waters in the West Coast production of *Mamba's Daughter,* a play that had won Miss Waters great acclaim on Broadway. Vincent reenacted the role played by Jose Ferrer in New York, and the company scored great success in Los Angeles, San Francisco, and Seattle.

At the end of the tour, Vincent again faced unemployment. Even radio seemed to be a dry well for him. Old friend John Houseman from the Mercury players had asked him to do a scene from his *Victoria and Albert* on CBS radio with Helen Hayes co-featured, but that had been months before. Price's career, frankly, was stalled, waiting for the right vehicle to carry him back to stardom. In the early winter of 1941, just as it appeared his professional drive might have dissipated completely, it was dramatically refueled.

Producer-director Shepard Traube sent Vincent a copy of a Patrick Hamilton play that was currently running with great success in London — *Gaslight*. Hamilton had earlier written the eerie *Rope's End* (1929) and like this predecessor, *Gaslight* gave its audiences very satisfying shudders. Traube offered Vincent the major role of Mr. Manningham, the sinister husband who almost convinces his wife she is mad, all in order to push her into real insanity and gain control of her estate. This was just the type of image-building role Vincent had been craving. He quite naturally grabbed this opportunity.

Sometime during rehearsals, the show's title was changed to *Angel Street,* and when it opened at the John Golden Theater on December 5, 1941, it quickly became the smash hit of the season. Vincent received such rave notices from the critics that he was again dubbed the toast of Broadway. "It is an astonishingly fine characterization; forceful, modulated, cerebral and hauntingly sinister." *(New York World-Telegram)* "It is a performance beautifully filled with menace, without ever seeming too melodramatic or extravagant." *(New York Herald-Tribune)* "Vincent Price is excellent, conveying suavely and powerfully the exact quality of the writing." *(New York Journal-American)*

Others in the cast who received terrific notices were Judith Evelyn as the victimized wife and Leo G. Carroll as the ambiguous inspector.

It is impossible to underestimate the effect that *Angel Street* was to have on Vincent's career. After the disappointing Universal cinema tenure, *Angel Street* pointed the way to a new, optimistic future. Even since his days as the good Prince Albert in *Victoria Regina,* Vincent had been cast as the heroic young man or the young man whose intentions had been sorely misunderstood. As he grew older, it was obvious these undernourished assignments were leading him nowhere. Unfortunately, Hollywood producers were loath to experiment by casting Price in different type parts. *Angel Street* changed all that. As Richard Lockridge *(New York Sun)* would report on the scare drama to his readers, "Vincent Price, of all people, is as sinister as villains need to be..."

The enormous acclaim Vincent received from *Angel Street* might have had an even greater effect on his career, had not the disaster of Pearl Harbor (December 7, 1941) launched America fully into World War II, thus robbing the theater of a public that luxuriated in its idolation of stage actors and actresses. As it was, *Angel Street* would enjoy a three-year Broadway run. (It would be translated into films twice, the first time in 1940 by the British Anglo company, with Anton Walbrook — who recently played Prince

Albert to Anna Neagle's Queen Victoria on the British screen — as the dastardly adventurer. Then, in 1944, MGM filmed the suspense tale, this time starring Charles Boyer and Ingrid Bergman.)

Vincent could only remain with the hit show for a year, but almost all of 1942 was busy and rewarding. He did a great many radio programs in this period. Six appearances on the "Philip Morris Show" with Tallulah Bankhead, plus four or five dramatic renditions, gave him variety, while another daytime audio serial, NBC's "Helpmate," gave him money. Judith Evelyn, his *Angel Street* co-star, was also featured in the soap opera, was were Arlene Francis and Myron McCormick.

Another vital activity performed by the star was in behalf of the USO and other service organizations aiding the war cause. Three days a week Vincent worked as a busboy at the local stage door canteen. Fellow busboys on his shift were such celebrities as Alfred Lunt and Philip Merivale, while among the notables on k.p. duty in the kitchen were the likes of Helen Hayes, Katharine Cornell, and Jane Cowl.

It was at the canteen that Vincent belatedly realized a startling fact of life. The people he considered real "stars" — Lunt and Fontanne, the Misses Hayes and Cornell, and others — were all but ignored by the mass of servicemen who came to the free club. The *actual* stars were luminaries like Linda Darnell and Betty Grable, the Hollywood personalities who were seen on the silver screen by millions each week. This appreciation certainly influenced Vincent's future show-business career, for after the war his acting activities would be confined almost totally to films (and later to television). Since Vincent has always believed in art for the common man, perhaps it is not all that surprising that he finally turned his back on Broadway. It seems that he relied upon the Broadway stage phase to obtain his acting refinements, and not for the personal glory.

Had Vincent sought only fame and financial return, there is little chance he would have participated in the Schubert Theater's experimental-theater program during the summer months of 1942. With three weeks of rehearsal and a limited-performance engagement that paid only a token salary, Vincent undertook the part of a wistful Civil War president in *Yours, A. Lincoln.* This production was displayed on Sunday nights for several weeks.

On December 8, 1942, John Emery replaced Vincent in *Angel Street,* and the show's ex-lead, his wife, and his son embarked for California. The year-long Broadway run marked the end of an era for Vincent. Although he would appear again on the New York stage, those appearances would be extremely infrequent and rather tangential to his professional standing.

Before he left New York, Vincent traded one of his favorite Bronzini portraits for Goya's small, but magnificent, *Old Man Looking for Fleas in His Clothes.* He also purchased a watercolor by Constantin Guys. He knew he would not be able to find such treasures in Los Angeles, for the Hollywood atmosphere, at that time, was not conducive to the flowering of the fine arts.

As Vincent and family headed for the West Coast by train, he little knew that the uncertain years of the "old" Hollywood days were about to begin.

Chapter Four

"The trouble with Hollywood is that it ain't got culture."

Vincent Price

When the Prices arrived back in Hollywood shortly before Christmas of 1942, the Fox executives to whom he was under contract were still uncertain about what they should do about Vincent's career. He presented a casting problem on the studio roster. It was easy enough to typecast Alice Faye, Sonja Henie, and Betty Grable into Technicolor musicals, or to cast Anne Baxter, Gene Tierney, Carole Landis, Joan Bennett, Linda Darnell, Nancy Kelly, Lynn Bari, et al. in more visually dramatic roles. Likewise, to situate such as Tyrone Power, Henry Fonda, Don Ameche, Richard Greene, Dana Andrews, and John Sutton in appropriate leading-men roles, and to vary the special talents of such players as bulky Laird Cregar, burly Charles Bickford, and aristocratic George Sanders between character leads and villainous secondary assignments required little special work by Fox's casting directors. The studio could even typecast Milton Berle, Charlotte Greenwood, Joan Davis, and Jack Oakie as comedy relief. But what to do with Price?

Certainly, his was a marketable talent, which had been proven on Broadway. For some reason, though, that commercial potential had not yet been tapped in motion pictures. Almost his whole career as a leading man at Universal had been disastrous. Twentieth tried to approach the problem intuitively, if not logically. In Mr. Price they had under contract one of the most popular matinee idols of New York. Consequently it seemed to them that they should cast him in film roles of a similar type. But Universal had tried that with little success. Vincent himself was aware of the problem, and when he reached the studio, he requested a meeting with his film-company bosses. During that meeting he reminded them of the type of role he had just accomplished on Broadway — a villain. He believed that his style apparently lent itself to an aura of make-believe wickedness and madness rather than the heroic celluloid mold that Universal had vainly tried.

Fox went along with Price's own reassessment. He was assigned to the studio's "big" film of the year, *The Song of Bernadette* (1943), based on the best-selling novel by Franz Werfel, and directed by Henry King. Whereas Vincent had spent every night in *Angel Street* methodically driving his onstage wife into insanity, in *The Song of Bernadette* he was given the strong role of the prosecutor attempting to commit the visionary Bernadette (Jennifer Jones) to the local asylum. Quite importantly, it was his first full-fledged screen-villain casting. Edith Barrett Price was also given a small role in the elaborate picture, so shooting was doubly pleasurable.

Production decisions on the expensively mounted *Bernadette* involved two main problems. How to handle Miss Jones — who, despite a few earlier screen appearances under the name Phyllis Isley, was making her official screen "bow" here — was largely left to her benefactor, producer David O. Selznick, who had placed the actress under personal contract. But the problem concerning the tasteful presentation of this story's religious subject baffled the studio executives. America in the 1940s was an extremely religious nation and about the only thing that could anger the nation as a whole, above and beyond matters central to World War II, would have been some sort of sacrilege or anti-religious comment. Indeed, many scholars believed the main motivation of the gregarious anti-Communist forces that descended on Hollywood less than a decade later was to place God and religion back into politics; Communism was equated with atheism, hence was automatically evil. Nevertheless, from a religious point of view, Fox wanted to please everyone with *The Song of Bernadette*.

These two factors, religion and Miss Jones, led to a great deal of indecision during the shooting of this big-budgeted picture. For instance, a dispute broke out among the creative forces over whether the visions seen by Bernadette at the grotto of Lourdes should also be witnessed by the moviegoers. Weeks passed before a final decision was reached, and even then it was settled for a reason that was largely negative. Fox decided that the vision (in the form of Linda Darnell) should be shown to the audience because it was feared that otherwise filmgoers might possibly infer that Bernadette was indeed a very deluded girl. To imply her insanity would, of course, be sacrilegious, and most assuredly bring the wrath of the Catholics down upon the moviemakers.

With such an array of production problems to resolve, it took an amazing nine months to complete the filming of *Bernadette*. This in turn caused the budget to soar, one factor being that actors were employed on a weekly salary basis. Vincent was getting restless during all these delays. Never one to be inactive for long, he made a move that rocked factions of Hollywood. Later, when asked his reason for his actions, he said, "The boredom of waiting for the studio to call began to pall."

What Vincent did that so shook the foundations of the staid, conventional Hollywood community was to start an art gallery right in the middle of Beverly Hills! It was something that no one else in the celluloid acting craft would have contemplated. Such an action failed to show proper respect for the almighty studio mogul who, once an actor was on the payroll, became ruler supreme of the performer's career and often life itself. Vincent refused to be cowed by such intellectual and cultural subservience. With George Macready, his erstwhile co-star from *Victoria Regina* and fellow art lover, he founded the Little Gallery. The two movie players found space in Beverly Hills for forty-five dollars monthly. They split the costs of redecorating plus the regular expenses of inaugurating a gallery. They hired Barbara Wolferman to supervise the shop when they were occupied on the sound stages.

In many ways, the Little Gallery was a big success. From the beginning, it was crowded, although sometimes only with browsing out-of-work New York actors homesick for their friends. But these convivial hangers-on eventually began examining the art works and were immediately impressed. Within weeks, it was apparent that Price and Macready had opened a bona-fide art gallery, and not one that reflected only the more dubious tastes of the meritricious elements in Hollywood. From the start, the two shop owners decided to showcase up-and-coming talents in the art world rather than play it safe with a roomful of Goya prints. They never sold an item for more than $150 even though they had to subsidize the gallery's operation solely from commissions. The store's percentage, as in other galleries of the time, was one-third of the selling price.

During the two years the Little Gallery remained open, Price and Macready presented twenty-two solo artist shows, giving each exhibition an approximate five-week run. They introduced to the West Coast artists such as Paul Burlin, Morris Graves, and John Whorf. Macready and Price also put together the very first shows of Howard Warshaw and William Brice. The Burlin show was of particular interest, since he was to attain overwhelming fame a few years later. Macready and Price allocated over five hundred dollars just for shipping some of Burlin's gigantic canvases to California, along with the normal expenses incurred in preparing for any art-gallery opening. They hoped to recoup their costs by selling most of the work, but at the end of the exhibition they discovered they had garnered not one sale. Apparently, the new "magic" realism was too advanced for the buyers in those days.

At each opening, the Little Gallery hosted between fifty to four hundred "customers." In such diminutive headquarters, there was often an overflow into the Beverly Hills streets, and automobiles that passed at these hours might have witnessed such celebrities as Fanny Brice, Katharine Hepburn, Aldous Huxley, Barbara Hutton, Greta Garbo, Franz Werfel, Rachmaninoff, Thomas Mann, and many others, all boosters of the establishment, waiting their turn to study the latest exhibition.

One of the shop's more commercially viable shows was a one-man display of the works of John Decker, famous Hollywood artist and iconoclast. Decker, who would be immortalized in Gene Fowler's book study of John Barrymore, was a very popular movie-industry figure and almost all his works for sale were purchased. The original Decker sketch of Barrymore's head that was world famous was purchased by the equally globally famous Tallulah Bankhead.

In October of 1944, the Little Gallery received page-one coverage in the local newspapers. Anthony Quinn was admiring some paintings in the gallery with Vincent as his host, when a stranger wandered in and said, "Hello, Mr. De Mille." Actor Quinn was at the time wed to Katherine De Mille, daughter of the famous producer-director, Cecil B. De Mille, and he was more than a little sensitive about this type of open taunting. Still, Quinn was the perfect gentleman, obviously thinking an art gallery is the last place in the world to indulge in bad taste. The intruder continued pestering him, until finally the interloper began pushing the actor. Quinn, in an effort to show the man he still possessed the common touch even though married into a distinguished family, gave the man a quick left to the head that dropped him immediately.

The fisticuffs disposed with, Quinn and Price walked on to

admire a Goya that Quinn intended to purchase. "A beautiful stroke," said Quinn, gazing at the painting.

"You don't do so bad yourself," replied Vincent, still looking at the fallen warrior behind them.

The circulation of this adventurous story did a good deal to increase business at the Little Gallery. It almost appeared that the shop might begin to turn a profit. However, in the spring of 1945, when the Office of Price Administration ceiling on rentals disappeared (following the end of World War II), the landlord raised the Little Gallery rent from $45 to $175 monthly. From that point on the gallery was doomed.

Still, the cultural venture had served a vital function. For the first time, art was brought to the movie community by two of their very own. Although it was readily admitted that Price had much more to do with the taste and operation of the gallery, Macready was essential in that he brought his many friends to the shop while, at the same time, bolstering Price's enthusiasm for the enterprise. When the Little Gallery closed, the two owners split the remaining stock among themselves equally, not by price, but by choice.

Another reason the Little Gallery was important, not only to Vincent but to the rest of southern California as well, was that it served to introduce Vincent Price to the public as a reliable and steady authority on the world of art. It was during these years that Vincent began seriously lecturing on art to different groups, and everywhere his message was the same: Art Is for Everyone.

This is one of the most important facets in Price's life. Before he appeared within the American art world, the collecting of art was considered by many to be an exclusive hobby of the wealthy. In addition, the art historians and dealers catered to this prejudice. Art lectures in this country had become pedantic monologues as boring as they were stuffy. Vincent believed that attitude was all wrong, and he set out, almost single-handedly, to correct it. He did away with the traditional hogwash about "classical" art that was priced out of almost everyone's means, and encouraged people to search their own towns for unknown artists and, more simply, to appreciate the beauty of the world around them. He informed his audiences that art was personal, that it could not be dictated by critics in Paris or London or New York. He stated that the first thing to seek when buying art was to uncover an appreciation of the world itself. In short, any buyer should and must *like* what he or she buys, no matter what it is. He proselytized for modern art, the nontraditional and the primitive; but also, in the broader sense, for anything that contained inherent beauty of any sort.

ABOVE: With Edward G. Robinson promoting their "$64,000 Challenge" quiz show appearances (CBS-TV, Sept.-Oct. 1956). BELOW: As Baka in *The Ten Commandments* (Paramount, 1956).

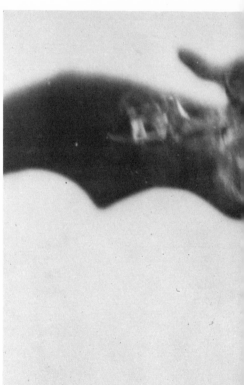

TOP: With Joan Fontaine in *Serenade* (Warner Bros., 1956). ABOVE: With Patricia Owens in *The Fly* (Twentieth Century-Fox, 1958). RIGHT: In *The Bat* (Allied Artists, 1959).

BELOW: With Brett Halsey in *Return of the Fly* (Twentieth Century-Fox, 1959). BOTTOM: With Patricia Cutts in *The Tingler* (Columbia, 1959).

TOP LEFT: With Luana Anders and John Kerr in *The Pit and the Pendulum* (American International, 1961). BOTTOM LEFT: With Jeanne Crain in *Nefertiti, Queen of the Nile* (S.F., 1961). BELOW: As Roderick Usher in *House of Usher* (American International, 1960). BELOW RIGHT: In *Master of the World* (American International, 1961).

RIGHT: With Giulia Rubini in *Rage of the Buccaneers* (Colorama, 1962). FAR RIGHT: With Ben Gazzara and Ray Walston in *Convicts 4* (Allied Artists, 1962). BELOW: In *The Raven* (American International, 1963). BOTTOM: With Michael Pate in *Tower of London* (United Artists, 1962). BELOW RIGHT: With Debra Paget in *Tales of Terror* (American International, 1962).

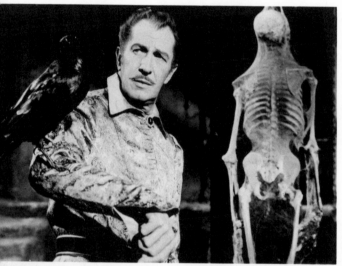

ABOVE: In *The Last Man on Earth* (American International, 1964). BELOW: In *The Comedy of Terrors* (American International, 1963).

Seemingly the public began to respond. He was asked to lecture, first at assorted colleges and ladies' groups, then at art seminars. Everywhere he traveled he urged his listeners, in the manner of the most ancient philosophers, to open their eyes and really *see*. Instead of strictly lecturing, Vincent threw open the symposiums to questions from the audience. In this way, he felt he could more personally involve people in the arts, as well as focus on individual points of interest. Such a concept also guaranteed interest in the lectures for both audience and speaker, in that everyone in the gathering had the option to participate and to challenge one another on any point in regard to the subject at hand. As Vincent would later pridefully admit, "I spoke everywhere on everything and have ended up with the satisfaction of being in love with my lecture audiences and hopeful that they love me, too."

Between filming *The Song of Bernadette,* running the Little Gallery, and executing the lectures, Vincent was a continually busy person, which was just what he liked to be. He also began serving on selected art juries here and there, nothing of major consequence, but a good beginning in that direction.

The post-*Angel Street* move to California was vital to shaping the rest of Price's life, and films were to be but a small part of the change that occurred. Because of the cultural wasteland that existed in many portions of southern California, Vincent found himself stimulated to help fill in the gaps, something he might not have found necessary on the East Coast. While he had been an appreciator of art while living in New York, he became an activist for art while residing in Hollywood. This was an important transformation in his character during the 1940s, one that has remained with him to the present.

When filming was eventually completed on *Bernadette,* Fox assigned Vincent to a good-guy role in the screen version of Maxwell Anderson's Broadway show, *The Eve of St. Mark* (1944). If the part of the rich southern boy had not been written as a comic relief in the plot, Price's part in the picture could almost have been considered sympathetic, but in no way matching the teary Americana performance of the picture's handsome lead, Fox player William Eythe.

While producer William Perlberg and director John Stahl were finishing *St. Mark,* studio boss Darryl F. Zanuck was guiding his personal project, *Wilson* (1944) to completion under the direction of Henry King. This multi-million-dollar feature, lensed in color, was aimed at being the studio blockbuster of 1944, a historical lesson that was supposed to be both edifying and entertaining for all Americans. Vincent was assigned the small role of William McAdoo, aide and son-in-law to Woodrow Wilson (Alexander Knox). This was neither a good-guy nor a bad-guy role, just one that played straight into the hands of furthering the action of the lengthy (154 minutes) plot line. It is interesting to note that Price offered one of his more restrained, yet telling performances here, and obviously felt at home in building a characterization around such an intelligent real-life figure.

When Price's latest Fox screen efforts finally reached the screen and began garnering quite respectful reviews for the actor, the studio took Price's career more seriously. The home-lot executives were particularly impressed that the critics had responded to Vincent's trenchant performance as the implacable, regal prosecutor in *Bernadette*. The *New York Herald-Tribune* was among many who singled out his acting as "excellent." The studio promptly cast him in a George Sanders-type cad role in the upcoming *Laura* (1944).

This picture, destined to become a screen classic, was plagued with troubles and delays from the start. Rouben Mamoulian walked off the project early in pre-production, and fellow director John Brahm declined the take-over offer. Only Continental director Otto Preminger was willing to guide the project. At this point, author Vera Caspary almost sued the studio to prevent the picturization. She had read the proposed scenario and flew into a rage with Preminger, who had agreed with this concept of the story line that was contrary to her original ideas. Finally Fox hired additional screenwriters to doctor the screenplay. The scenario ended up being a compromise: Caspary was victorious in having the characters fleshed out, while Preminger won the battle of plot details. Regardless of the in-fighting, when *Laura* was released, nearly everyone connected with the picture received proper acclaim. Vincent, portraying the lily-livered, lay-about Shelby Carpenter, further convinced his film bosses that he should continue to portray more villainous, acerbic roles. His scenes with co-star Clifton Webb were often pointed out as some of the picture's highlights.

Price was next rushed into *The Keys of the Kingdom* (1944) as a vanity-ridden priest, rightly named Mealy. Because this was only Gregory Peck's second (starring) film role, and since his first film had yet to be released when this was shot, Fox surrounded the new leading man with an exceptionally strong support cast, including Price, Thomas Mitchell, Edmund Gwenn, Sir Cedric Hardwicke, and Anne Revere.

VINCENT PRICE UNMASKED

Fox had recently paid a great deal of money for the screen rights to Lajos Biro's past stage success, *The Czarina,* believing it was an apt vehicle for director Ernst Lubitsch to display his very commercial "touch." Lubitsch worked on pre-production of the feature, but when he became to ill to direct, Fox substituted Otto Preminger as director. It was hoped that Preminger would do for this film, called *A Royal Scandal* (1945), and its star Tallulah Bankhead what he had just accomplished for *Laura* and Gene Tierney. Sadly, he did not or could not. Preminger has never been truly capable of a light touch either in cinema or on the stage. Unfortunately, this frivolous script badly needed just that, and this had been the reason why Fox had initially turned the property over to Lubitsch. The lethargic pacing of the intrigue at the court of Catharine the Great received a colder welcome from filmgoers than anyone could have imagined. A few kindly critics noted that Vincent, as the French ambassador, was "extremely amusing." (*The New York Daily News)* At this point, it was back to menacing meanies for Vincent. In *Leave Her to Heaven* (1945), he was cast as the evil prosecutor. In this film version of Ben Ames Williams' popular novel, he was co-featured with Gene Tierney of *Laura* fame, and again he met with great success. Director John Stahl was well aware that if given an occasional free rein, Price could enliven the proceedings with an element that *The New York Post* chose to call the "luxury of the bravura." As Tierney's former beau and the relentless district attorney, he made his relatively few on-screen moments count heavily.

Leave Her to Heaven probably guaranteed for Vincent his growing identification with villainous theatrics. Since coming to Fox he had appeared in three astonishingly successful features: *The Song of Bernadette, Laura,* and now *Leave Her to Heaven.* In all three he had played either the villain or a complete wastrel; in short, a cad. Vincent was becoming the country's favorite bad guy, and one of the most persuasive actors of his type.

Naturally enough, Fox wished to take advantage of this public acceptance, so they provided him with his first solo starring part in a modest vehicle called *Shock* (1946), directed by Alfred Werker. As Dr. Cross, Vincent played a homicidal physician who finds that the sole witness to his crime is now a patient (Anabel Shaw) under his care. Admittedly the film was a "B" picture, with a cast that featured Lynn Bari and Frank Latimore, but for Price it was at least some kind of a bid for cinema stardom.

When *Shock* debuted at New York's action-film house, the Rialto, it met with some rough critical forces who took high exception to the movie's premise. Bosley Crowther (*The New York Times*), for one, objected to the fact that this dual-bill item had done psychiatry a great disfavor by making the arch foe (Price) a doctor of the mind. Crowther argued that this relatively new medical area needed a great deal more public understanding rather than demeaning at the hands of the entertainment world. John McManus (*PM*), for another, was even more outraged. He alerted his readers, "I have seen many irresponsible, meretricious and sometimes sickening films in my time but *Shock* is the first one that ever literally turned my stomach."

Above and beyond this understandable carping (Anabel Shaw played the distraught wife of a World War II P.O.W. who is on the brink of a nervous breakdown as she doubts whether her G.I. husband is still alive), Price received mixed reviews for *Shock*. "He plays it with a dazed intensity which makes one suspect that he is sleep-walking in several scenes." (New York *Herald-Tribune*) On the other hand, *The New York Post* applauded, "I like the Vincent Price type of killer-medico better than the grosser examples by men like Lionel Atwill, John Carradine and Bela Lugosi."

Price could have thereafter returned to the ranks of supporting parts. However, the timing was right for choicer parts. Fox had again paid a large sum for a novel, this time Anya Seton's Gothic romance, *Dragonwyck,* which studio head Darryl F. Zanuck decided to personally supervise as a massive 1946 release. He chose Joseph Mankiewicz, producer of *The Keys of the Kingdom,* to make his directorial debut with the thriller. When Zanuck's actress favorite, Gene Tierney, was selected to portray the nine-teenth-century heroine, it was felt that Price, who had played so well with her in previous films, would make the perfect foil for her. If Price had been hesitant about dominating the proceedings in *Shock,* he exhibited no such timidity in *Dragonwyck,* providing a fully shaded, yet oversized portrayal of the upstate New York patroon who is tyrannical, sensitive, and deranged. The studio's faith in Price's potential was well founded, for the majority of critics were mightily impressed by his portrayal of the peculiar Nicholas Van Ryn, the last of the Dutch patroons. "Vincent Price's characterization of a proud, cultured man disintegrating into a crazy drug fiend is the most arresting performance in the film." (*The New York Daily News)* The New York *World-Telegram* was even more prophetic in its praise, "Vincent Price, who has become Hollywood's great master of these roles of slinking suave villainy, bolsters his standing still further as he moves through the turbulence of this picture."

VINCENT PRICE UNMASKED

Industry observers who had been following Price's Hollywood sojourns for the last several years were not amazed when Vincent was touted as a likely contender for an Academy Award nomination. Sadly, he was not nominated. However, looking at the situation realistically, it would have been nearly impossible for Price to beat out that year's actual Best Actor winner, Fredric March of *The Best Years of Our Lives*.

During the making of this stream of Fox features, Price continued to give lectures and appear on art juries, although his free time for such cultural outlets was quite limited. He was in great demand on his studio home lot, and in the three years since he had come to Hollywood to stay, he had appeared in nine features. After *Shock*, Vincent had requested studio permission for a leave of absence to go to New York to appear in Jerome Chodorov's *Comedie Francaise*, but Fox refused, citing the pending *Dragonwyck* as the reason. Fox had also assigned him the only lead in *One-Man Jury* to be filmed by low-budget Fox producer Aubrey Schenk (of *Shock*). Price was to have played an idealistic newspaper publisher who becomes involved in a murder. Vincent dropped out of this picture when *Dragonwyck*'s production schedule was established.

More disappointing was Price's actual work on *Forever Amber*, in which he played King Charles II, a repeat performance from his 1940 film, *Hudson's Bay*. He had been working for seven weeks in the gargantuan version of Kathleen Winsor's sexy, historical, best-selling novel of Restoration England when Darryl F. Zanuck decided that director John Stahl had to be replaced and that British import Peggy Cummins was not living up to expectations as the infamous hussy. When the three-million-dollar movie went back into production, Linda Darnell was playing the blonde-whore lead, Otto Preminger was directing, and George Sanders, long a competitor of Vincent's for choice movie roles, had inherited the part of the foppish British monarch. When the much-heralded picture was finally premiered in October, 1947, its built-in box-office appeal carried it to financial success. While the film itself and Darnell in particular were scorned for their ineptness, Sander's epicene performance* received its critical due as one of the epic's few genuine bits of entertainment, even if the characterization did border on the excessive. One can only wonder how Price's interpretation of the British monarch would have been greeted by the critics and public alike, and how that reception might have affected the future shape

Sanders would again play Charles II in "The King's Thief" (MGM, 1955).

65

of his screen work. As it was, rumors were adrift in the movie colony that Price's inadvertent disagreements with a faction of the Fox hierarchy had been at the root of his replacement in the *Amber* reorganization.

After leaving *Forever Amber,* Price and Peggy Cummins moved over to *Moss Rose* (1947), a far less important property, but one that had its own merits as a leisurely paced whodunit. Victor Mature of the rippling biceps and the sneery smile was cast as the handsome menace of this period thriller, with Ethel Barrymore and Price (as a polite, patient Scotland Yard man!) present to give the leads more than adequate on-camera support.

For personal reasons, *Moss Rose* is a key film in the Price canon, for it marks the final picture under his Fox contract. In the post-World War II changeover on the studio lot, he was considered a dispensable, too costly asset.

During his Fox years, Vincent had not only been prolific in his movie career, but he had performed on a score of radio dramas as well. Often on these anthology programs he had the opportunity to try his hand at enacting parts handled on-camera by his professional rivals, as with *Hangover Square, The Lodger,* and *A Scandal in Paris.* One of these radio outings was of particular interest and pleasure to Price. In the summer of 1945 he did *Flesh and Fantasy* for the "Screen Guild Players" on CBS radio, and he had the chance to work with Edward G. Robinson. He had had frequent meetings with Robinson during the life of the Little Gallery, and until Vincent arrived on the Hollywood scene, Robinson had been considered the number-one authority on art in the movie community. Along with Donlevy, Hardwicke, and Macready, Robinson and Price shared the intrinsic love of beauty that was so absent in the glib surface of Hollywood. Over the years, Price and Robinson became close friends, even though Robinson's taste in art was much more classical than Vincent's.

During these busy California years, Vincent and Edith Price had set up a permanent home in the Los Angeles area. They bought the old Walter Lang mansion in Benedict Canyon, Santa Monica. It was flat-roofed, a combination of the rustic and Spanish styles of architecture and made of rough pieces of cement. The couple repainted and redecorated the entire place by themselves, even taking turns pillaging the vegetable garden for sweet returns.

Aside from his growing renown as both actor and art historian, Vincent was also acquiring quite a reputation as something of a gourmet chef. He and Edith entertained royally and often.

Frequently the invitees were the delighted guinea pigs for one of Vincent's most recent gastronomical discoveries. The Price heir, Vincent Barrett, who was called Barrett, was fast maturing. Vincent was deliberate in spending a great deal of time with the lad, often driving down to San Diego to tour the marvelous zoo with him. Vincent combined the education of religion and art by telling his son parables from the Bible while showing him some of the great works of art depicting the various Christian scenes. He and Edith encouraged Barrett to follow whatever interests came naturally, and neither parent forced their son into preconceived molds.

When his Fox contract expired, Vincent was offered the continuing radio role of Simon Templar in the popular series, "The Saint," a sleuth character made most famous by none other than George Sanders in a series of early-forties RKO "B" pictures. Price accepted the offer, which guaranteed him financial remuneration on a continuing basis between free-lance assignments for the next several years.

Money was certainly becoming more important to Vincent, but not for the obvious reasons. During the Fox years he earned approximately $100,000 annually from all his assorted activities. Never a miserly type, Price deployed the income to enjoy the good life. In addition to the Benedict Canyon home, Vincent was building one of the finest collections of art in the United States. He was constantly buying or trading new acquisitions, or exploring the galleries in many cities for likely future purchases.

Vincent, if not the biggest star in the Hollywood galaxy, was definitely one of the most popular with the people in the industry. His keen intelligence and outrageous sense of humor marked him as a constant companion for the most amiable of the film and art crowd. His lack of pretension was much appreciated, and a dinner party at his home would include as many people from the crew as from the cast and management.

Perhaps his likability was vital in his wavering career as a free-lance performer. Universal gave him a role as a treacherous guy in Michael Gordon's first film effort, *The Web* (1947), released after *Moss Rose*. After that disappointing, yet commercially viable, assignment he was hired by RKO to play a wicked magician opposite Henry Fonda's upstanding ex-G.I. in *The Long Night* (1947). Even overlooking the fact that it was a slavish, pale remake of the French *Le Jour se Leve* (1939), the film lacked proper pacing. Director Anatole Litvak was so consumed with his passion for creating the appropriate atmosphere of tawdry evil surrounding a bleak middle-eastern mill town, that he devoted too little energy to coaxing coherent performances from his male players. For the first time in years, Price floundered in front of a camera, and it showed in his filmed performance.

Universal got Price back to appear in what would be his first film musical, *Up in Central Park* (1948), starring Deanna Durbin and Dick Haymes. Vincent was cast to type, if not to physical mold, as the corrupt Boss Tweed in this sloppy rendition of a recent Broadway hit. Said one New York daily of Price's impersonation, "Vincent Price, tall, aristocratic, and British accented, is surely the strangest portrait of short, squat, bearded and grafting Boss Tweed ever offered to a bewildered citizenry." Physical resemblance to one side, Price provided an interesting combination of hissable villainy with occasional shades of a cultured, sympathetic ideology. He even had occasion to talk-sing a bit of a song with a title he must surely have appreciated, "May I Show You My Currier and Ives."

While Price was on the Universal lot making the disappointing *Up in Central Park,* Bud Abbott and Lou Costello were on adjoining sound stages preparing the first of their mock-horror screen exercises, *Abbott and Costello Meet Frankenstein* (1948). With Price so readily available, it was decided to shoot a sight gag using the Invisible Man character Price had last played in 1940. For the joke finale scene, he did a few days work, mostly dubbing in the voice of the transparent figure, picked up his pay check, and walked away from the effort.

During and after his artistically unrewarding Universal chores, Vincent went on an art rampage, scoring the citizens of Los Angeles for their seeming lack of overt interest in art, and helping to organize a West Coast Modern Institute of Art. Both extracurricular activities went hand in hand, each contributing to the other.

When Walter Arensberg's collection of early Cubist art was being heralded as one of the "wonders" of Los Angeles, Vincent became friendly with him and increasingly aware of the fact that Los Angeles really had no suitable place to store a collection such as Arensberg's. For this reason he enlisted the aid of Richard Sisson to devise a scheme that would hopefully rectify the situation. The two hatched a plot to inaugurate a museum devoted primarily to contemporary art. For weeks Vincent covered all bases in an attempt to start the project rolling, i.e., raising money, arranging space, and negotiating for possible art pieces for the collection. Edward G. Robinson helped a great deal, as did Fanny Brice, but from the beginning it was Vincent's project. In the end, Price raised the necessary ten thousand dollars and acquired an empty loft next door to Romanoff's restaurant. Kenneth Macgowan, later of UCLA, was selected to head the project on a full-time basis, and soon the Modern Institute of Art in Los Angeles was a reality. Ironically, it was by then too late to make a bid to acquire the Arensberg collection, which eventually was housed in the Philadelphia Art Museum.

Vincent had to browbeat quite a few Los Angeles citizens to propel the museum project forward, and the particular target of his scorn was the upper echelon of the motion-picture industry. Whether the purpose was to embarrass them into giving money to the arts or whether he was just speaking his mind, his remarks about Hollywood, tainted with his rapacious humor, became front-page news around the country.

"The trouble with Hollywood," he stated, "is that it ain't got culture. It's a band of characters with pretty faces or broad shoulders who don't give two cents about the higher things in life. Most movie stars just pretend to be highbrow because they figure it's the smart thing to do. But it's just lip service."

This unvarnished allegation by Price surprised much of middle America, which naturally assumed the movie people were as interested in art as they generally professed to be. His irate comments even might have raised the hackles of a few inmates of the film colony, but the important thing as far as Vincent was concerned was that he had raised the needed museum money. Perhaps the blow was softened by a diplomatic rejoinder.

"Many Hollywoodians may have good taste and an interest in culture, but they certainly hide it. They're afraid they'll be branded as sissies if someone finds out they write poetry or own a painting. They're so timid about culture."

Excluded from this tirade were Miss Brice and Mr. Robinson, of course, and some surprising art lovers like Burgess Meredith, John Hodiak, and Joan Crawford.

After the money was raised, volunteers helped to organize the new cultural mecca. People from the community helped paint the walls and build partitions and scrub and wax the floors. It was like a ground-swell movement on behalf of the arts. At one committee meeting it was decided that the beige in a dress worn that day by Fanny Brice was perfect for the walls. Miss Brice then removed the garment and left it for the painters to match the color.

Price and Macgowan and the rest of the board huddled together to select a director. They decided upon Kenneth Ross, critic and one-time galery director. Before long, the institute was officially open. Its first show was "Modern Artists in Transition," and it fulfilled the expectations of all. It was daring, original, bold, and beautiful. Most of all, it was art, an art that the local people had a hand in creating.

True to form, the memberships at the two-, five-, and ten-dollar levels boomed. Within a year, over five thousand memberships in those categories were filled. Even the newspapers supported the institute, so much so that Kenneth Ross was named City Art Commissioner a year after getting the institute under way. Ross was succeeded by Dr. Karl With. Unfortunately, Dr. With did not have much occasion to innovate, since the wealthier members of the community persisted in shunning the cultural center. The institute was forced to close about two years after its opening. There were two basic reasons for the failure. The first fault was that few people in Hollywood would loan paintings from their personal collections for exhibit at the museum. That meant the museum was forced to borrow most of its works from outside the community and to constantly barter with other institutions for exchanges. The second factor had been foreseeable at the start, namely a lack of perpetuating funds. Although the general citizenry supported the establishment, the wealthier members of the Los Angeles environs would not pledge enough money to nurture the modestly budgeted foundation.

Nevertheless, it had been a grand time while it lasted, and Vincent had poured considerable money, time, and soul into the project. Still, when the end came, Price almost expected it. He knew that *all* members of the public needed to be educated in the arts before they would support a museum that reflected the non-traditional approaches. For that reason, he continued to accept as many lecturing spots as he could. He felt that would be the territory where the battle finally could and would be won: the interpersonal exchanges of different points of view contributing to the eventual awareness of the masses.

In this period he was also being asked to serve on more art juries, a duty he always accepted with delight. One such chore in 1948 led him into deep water again. He and co-jurors Donald Baer and Earl Loran chose fifty paintings to represent a Los Angeles show featuring West Coast artists. This period saw the beginning of Senator McCarthy's Communist witch hunts, and this irrationality tainted this art show almost as much as it did the film industry a few years later. What happened was that a beautiful rendition of *A Ruined Church with Figure* was termed by some as anti-religious and, therefore, Communist. A New England primitive much in the Grandma Moses mold, entitled *Little Red Schoolhouse,* caused the biggest furor. Critics felt the schoolhouse was *too* red, and labeled the painting an out-an-out Communist work. Needless to say, the show was a disaster. But Price was beginning to accustom himself, and those who worked with him, to the violent reactions provoked by art.

Later in 1948, Vincent served with other celebrities as an auctioneer for a Bonds for Israel "Art Affair," and again was responsible for bringing a great deal of money into the till, a sum estimated at over $50,000.

As busy as he was with motion pictures, art, lecturing, plus the almost constant radio appearances, it was little wonder that things were functioning less well on the home scene. On May 10, 1948, Edith Barrett was granted a divorce from Vincent, winning custody of Barrett, plus $330 monthly alimony and $330 monthly child support. Also included in the settlement were the Benedict Canyon home and a $25,000 insurance policy.

Suffering from the post-divorce blues, Vincent, in the winter of 1948 purchased a dog named Joe, whose breeding consisted of "57 varieties." Joe was a dog like most any other, except perhaps his master loved him more. Years later, Vincent would write an entire book devoted to Joe, singing his praises to the world. The animal lover in Price is perhaps the most difficult to establish on paper. One would appear a bit foolish listing the acquisitions of various pets and describing how kind the owner was to them. But Vincent has spent his entire life in the company of animals of all different shapes and sizes. He has cared for them and loved them, above and beyond the call of any duty.

Another companion during this difficult time, beyond his occasional visits with son Barrett, was fashion designer Mary Grant. Vincent was regularly seen in her company and rumors floated through Hollywood about a possible second marriage. After all, gossips insisted, Vincent and Mary shared a love of art, a love of fine cooking, and a love for their work. Finally, the insiders-outsiders were proven right. On August 8, 1949, Vincent and Mary were wed in Tijuana, Mexico. Perry Rathbone, distinguished director of the St. Louis City Art Museum, served as best man.

In the meantime, Vincent had done more films. In 1948 he played Richelieu in MGM's colorful rendition of *The Three Musketeers,* a lavish version more noted for its trappings than verisimilitude. Price's part, as directed by George Sidney, carefully disguised the fact that he was a cardinal in the French court, so that religious-oriented moviegoers would not be offended that the character was such a grasping soul. Far less prestigious was Vincent's work in Universal's *Rogue's Regiment* (1948), a potboiler showcasing hard-boiled Dick Powell. In this silliness that few on either side of the camera could take seriously, Price performed as an antique dealer, who was the villain, but an aesthetic one. He went back to MGM for *The Bribe* (1949), which attempted to make box-office magic of the new screen team, Robert Taylor and Ava Gardner. One of the picture's few unique qualities was that three of its supporting stars were all art lovers: Price, Charles Laughton, and John Hodiak.

Every actor has certain films in his career that he hopes will be lost for all time through some kind act of God. One of Vincent's is surely his next, Universal's *Bagdad* (1949), a cloak-and-dagger entry geared to show off the cinematic beauty of redheaded Maureen O'Hara in a juvenile romantic adventure yarn of the desert country. Price, however, unlike his prior Fox films, displayed no restraint in enacting the wicked Pasha, a lascivious, avaricious, comic-strip figure. It seemed the worse the caliber of a film, the more outrageous would become Price's interpretation of the character. And no one seemed to complain too loudly, least of all the kiddies and action-filmgoers for whom such pictures were hastily constructed. As Price reasoned, "People love to see a man enjoying his work."

After a run of some eight rotten films, Vincent finally won a few decent roles. The first was *Champagne for Caesar* (1950) made with director Richard Whorf at United Artists. A witty satire on radio giveaway shows, Vincent gave an alarmingly satirical performance that helped balance Ronald Colman's suave underplaying as the genius.

Another even more robust entry was entitled *The Baron of Arizona* (1950), done for the Lippert independent company. Young Samuel Fuller, presently a cinema cult figure, was given his first opportunity to direct a feature, and the budding craftsman made much of the opportunity, embellishing his account with solid cinema values. Although the black-and-white feature was not received with hosannas when it was initially released, it has gained in international reputation since then, perhaps in Europe more than America, or in *auteur* circles rather than with the general film audience. *The Baron of Arizona* rightly remains one of Price's personal favorites. Again, he was a villain, but this time he was also the protagonist of the piece, a con man who nearly steals the whole territory/state of Arizona from the United States of America. At the film's conclusion, he confesses his ingenious crime, thus making himself a celluloid hero of sorts. In the expansive characterization, Price played the complex role with intensity and variety.

Thereafter, Vincent returned to Universal to make a bread-and-butter picture, *Curtain Call at Cactus Creek* (1950), which allowed him, Donald O'Connor, Eve Arden, and other members of the cast to overact as much as they wished. It is interesting to note that Price never displayed any visible embarrassment in tackling these undemanding, childish screen assignments. There was never a tinge of condescension or unbridled superiority about his jovial capering in such lackadaisical double-bill fodder.

Vincent and his new wife Mary had been house hunting during this period, and they finally selected and purchased a seventeen-room Beverly Hills mansion that had once belonged to a Texas oil man. The newlyweds were kept busy converting this gigantic house into a true home. Vincent installed bookcases throughout the house, and moved his private collection to this new "museum." A few years later, when the pair were being interviewed on television's "Person to Person," host Edward R. Murrow termed their home "the biggest do-it-yourself project in America."

It was also in 1950 that Vincent was elected to the Board of Directors of the Los Angeles County Museum. This was a post he held for many years.

But perhaps the most dramatic development of Vincent's life at this time was the advent in Hollywood studios of television production on a full scale. Indeed, there was not one performer in Hollywood who was not affected by TV in one way or another. Vincent believed television would prove a good medium for him, and he promised himself he would appear on the home screen whenever possible. He launched his new career by appearing as a celebrity guest on "Pantomine Quiz" and in a few episodes of "Saturday Night Revue with Jack Carter." As the video industry grew, he would take an active part in many of the early "live" dramas, as well as literally hundreds of single episodes in the filmed series that followed. In many interviews he gave during the 1950s, Vincent continually stressed the point that right away he decided to work on "whatever television shows would have me." He went on to emphasize that television gave the actor an opportunity to play many varied roles in a short period of time. And, of course, it gave the player both tremendous professional exposure and a lucrative adjunct to his yearly income.

But at this point, it was radio and not television that was pointing the way to Vincent's professional future. Although he continued as Simon Templar in "The Saint" on NBC, he did three CBS radio dramas that were significant: *Bloodbath, Three Skeleton Keys,* and *Present Tense.* All were dramas of the macabre, a form in which Vincent excelled because of the rich deepness of his voice. The subtle menace contained in his full-bodied voice was naturally suited to scaring the wits out of most pliable souls, a fact that moviemakers had not as yet comprehended. Certainly he was playing villains in films, but these parts tended to resemble the Sir Jaspers of Victorian melodrama more than the frightening bogeymen of the macabre.

On the film front, producer Howard Hughes cast him in *His Kind of Woman* (1951) with Jane Russell and Robert Mitchum. Miss Russell was still under an exclusive contract to the eccentric billionaire-film mogul, and this feature was just another in a line of vehicles designed to exploit her famed bustline. Critics might have carped that the on-camera combination of Russell and Mitchum was animally magnetic but dramatically deficient, but they had to admit that Price as a narcissistic Hollywood matinee idol was keeping one jump ahead of the film audience in laughing at this very oversized interpretation.

To keep his hand in stage work, Vincent performed at the Las Palmas Theater in Los Angeles in *The Winslow Boy,* with Jane Wyatt as his co-star. The show ran for three weeks in November, 1950, which included extra performances added because of the production's popularity with theater-goers.

In December of that year, he launched a West Coast lecture tour, speaking on "The Responsibilities of the Actor and Citizen Today." Part of the responsibilities detailed in his prepared talk was the actor's obligation to sensitize himself to the beauty in the world — in other words, man's attempt to express himself in art.

At about the same time, the collector side of Vincent Price inspired the celebrity to acquire a painting by a young unknown American for two hundred dollars. The artist was Jackson Pollack. An oft-told anecdote about Vincent and Mary Price involves another painting by an equally then-unknown craftsman, one Richard Dieberkorn. One night one of the guests at a dinner party given by the Prices stared at the Dieberkorn canvas for a long time, displaying obvious disdain. Finally, the guest turned to Mary and asked, "What do you call this?" Mary turned on one of her sweetest smiles and demurely replied, "We call it 'We Like It.'"

Vincent was lured to France in the summer of 1950 to begin filming *The Adventures of Captain Fabian* (1951) for Republic Pictures. This mini-swashbuckler was completely packaged around star-(alleged) scripter Errol Flynn, who had associates filling each production job. Flynn himself was late in arriving, and since he was the unofficial producer as well as the potentially lucrative star, the film could not go on without him. This situation was quite all right with Vincent, because the four weeks he spent with Mary waiting for Flynn to appear on the sets was like a paid vacation. He and Mary rented an automobile and spent the weeks exploring the back roads of France, stopping at interesting small villages to satisfy either their artistic or culinary appetites. They did not hesitate in purchasing several art works and shipping them back to their California home. Vincent once described this idyllic period "the last gasp for the middle-income collector." Indeed, those were the days when one could still buy art at amazing bargains, if one bothered to seek out such "steals."

Flynn finally arrived on the set, and the one-hundred-minute feature was shot, to the misfortune of all. Upon its release the following Christmas, *The New York Times'* critic described the costume drama of nineteenth-century New Orleans as "an absurd, yawn-provoking hodgepodge of romance, intrigue and swashbuckling capers." Not uncharacteristically, though, Vincent remembers the movie with fondness, but only because it provided him with an ideal occasion for a French art tour. Even the business side of the film did not work out well for most concerned. Vincent had been hired to perform in Fabian for thirty-five thousand dollars and when Flynn and company only paid him twenty thousand dollars, he had to go to court to recover the balance. It was well into 1954 before Price obtained the sum owed him.

The money dispute with Flynn et al. was not personal in any way, for Vincent and star Flynn were amiable co-players throughout the lensing and even afterward. If anything, this legal squabble just illustrated Vincent's (and his agents') practical side. He never deceived himself with illusions that he was appearing in movies to make important artistic contributions. On the contrary, Vincent was always the first to mock his own bad pictures. Since Vincent loved working and since his life-style demanded certain sums of money to maintain his interests, he has often agreed to appear in entertainment ventures of very dubious value. For a long time many people involved in the film industry have been convinced that Price makes movies only to support his artistic interests.

It was also at this time that the Prices took an extended trip through Central and South America to further explore the art of those areas, most particularly, Mayan, pre-Columbian, and primitive. Their first stop was Mexico City for a tour of the galleries and museums, which have long been the repositories of some of the most vibrant art in the world. Vincent loved the city and stayed long enough to survey a good deal of the city's magnificent range of art and architecture. Next was a flight in a private plane to Guatemala, with low flying over the archeological sights of Monte Alban and Mitla near Oaxaca. The museum in Guatemala City only served to tantalize Vincent, and he chartered a small plane for a dangerous jaunt to the heart of Mayan country — Quirigua. Vincent was completely awestruck by the Mayan ruins and remains. To this day he considers the Mayan culture to have been the most creative and productive art community in the history of man.

While in Quirigua, Vincent decided he would enjoy living in one of the nearby peasant villages for a few days, to observe at close hand the regular life of the native people. None of the natives had the slightest notion that Vincent was a famous man. They saw him only as a kind and curious foreigner who was as sensitive to their poverty as he was to their art.

Finally, though, the Prices had to continue their journey, thereafter flying to Merida in Yucatan, where connections to the centers of the Mayan culture, Chichen Itza and Uxmal, could be made. The Prices, overwhelmed by Chichen Itza, agreed that it was "a wonder of the world," a wonder that Vincent has since revisited whenever time permits.

Marina Cisternas, then the leading Spanish-language columnist in Hollywood, had been instrumental in having Vincent chosen as one of the art jurors at the first Peruvian World's Fair. He and Mary flew to Peru, where Price learned he had been scheduled to deliver a talk on Peruvian art. It also seemed that the Peruvians were raising his status in the art world, since all of them addressed him as "Dr." Price. Vincent was stunned by the news of his impending lecture, but Dr. Walter Guiezieke, an American archeologist who lived in Peru, came to his timely rescue. For the next few days, Dr. Guiezieke escorted the Prices through the wonders of Peruvian art and culture, especially the Incan art in Machu Picchu and Cuzco. Vincent was most impressed with the architecture of the Incas, the polychromed pottery of the Nasca and Chimu peoples, and the textiles of Paracas stored in the museum at Lima. In a little over a week, Vincent absorbed enough to deliver an extremely well-received lecture. "Dr." and Mrs. Price returned to Los Angeles for a rest from their "diggings."

Back in Hollywood, Vincent found himself in demand. Howard Hughes had been rather impressed with Price's job in *His Kind of Woman,* and offered him a RKO contract. Although the actor was pleased with Hughes' offer, he demanded two stipulations: that the contract must be nonexclusive, and that it must give him the option to direct a picture if he so desired. Hughes agreed to both terms, and a contract was signed promising Vincent's services to the RKO lot for one picture per year.

Vincent began seeking a property he might produce and direct under his new studio agreement. Studying the RKO archives, he came across a property called *The Great Man Votes,* which John Barrymore had filmed in 1939. The story appealed to Vincent and plans were made to go into production. Unfortunately, it never reached the sound-stage level. Instead, Vincent was cast in *The Las Vegas Story* (1952) as a ne'er-do-well gambler. Jane Russell, of course, was top-billed as the sultry songstress who rekindles a romance with brawny Victor Mature. Price was given the secondary role of Russell's blue-blooded, but unscrupulous, husband. This time the RKO formula of sex and action in yet another locale met with generally unfavorable notices.

Vincent fared far better on television during this period. In 1952, for example, he appeared successfully on seven teleplays, compared to his one unheralded film appearance. As a touch of nostalgia, Price repeated his famed role of Mr. Manningham in *Angel Street* for the NBC "Best Plays" radio show.

Another factor in Price's movie slowdown during 1952 was the illness he suffered at Christmas time in 1951. Vincent was touring with a West Coast road-show company of T.S. Eliot's *The Cocktail Party.* When the show reached Tacoma, Washington, for a one-night stand on December 21, 1951, Vincent collapsed after the performance and was rushed to the local hospital. The next day's newspapers carried a story that reported that Price had a "potentially dangerous ailment." Later that day Vincent's malady was diagnosed as a perforated, duodenal ulcer. Vincent was released from the hospital on the day before Christmas. He returned to his California home and stayed there recuperating for many weeks. It is typical of this man with his boundless energy that he would turn even this mishap into a creative adventure. A few months after hhe unpleasant episode he composed a tongue-in-cheek article detailing the joys of living with a painful ulcer.

Vincent was now convinced that he should immediately resume his Broadway stage career, and when able, he rejoined the tour of *The Cocktail Party,* hoping that this might lead to some New York offers. He later undertook a summer-stock program at the famous LaJolla Playhouse, the highlight of which was his performance in *The Lady's Not for Burning.*

When Charles Laughton dropped out of the cast of George Bernard Shaw's *Don Juan in Hell,* a concert-reading version starring Charles Boyer, Sir Cedric Hardwicke, and Agnes Moorehead, Vincent was asked to replace Laughton in the key part of the Devil. This venture proved a delight for Vincent, partly because he adored Shaw's writing, but mostly because of the companionship of two fellow art lovers, Boyer and Hardwicke. As Vincent recalls, "Every town we visited, all three of us went to the museums, to every place of interest. It was a fabulous experience."

Eventually, Hardwicke tired of the constant motion and begged off the daily extracurricular treks. But when the successful tour reached Philadelphia, Vincent and Boyer were determined to have a solid look at the famous Barnes collection located within the sacrosanct walls of the Barnes Foundation in suburban Merion, Pennsylvania. As the story goes, the founder of the museum was a bit eccentric and had established the proviso that no one could view his collection without a special pass. Rumor had it that one art lover had obtained entrance to the "shrine" by impersonating a garden-supply truckdriver. Price and Boyer were convinced a more direct approach was in order. They spread the word among all their Philadelphia friends (including Vincent's past Yale roommate, Ted Thomas) that they would like to see the collection. Someone at the foundation apparently sympathized with their plea, and they were summoned to the private museum. They spent hours studying the ninety Cezanne paintings, one hundred and fifty Renoirs, and scores of other great masterpieces created by Matisse, Soutine, and many, many others. An added treat for Vincent was the collection of African Primitive pieces. Price would often retell this adventure as just one example of how his acting career served as an entrance to the out-of-the-way art world.

During the remainder of this stimulating tour, Vincent was able to familiarize himself more completely with the local museums in such cities as Toledo, Portland, Kansas City, and Boston. Once again, it confirmed Price's notion that there was a great deal of art available to the ordinary citizen throughout the United States.

When he returned to California, Howard Hughes informed him that he was to play the male lead opposite Jane Russell in the forthcoming *Topaz*. This pleased Price, for unlike many other members of the movie colony, he believed that the curvacious lady had far more acting skills than she was ever credited with by her peers. While *Topaz* did not come to be, Jane Russell and the Prices remained good friends, with the celebrated glamour girl often a dinner guest at the Price home.

Also in 1952, Price provided the narration for two art documentaries, *Pictura* and *The Ancient Maya*. In *Pictura*, Vincent redubbed a sequence originally done by Jean Servais in French. Unlike most art documentaries, *Pictura* had its own opening at a New York theater, the Little Carnegie, and enjoyed a first-class, well-reviewed run. *The Ancient Maya* had been sponsored by the United Fruit Company, and after a few theatrical releases in America, the short subject was dispatched for video showings.

Toward the end of 1952, Vincent had a choice of two professional options. Jose Ferrer offered him one of the lead roles in the Broadway-bound comedy, *My Three Angels,* while Warner Brothers came to him with the idea of a three-dimensional film remake of the 1932 classic, *The Mystery of the Wax Museum.*

Another major turning point in his career was at hand.

Chapter Five

"I'm sure if I'd done other things in my career, I could be more distinguished. On the other hand, of course, I could also be starving to death."

Vincent Price

Michael Curtiz, the Hungarian director who had guided Vincent through his first Warner Brothers picture in 1939 *(The Private Lives of Elizabeth and Essex)* had also directed the famous *The Mystery of the Wax Museum* for the studio in 1932. Lionel Atwill had excelled in the part of the mad doctor on a murderous revenge rampage, with Fay Wray as the screaming heroine. When Jack L. Warner, head of production for Warner Brothers, decided to combat the threat of television with a newly perfected motion-picture development called 3-D, he reviewed this old feature and chose it as the perfect vehicle to launch his studio's use of this new commercial process.

Warner was not reaching to wipe out the inroads television had made on moviegoers' habits. Rather, he hoped to counteract some of its competition in much the same way Warner Brothers had "saved" the film industry from radio with the promotion of real sound pictures such as *The Jazz Singer* (1927) with Al Jolson. The various three-dimensional systems, all of which gave the illusion of adding startling depth to a movie, had been passed around the Hollywood studios, arousing little interest, until Arch Oboler's *Bwana Devil* in the Polaroid process was released in late 1952 and made a tidy profit for United Artists.

Warner offered Price the part of Henry Jarrod, the lead role in the proposed color feature. When Jack Warner made the bid, Vincent took the whole scheme as a joke, especially when the executive went into a detailed explanation about the 3-D process, which required the movie patrons to wear funny little glasses with two differently polarized lenses. It took a firm money offer by Warner to convince Price of his serious intent.

Later, when a reporter asked Price why he had selected the revival of a once-famous horror picture over another crack at Broadway, he simply told the newsman that he had grown used to the sunny California climate. Had Vincent been in a more serious mood at the time, he probably would have explained that his intellectual roots were now in Los Angeles. He was involved in many art programs and organizations on the West Coast, and it would have been extremely difficult to leave them for an entire year, the minimum contractual obligation attached to the contract offer for *My Three Angels*.

Although the 3-D process would have a short-lived success, Warner Brothers' *House of Wax* (1953) made movie history as a box-office bonanza. In retrospect, its success was largely due to the fact that it was one of the few films made in the process with a script that would stand up on its own.* In *House of Wax,* 3-D became an extra ingredient instead of the film's only asset. Indeed, 3-Dimension was only one of the spectacular production values thrown into the picture (WarnerColor, stereophonic sound, magnificently gaudy sets, a consuming fire sequence, and dazzling camera work that fully utilized the new filming process were among the others.) An irony of this production was that the picture's director, Andre de Toth, had only one eye, making him one of the few people who could never properly see the final outcome of his film.

When the film with its stereophonic sound was released in April of 1953, Warner Brothers outdid itself in publicizing the property. They held a big premiere at New York's Paramount Theater, one that seventy-year-old Bela Lugosi attended in the company of a live gorilla on a leash! "It Jumps off the Screen into Your Lap!" screamed some advertisements, while others warned "Explore the Ultimate Dimension of TERROR!" Even sex was worked into the Warners' hard-sell campaign. "SEE Crazed, Lustful Monsters Leap from the Screen INTO THE AUDIENCE!" "SEE a Fog-Shrouded City in Terror as Crazed Monsters Stalk for Revenge, Beauty, Lust!" (Instead of having lustful and/or loathesome creatures molesting certain members of the audience from the screen, patrons were subjected to the optical illusion of a bouncing

---

MGM's musical "Kiss Me, Kate" (1953) and Alfred Hitchcock's "Dial M for Murder" (1954) were both superior properties lensed in 3-D, but released as "flat" features.

paddle ball jumping out at them, as well as an unheralded assortment of furniture and bric-a-brac thrown at them.)

Except for Bosley Crowther's withering review in *The New York Times,* the critics seemed to realize that audiences were going to become devotees of the film in no uncertain terms. *The New York Daily News* gave the picture three stars, even while admitting the film was a "synthetic spine-chiller" and the action was "ridiculous." The best reviews, though, were the notorious word-of-mouth raves that circulated through the small communities of the country as well as the metropolitan centers. The film registered a tremendous box-office response for Warner Brothers, grossing about $4.3 million in the United States and Canada, and $9.2 million world-wide. (In late 1971, *House of Wax* would be reissued in an improved single-image 3-D process, and would garner new profits for its latest distributors.)

No small part of the initial success of *House of Wax* was due to the fact Vincent went on the promotional trail to promote the shock feature. Typically, his offscreen sense of humor was obvious in his talks on this successful promotional trip. One day Price was making a well-advertised appearance in the Buena Park Wax Museum near Los Angeles. He took the place of a wax figure of himself in a scene from the movie. "I was standing in a menacing pose with a hypodermic needle," he described. "As the people came closer to look, I squirted water from the needle at them. It was great fun."

Not only was it enjoyable, but more importantly it thrust Vincent, who had been in danger of being relegated to the confines of a screen supporting player, back into the top rank of Hollywood performers. His name was once again in prime spots in all the columns and on the lips of more adventuresome producers. The success of *House of Wax,* which owed a great deal to Price's oversized, outrageous, but spellbinding performance, gave Price's professional career as big a boost as Broadway's *Victoria Regina* had done nearly two decades before.

After the fabulous response to *House of Wax,* it was quite natural for others to wish to jump on the bandwagon, and Vincent was deluged with offers to appear in more "horror" films, that in previous years would have automatically gone to Boris Karloff, Bela Lugosi, Lon Chaney, Jr., John Carradine, Lionel Atwill, or George Zucco. It was a tricky situation for Price. Although he had been playing cad roles for years, he feared he now might be relegated to starring in grade "B" horror flicks the rest of his life. Reportedly, he felt this was not why he had spent all those years training on the stage. Therefore he refused these offers, and the Karloffs and Carradines were hired as "second best."

Price also now bridled at the thought of committing himself to a long term on Broadway, despite his avid desire to participate once again in a New York stage production. The solution came in the form of an offer from Jose Ferrer to appear in the New York City Center's production of *Richard III,* a deliberately limited run. Vincent started playing the duke of Buckingham in that elaborate production which opened on December 9, 1953. Director Margaret Webster's production was heavy on atmosphere, but short on originality. The reviews were respectful — of both the Bard's text and the array of well-known stage names (Ferrer, Florence Reed, Jessie Royce Landis, Margaret Wycherly, Maureen Stapleton, Philip Huston, Staats Cotsworth, Price,) — but quiet in tone. Ferrer was, admittedly, badly cast as the treacherous, usurping king, and the play tended to flounder around his central role. Of Price, Brooks Atkinson (*The New York Times*) reported. "........(he) gives a weak performance in a style that is almost conversational." Luckily, by Christmas, Price was back in Los Angeles.

As a lark, Price made a short, unbilled appearance as the great Renaissance lover in Bob Hope's *Casanova's Big Night* (1954). Even though the picture incorporated such other tried and true "horror" staples as Basil Rathbone, John Carradine, and Lon Chaney, Jr., the movie emerged as a much inferior Hope costume satire, demonstrating that the cinema medium of the 1950s was leaving the ski-nosed comedian far behind.

To comply with his RKO contract, Vincent struggled through *Dangerous Mission* (1954), which relied on the glories of Glacier National Park as seen in 3-D to compensate for the impoverished who-is-the-killer plot ploy and the undernourished enthusiasm of star Victor Mature and co-lead William Bendix. Only young Piper Laurie, playing the murder witness who has fled New York to avoid gangland reprisals, provided a well-modulated acting treat for discerning filmgoers. And with a title like *Dangerous Mission,* many people assumed the film was a Korean War story, which dimmed the prospect of audience attendance even further.

Columbia Pictures had been anxious to skim some of the box-office rewards of *House of Wax.* Studio boss Harry Cohn hired producer Bryan Foy and screenwriter Crane Wilbur, the two collaborators on *House of Wax* to film *The Mad Magician,* another 3-D color horror entry. It was natural that the production chiefs went to Price to collaborate in their repeat effort. As is the case with most attempts to copy successful picture formulas, *The Mad Magician* was a poor stepchild to *House of Wax.* Production values were niggardly restrictive, and the shaky script made the use of visual gimmicks even less likely than in *Wax.* Price did his best to cover the production with his special brand of scariness, but the best trick of this magico movie did not come until seventy-two minutes after it started, when the screen finally flashed a "The End" title card.

Apparently regretting his appearance in another macabre film entry, Price reversed his decision about contracting for a possible long-run Broadway show. He selected A.B. Shiffrin's comedy *Black-Eyed Susan,* directed by Gregory Ratoff, the latter having helmed *Moss Rose* back at Fox in 1947. Appearing with Vincent in this play, besides Kay Medford and Dana Wynter, was another Mercury Theater alumnus, Everett Sloane.

The comedy opened its tryout run in Hartford, Connecticut, on November 11, 1954, then moved to Boston for a very successful month. Elliott Norton, critic of the *Boston Post* and traditionally known as a tough reviewer, reported, "...the wickedest show of the season is also the funniest." In the play, Vincent played a middle-aged neurologist, Dr. Nicholas Marsh, searching for the fond memories of his youth, along with a gaggle of nineteen-year-old girls. It was the type of harmless play that could be typed as a "sex comedy," and although it appears extremely tame by today's standards, it vied only with *The Moon Is Blue* for the status of most controversial new play of the early 1950s. The implications of a middle-aged doctor carrying on with teen-aged girls were too much for some staid viewers, who obviously considered this production more of a moral "horror" show than any of Vincent's insane celluloid antics.

When *Black-Eyed Susan* opened at Broadway's Playhouse Theater on December 23, 1954, it garnered mostly bad reviews. John McCain *(New York Journal-American)* alerted, "A new high in low taste was achieved last night," and labeled the show a "consignment of soiled linen." An incensed William Hawkins *(New York World-Telegram* and *Sun)* charged, "This exhibition at the Playhouse could make all the Puritanical hypocrisy of the Victorian Age seem welcome back. Fortunately it is so tasteless, inept and humorless, that it is not likely to infect many people with such reactionary pipe dreams."

Price did not emerge unscratched from the critical roasting. Granted he had some overripe (burlesque) moments in his part, as when a pregnant woman charges him with having fathered her child. He executes an oversized double-take, and then mumbles, "I guess this is what is known as a pregnant pause." Later Price rather rudely alerts a patient, "Your spinal column is upside down, which is why you're getting all your messages at the wrong end." And so it went, with Price, according to observers on the scene, doing an elaborate imitation of how farceur Edward Everett Horton might have handled the Broadway assignment. Perhaps the most chiding comment about Price's performance in this dubious vehicle was offered by Brooks Atkinson (*The New York Times*) who pondered within the confines of his review: "It would be interesting to know what actors think about when they play in comedies as distasteful as this one. Vincent Price, for example. Do you remember when he played the rapturous Prince Albert in *Victoria Regina*? What's more to the point, does he?"

Expectedly, at least by those who witnessed the show, *Black-Eyed Susan* folded after four performances. Undoubtedly Vincent was hurt by this failure. It would be many years before he would again return to the Broadway stage.

Back in 1953 Vincent had performed in an abysmal RKO feature entitled *Son of Sinbad* (also known as *Nights in a Harem*). Because of its allegedly titillating nature, a fact played up by the Hughes publicity machine, the picture was temporarily shelved, and did not see full-scale release until 1955, by which time it had gathered a sizable, far-flung reputation as being a "hot" little picture, filled with enticing skin-and-veil sequences. If less-knowing critics wondered why RKO had manufactured this half-baked sword-and-sandal entry starring Dale Robertson and Sally Forrest, Vincent could have explained the production's *raison d'etre*. "The film was simply a write-off for Howard Hughes. He needed a vehicle in which to fulfill his obligations to a swarm of ladies who had been brought to Hollywood over the years as beauty-contest winners — and perhaps other reasons — and they were legally entitled to one film appearance. The film with the harem scenes was the obvious way out of Mr. Hughes' predicaments."

To further promote *Son of Sinbad,* in which Vincent capered about as a sassy, foolish Omar Khayyam, Hughes went so far as to hire a cross-country train car to carry his "Sinbadettes," four luscious harem girls sent out to publicize the picture. As usual with a Hughes promotional campaign, the extra public relations paid off dividends, insuring that the color feature at least would turn a profit, if gain no critical respect.

At this juncture, Vincent had been making regular guest-star appearances on some of the network television shows, along with dramatic appearances. Three popular dramatic entries came as Gideon Rome in *Night Execution* on "Climax," as John Hayes in *The Brainwashing of John Hayes* on "TV Reader's Digest," and as Dr. Sloper in *The Heiress* on "Lux Video Theater." He also continued his radio career by acting as a substitute host for friend Herbert Marshall on "Your Radio Theater." This guest host job lasted about three months, while Marshall was busy at 20th Century-Fox filming *The Virgin Queen* (1955), a partial remake of events encompassed in Vincent's *The Private Lives of Elizabeth and Essex.*

After director Michael Curtiz finished editing *The Vagabond King* (1956) in VistaVision and color at Paramount, he requested Price to come in as a narrator on this ill-fated movie operetta starring Oreste (Kirkop, also known as Kirk Oreste) and Kathryn Grayson. Thereafter Price was teamed on camera with another opera star, Mario Lanza, and the results were not any better. The film was Warner Brothers' *Serenade* (1956). The studio advertised the Lanza—Joan Fontaine feature by highlighting "The Incomparable Singing of Mario Lanza" and "The Thrill of His Voice!" While the picture received generally poor notices, *Variety* did judge, "Vincent Price, equipped with some sharp dialog by the scripters, stands out as a caustic concert booker."

During production of the expensive *Serenade,* Vincent saw another side to the famed tenor. As Price remembers it, "Lanza, who was, shall we say, not a very gracious man, was at the time dieting — it seems he was always dieting — and apparently living on whiskey and garlic. To put it bluntly, he reeked. Poor Joan had to be almost pried from her dressing room to do the love scenes. I can remember an assistant director knocking on her door and telling her she was wanted on the set. There was a pause, then her voice asking 'Now?' "

Lanza's brilliant tenor notes were his primary claim to fame, but Vincent's baritone nonsinging voice was also in great demand. Not only had he done narration for *The Ancient Maya* and the foreign-packaged *Pictura,* but he also narrated a film for the British Film Institute called *Notes on the Port of St. Francis* based on a Robert Louis Stevenson text. In 1955 Price narrated and made an appearance in a thirty-minute documentary short called *The Story of Colonel Drake.* Financed and sponsored by the American Petroleum Institute, this film told the story of the first man to drill successfully for oil in America. Vincent also went to Australia during 1955. While there, he did a radio show based on George Orwell's famous *1984* and explored his main interest, primitive art, in this case the art and crafts of the aborigines and other local tribes.

Back on the RKO lot, and under the direction of Fritz Lang, Vincent was put into the black and white *While the City Sleeps*. As an indolent newspaper columnist, Price held his own with the "Ten Top Stars!" (most of whom had passed their cinema prime). This feature concluded Price's RKO pact, for not too long afterward the RKO combine went out of the feature-film-making business.

It was a distinct and prestigious move upward when Vincent was next signed by producer-director Cecil B. De Mille for his spectacular remake of *The Ten Commandments* (1956). In this VistaVision, Technicolor, road-show epic, Vincent was assigned the showy support role of an Egyptian architect. Predictably, the characterization was geared to be sinister. Price was not a little astonished at the scope of De Mille's own engineering during this mammoth undertaking in Egypt. As he later recalled, "I remember having to show Cedric (Hardwicke), Yul Brynner, and Charlton Heston the city, pointing at this huge empty cyclorama and saying, 'Yonder is the city of Sephi!' De Mille (then) said did we want to see what I was pointing at and showed us this scene with 13,000 people. He had just commandeered whole villages of people in Egypt."

With his customary modesty, De Mille heralded the Biblical entry as "The Greatest Event in Motion Picture History," and indeed, the movie did do overwhelming business, despite critical and withering reviews. The passage of time has shown what a superb huckster De Mille was, for when *The Ten Commandments* was re-released in the very late 1960s, audiences around the country almost hooted the puerile charade off the screen.

From a speciously pious success to a philosophical flop was Price's fate in moving from *The Ten Commandments* to Irwin Allen's *The Story of Mankind* (1957) at Warner Brothers. Price was given the role of the devil, the same part, in a different form, that he played in *Don Juan in Hell* on tour. The picture was amateurishly directed by Allen, with a stable of superannuated star names set to portray silly cameos from the history of civilization. Even before he began shooting this picture, Price must have been aware that it was going to be an artistic bomb. With tongue planted firmly in cheek, he told a reporter, "It will probably be the last movie ever made because it covers everything."

A small consolation in toiling in *The Story of Mankind* was that it provided Price with an occasion to again work with Ronald Colman, the star of *Champagne for Caesar*. Of their unfruitful professional reunion, Vincent said, "He was a marvelous gentleman, quiet and charming and with a delicious sense of humor. We knew during the filming that the picture was heading downward, the script was bad to begin with and it worsened with daily changes. I remember one puzzled visitor asking Ronnie if the picture was based on a book. He replied in that beautiful, soft diction of his, 'Yes, it is, but they are using only the notes on the dust jacket.'"

After the *Mankind* debacle, Price took a reprieve from film work. He was enjoying working more and more on television, and in 1956, logged a staggering total of thirty dramatic show appearances. More important than any of the televised plays, though, was a surprising appearance on a video quiz show.

Jockey Billy Pearson had recently made a smash hit on "The $64,000 Question," the nation's most popular television program, with an estimated viewing audience of over fifty million persons a week. The producers of the show thought it might be a lively idea to have Vincent contest Pearson on the sister show, "The $64,000 Challenge," then the nation's second most popular video show. Although well-known in show-business circles as an art connoisseur, Vincent was still known to the general public as an actor and nothing else. Price was thus booked on the show, and the audience immediately warmed to the contest between the lanky, six-foot-four actor and the minute, five-foot-three jockey.

The first three weeks of rivalry, or up to the $8,000 level, went rather routinely. Price and Pearson quickly answered all the questions thrown at them. Whether motivated by a sense of the dramatic or by more difficult queries, both contestants started to take more time with their replies at the $16,000 level.

The grand theatrics, though, actually began at the $32,000 plateau. Several lovely showgirls brought out seven unidentified small pieces of sculpture on individual trays. The object was for Price and Pearson to state the country of origin of each work. Price, as challenger, went first. Vincent went through them all once, silently, then went back to the first object and began to rattle off the nations rather quickly: Panama, Egypt, Mexico, Greece, Cyprus. Then a very long, suspenseful pause as he held the sixth *objet d'art* in his hands, giving it one last look. He hesitated, then said, "I don't know anything about it, except that it's Chinese." Quizmaster

Sonny Fox excitedly told him he was correct, whereupon Price moved on to the last piece and quickly stated the item was from the Marquesas Islands.

Then it was Pearson's turn, and the routine was much the same, except Pearson paused on the Egyptian piece rather than the Chinese work.

The next week, the two experts went for the top prize. Eight paintings resting on movable easels were wheeled out on stage. The two combatants were then told they had to name each artist responsible for each work. Again, as challenger, Price went first. To make sure of his crucial answers, Vincent paced himself through all his decisions, before he gave his first answer out loud. Then, offhandedly, he went through the works in rapid succession, identifying the works of Toulouse-Lautrec, Rembrandt, Daumier, Durer, Gauguin, Whistler, Hals, and Michelangelo.

Sonny Fox then moved over to allow Pearson the opportunity to identify the works. Like Price, Pearson perused each of the objects before vocally responding. He rattled off the first three answers without a miscue, then stood deliberating over the Durer. Sonny Fox, nervous perhaps at the thought of all that money, said, "The next work, the Michel——," stopping before the entire name was blurted out. Pearson did not even blink an eye. He was concentrating on the Durer so hard. When he said, "Durer," then moved on to guess the following Michelangelo and the rest of the works, the contest was called a tie.

Sonny Fox was then forced into an on-camera decision, based on whether he felt Pearson had heard the possible hint or not. His judgment was that the jockey had not heard him, so the $64,000 was split between the two contestants. As soon as the show was concluded, the CBS telephone lines were flooded with calls protesting the decision, saying that Pearson must have heard the clue. The producers and the sponsors reviewed the videotape the next day and announced, in widely proclaimed newspaper headlines, that Fox's judgment was correct. For his part, Pearson swore he did not hear Fox's outcry. And Vincent agreed, thinking the settlement "perfectly fair." As an added rejoinder, Price nixed the idea of a rematch at the same plateau, admitting "My wife has already spent the winnings." On art, no doubt.

Immediately upon completing "The $64,000 Challenge" stint, Vincent left for South Africa to conduct a cerebral-palsy benefit show. While in The Dark Continent, he enjoyed some sightseeing and the expected art-treasure hunt. When it came to primitive art, there were very few obstacles that could stand in his way, and Vincent went among the native people in earnest search of their crafts and cultures.

On returning to the United States, Price learned that he had been matched against Edward G. Robinson in yet another challenge for the $64,000 prize. The producers of the TV show had found the Price-Pearson match among their most popular, and now recruited the old Hollywood "gangster" to show his cultured side on the air. It was the perfect competition in many ways. While Robinson toiled in countless films as the rough-hewn, barely literate mob figure, a decade later Price was establishing himself as the meanest man in the movie world. And in real life, the two were probably the most gentle and cultured men in the motion-picture industry!

In almost a rerun of the Price-Pearson match, Robinson and Price breezed through the first few levels, then experienced troubles on the upper plateaus. The two actors battled for six weeks, reaching the $64,000 questioning on the last night. Instead of having a tie result from two correct answers, the two men drew the match when both gave wrong answers. Robinson said a painting done by Bellini had been the work of van Eyck, while Price was forgetful of the fact that Daniele da Volterra had painted draperies on the nudes in Michelangelo's *Last Judgment*. The two movie stars split the top prize, $32,000 to each, and the match was over.

Although Vincent received $64,000 from the results of the two matches, the money was hardly the most important feature of the shows for him. Not to say that $64,000 in the mid-1950s, or twenty years later, is not very serious money. However, the additional benefits that accrued to Price stemming from his guest appearances on that show proved invaluable.

Following the Price-Robinson match, Aline Saarinen wrote a column in *The New York Times* that mirrored public reaction to the two actors.

> ...what was exciting...was the contestants' attitude about their subject and the fact that this unbelievably vast audience inescapably learned that art is something significant and enriching and that enjoyment of it is within everyone's reach....
>
> It was Mr. Price, however, who was the real hero. At once urbane and appealing, he communicated to millions an infectious enthusiasm and an adventuresomeness into modern art. His reactions seemed fresh and unhackneyed. When he said, "You don't need sixty-four thousand dollars

to be a collector or enjoy art — it doesn't even cost sixty-four cents to go to a museum" or "The artist is a reporter on civilization in any era — and I am interested in the art of my time," he took art off its pedestal and showed it to be alive and pertinent. That he should have grasped every opportunity to say these things is not surprising...he fights for modern art — whether by raising scholarship funds, standing up to the American Legion's sporadic, extraneous attacks, or sparking efforts to form a museum of modern art in Beverly Hills. His approach to art is down to earth and glowing and he is secure enough in it to have humor about it.

Ms. Saarinen continued on for another six paragraphs discussing Price's affable nature and his extensive knowledge and love of art. More than any prior notices he had received for his stage or screen work, the Saarinen review was perhaps the most important he would ever receive. The TV program had thrust him forward as one of America's most popular art connoisseurs, and the Times write-up had now established him as both knowledgeable and respectable.

Still, Vincent was amazed to find literally barrels full of mail on his return to California, and none of it fan mail connected with his recent films. The public had obviously latched onto him as their popular guide into the world of art. Typical of the letters he received were notes such as the ones that asked, 'My daughter has sixty dollars and wants to buy a drawing. Where should she go?" "Can I buy anything good for forty dollars?" He also received a few impossible questions, such as, "Could you identify a painting I found? It is of the sea and has a ship sailing."

The significance of this response was not lost on W. Colston Leigh of the Leigh Bureau in New York. The Leigh Bureau was the largest lecture agency in America, booking lecture tours by interesting people whom the agency represented and the public, hopefully, wanted to hear speak on a variety of topics. Using as an introduction the name of his father, W. R. Leigh, one of the very good Western artists of America, Leigh approached Price with the idea of becoming an art lecturer. He told Price he was convinced that the public would welcome enthusiastically the actor in a series of lectures on art, or on any other topic Price felt inclined to handle. Although skeptical, Price decided to try it. After all, he must have reasoned, he had been lecturing informally for years.

The first program he devised was "Dear Theo," a dramatic reading of the letters of artist Vincent van Gogh to his brother

Theo. The letters, which Price called "one of the great nine-teenth-century spiritual records" vividly depict the hopes, ambitions, disappointments, and frustrations of van Gogh, whose relationships with his family, friends, and women were ill-fated. Van Gogh proved to be one of the loneliest men in history, and he turned all his love to Theo and respected his brother more like a father. To this surrogate father, therefore, van Gogh revealed his innermost feelings and desires, usually via his letters.

Concomitant with the assortment of letters, Price told the history of van Gogh, an artist who sold only one painting during his entire life; he told how after his death, and the demise of his brother as well as his dealer, his paintings became quite the collectors' rage of Europe, and many of the great art movements were patterned after his style.

Intertwining the letters with history gave Vincent an unparalled ninety-minute program. It was educational, heartrending, and very entertaining. When he embarked on the first of his lectures under the Leigh banner, he quickly became a sensation on the lecture circuit. Even though his appearances were infrequent the first year, both reviews and word-of-mouth criticism were so good that groups from all over the country began requesting him. Almost overnight, he became one of the highest-paid and most popular platform performers in the business. In 1959, he became the number-one speaker, overshadowing the likes of Eleanor Roosevelt. He has held that top spot ever since. He is, in the words of W. Colston Leigh, "the most consistent performer on the circuit."

Obviously Vincent was gathering unto himself a great deal of personal publicity at this time, what with the movies, art lectures, and television quiz shows. It came out that he had been a member of the Pomona College Art Historian Society, and he was quickly invited to become a member of the Art Council at UCLA. He was given an honorary doctorate in art by the California College of Arts and Crafts. The public was honoring him as never before, and in return for this outpouring of love and respect, Vincent and Mary Price began opening their home for art tours. They had built a substantial collection of primitive and modern art, ranging from a thirty-foot totem pole to the works of Richard Diebenkorn. Although an admission price was charged for these tours, Price donated *all* the proceeds to different area art projects. One of these tours brought three thousand people through the Price home in one day, and Vincent was gratified by the fact that the public was not only interested, but extremely polite and considerate. "There was never as much as a discarded match," Price said in describing the clean condition of his home following the tours. Unlikely as it sounds, nothing was stolen either. Of course, Art Linkletter, a friend of Price's, once looked at his collection of primitive art and told him he did not have to worry about burglars. "This stuff is so ugly," said Linkletter, "nobody else would want it."

Newspaper reporters often came to Vincent for interviews on art, since the statements he made were always good copy. One time Vincent assailed the snobbery connected with most art. "Art is something that's moved from 57th Street to Madison Avenue, and soon it will hit the Bronx. As a matter of fact, you've no idea how many painters I've wanted to see who are now in the Bronx." Another time, he was asked for the definition of art, and he bridled, "Good heavens, let's not refer to it as art. It has a dreadful connotation, and it really should be stricken from the dictionary. I'd rather call it a 'creative act.' " Another quote of his that saw nationwide print was in response to his anti-classical approach to art, "I love to buy paintings and sculpture by struggling young American artists no one ever heard of. It's not inverse snob appeal, really, but the satisfaction I always feel I will have in the future when everyone else recognizes these artists as tremendous talents." Vincent was fast becoming one of the most popular figures in the art world because of both his friendliness and his brutal honesty.

When the scandals concerning such television shows as "The $64,000 Question" rocked the nation a short time later, Vincent was one of the contestants untainted by the uproar. "I wasn't coached," he declared. "After all, I am an art historian." And as the lectures and public display of his erudition in the field have proven, Price did not need help from anyone concerning the world of art.

Of course, the motion-picture industry wanted to take some advantage of Vincent's new-found popularity. During this time, Vincent made *The Fly* (1958) for producer-director Kurt Neumann at 20th Century-Fox. *The Fly* was based on a story of the same name that had won the award for the best work of fiction in *Playboy* magazine, and executive producer Buddy Adler of Fox had bought the George Langelaan property especially for Neumann's low-budget production unit. While Adler doubted Price's marquee value after his last few pictures, Neumann was certain that the Price name still held magic in the horror market. Price accepted the film offer, and even had fun doing the film. He recalled later a hysterical day spent with co-star and friend Herbert Marshall. "In one scene, Herbert and I had to examine a spider's web which held the small fly which was supposed to be my brother. It took a whole day to film the scene and we kept laughing ourselves sick. In the end, we had to film it standing back to back — we just couldn't look each other in the face."

Upon release *The Fly* garnered exceptional reviews for a picture of its type. The Hollywood *Reporter* hailed it as a "weird masterpiece," while *The New York Times* ranked it as "the most originally suggestive hair-raiser since *The Thing*." A heavy promotional campaign followed fast on the heels of these potent reviews and the film went on to gross over $1.7 million in distributors' domestic rentals. Vincent's ability to emulate a grand style of macabre vivacity without being foolish was again paying very rich dividends for all concerned. His stock as a movie "name" soared again.

Before the release of *The Fly,* William Castle hired Price to appear in his *House on Haunted Hill* (1958). Castle was the type of energetic producer-director who relied on absurd but commercial gimmicks to publicize his often low-class product and bring it into the public limelight. *House on Haunted Hill* was no exception. It had "Emergo," one of the corniest gadgets ever imagined. Wanting to capitalize on the former popularity of 3-D, Castle's advertisements for *Haunted Hill* promised that the "thrills fly right off the screen." What actually happened during a showing of the picture was quite different. A skeleton was hooked onto wires leading from one end of each theater to the other. At the right psychological moment, the projectionist pushed a button and the skeleton went zipping along the wire track. Glowing with luminescent paint, it was supposed to scare the wits out of the audience. That it certainly did not live up to its publicized expectations was obvious, but the gimmick was lowbrow fun, and served its basic publicity purpose.

Vincent, meanwhile, continued his array of guest-star appearances on television's various dramatic shows, ranging from "Lux Video Theater" to "G.E. Theater" to "Playhouse 90" to "The Alcoa Hour" and "Alfred Hitchcock Presents." Two additional shows to bring Price to TV's home viewers never came to pass. In 1957, CBS approached Price with the idea of co-starring with Peter Lorre in a series entitled "Collector's Item." In the proposed series, Price and Lorre would play adventurous art dealers who continually encounter dangerous situations in their quest for art discoveries. The filmed episode, *The Left Hand of David,* is currently available on the sixteen-millimeter black-market home-movie market for a price of forty-two dollars. The other unsold project was conceived by actor-producer Mark Stevens who offered Price the chore of hosting "The Mysterious Traveler," a video spin-off on the veteran radio show. In it, Price would have emerged as the elegant host. Price explained further to the trade press, "I'll provide the narration as well as pop in and out of the story, and do my very utmost to scare the living daylights out of the viewers. People love that sort of thing."

With two potential series cancelled before they began, Vincent took his own idea of a show format to the networks. Price was convinced, based on the ratings of his quiz-show appearances, that the time was ripe for a weekly series on art. "I'd like to combine information with entertainment," he said. "I want to go to every museum in the country and show the vitality of the cultural centers in each city. The idea particularly intrigues me because I'm one of those 'Have tux, will travel' actors." The networks remained cool to Price's program notion.

Instead of the weekly art series, Vincent contented himself with co-scripting and narrating the widely popular *Revolution of the Eye* (1959), a film documentary that was made and financed by the Museum of Modern Art. As Vincent explained, "Its purpose was to show how people see things today they never knew existed fifty years ago." After a few special showings at different museums and forums, the documentary was aired on CBS-TV. From the mail the show sparked, it was apparently quite popular with the masses, but that did not alter the minds of the network heads who had vetoed Price's suggestion for a weekly series on the subject.

Vincent did get a firm offer for a different type of weekly series, this one called "ESP," which explored the mysterious powers of the inner mind. Not a dramatic show, Price served as moderator for this weekly excursion into the unknown. Of all the shows that had been proposed to the actor, this one was probably the least interesting and the most unworkable. Ironically, it was the one that did get on the air, but not for long. After only three weeks of telecasts, it was cancelled. Upon being told of the decision, Price told the press, "Unquestionably, the series represents my one big flop, but I never had a more exciting time. It's been a tremendous experience. My one regret is that ESP wasn't given a chance. Our audience was building, our rating had doubled. In our third week, we had, I think, a clue as to how to make the program a hit, but unfortunately, the cancellation came before the possibilities could be explored. Nevertheless, I've enjoyed the experience so much that I welcome further work in television."

Vincent did obtain much more work in the medium. Since he was one of the special breed of performers who are as interesting offscreen as well as on, he guested on many video outings as a pure and simple personality. He was also a good game-show contestant and continued to ply that fertile field of endeavor, as well as the realm of TV anthology dramatic shows.

On the film front, he went into Irwin Allen's *The Big Circus* (1959). Allen, of course, was the producer who had fared so badly with *The Story of Mankind*. For this new color venture, Allen chose to imitate Cecil B. De Mille's *The Greatest Show on Earth* (1952), on a very low, low budget indeed. With unsubtle Victor Mature as the John Ringling North figure, *The Big Circus* tossed into the melee every cliche imaginable both in and out of a circus atmosphere. Price was put into this mess as the ringmaster. Vincent then moved over to another Allied Artists' sound stage to do *The Bat* (1959) for director-scripter Crane Wilbur. Although the title immediately connotes another monster horror tale, it was actually based on the famed Mary Roberts Rinehart whodunit. With Mercury Theater alumnus Agnes Moorehead, who had been part of the *Don Juan in Hell* touring troupe, Price was again a suspected evildoer, and again, he was proven innocent at the finale.

After filming *The Bat*, Vincent served as master of ceremonies on the television quiz show, "Keep Talking." Like "ESP," this program chore was short-lived, and did not interfere a bit with Price's film work or art collecting.

Continuing his film career, 20th Century-Fox signed him to a hefty contract for *Return of the Fly* (1959). Unfortunately, Kurt Neumann, who produced-directed *The Fly,* died of natural causes some weeks after that picture's debut, and the sequel was assigned to producer Bernard Glasser and director Edward Bernds, who managed to excise whatever originality the film promised. Price thought the whole effort a shame, saying, "The script was one of those rare cases when the sequel proved to be better than the original. When I first read it, I was very excited about the possibilities. Then the producers, in obvious bad judgment, proceeded to put in a lot of gimmicks in the belief that films need gimmicks to be popular. In the end, they lessened and nearly ruined the dramatic effect that could have made a truly superior picture." As predicted, this film drew a large carry-over audience from the original entry, so it did make some return on the investment.

With *The Tingler,* his fourth and final release of 1959, Price returned to the William Castle fold. It was another of Castle's gimmicky, but successful, shock features. The picture proved to be an accidental forerunner of primal therapy, having Price's mad doctor exploring the connection between loud screaming and the release of all anxieties. Where Emergo had been the crowd-gathering gimmick in *House on Haunted Hill,* Castle pulled out of his hat a new lure called Percepto to bolster *The Tingler*'s box-office take. Unlike its predecessor, however, Percepto actually enhanced the viewing for many. Certain rows of theater seats were wired with electric motors, and near the end of the film, when the creepy-crawly menace broke loose in the imaginary theater (on the screen), (off-screen) patrons were suddenly startled by an unnerving shake, rattle, and roll of their seats. Timed precisely, the incident synchronized beautifully with a similar moment on the screen in which a woman was attacked by the mad tingler.

Dramatically, *The Tingler* scored below even Castle's modest standards and Howard Thompson of *The New York Times* wrote, "It failed to arouse the customer seated in front of this viewer yesterday — a fearless lad who was sound asleep, snoring. Just keep us awake, Mr. Castle." Despite the withering glances the critics gave this film, Vincent was cited for his courage in appearing in films that had hopeless scripts. Bob Thomas, a syndicated columnist was one of the first to dub Price the "king of the shock pictures." Thomas noted, "Probably no actor is working more steadily in feature films, and the moola helps add to his collection of canvasses, already numbering 700." Thomas was correct on both counts, and to insure that he had no idle time during busy 1959, in October of that year Vincent embarked on a lecture tour that covered fifty dates in fifty-five days.

During the three years that Vincent had been associated with the Leigh Bureau, he had worked extremely hard refining his lectures and creating new ones. Along with the "Dear Theo," Price prepared a lecture entitled "An Actor's Life for Me," a bitter-sweet reminiscence of his almost twenty-five years in show business. Relating the comic and serious incidents that had made his life as an actor exciting, he sprinkled the talks with revealing, yet innocent, anecdotes of the personalities in the entertainment world.

The third program he prepared for his platform appearances was "Three American Voices." This evening talk featured the works of Walt Whitman, James McNeill Whistler, and Tennessee Williams. In a blend that was both enriching and exhilerating, Price combined some of the best passages from each artist's works. The majestic sweep of Whitman's alliterative free verse was glorified by Price's full-bodied readings from *Leaves of Grass.* And Whistler, although primarily a visual artist, was discovered as a controversial and bitterly caustic essayist when Vincent offered his rendition of "The Gentle Art of Making Enemies." The last portion of the three-fold evening was devoted to a one-man presentation of Williams' *The Last of My Gold Watches*. Although the entire program was effective, the Williams' episode, perhaps because it was written for performance in the first place, received the bulk of the accolades. The "Three American Voices" program vied with "Dear Theo" as Vincent's most effective lecture piece at this time, and when the Library of Congress invited Price to present a lecture on February 15 and 16, 1960, he performed the Whitman-Whistler-Williams trilogy.

"Three American Voices" was quite indicative of Price's method in that it brought together seemingly disparate elements — painting, theater, and poetry — and wove them into one inseparable unit. The evening's talk was structured much in the way Vincent had built his own life, with a gentle, yet steady, intertwining of art, theater, literature, cooking, and all his other interests. When asked once how he could do so many different things, Price responded, "They are not as different as they seem." For, at the core of Vincent's life has been an aesthetic sensitivity to beauty and craft, and everything in which he has ever exhibited profound interest requires only an awareness of beauty and skill.

Yet another Price entry on the platform trail was "The Living Ideas of Democracy." Instead of the hackneyed flag-waving exercises in which many celebrities indulged, this talk included the writings of many statesmen-philosophers like Thomas Jefferson, Henry David Thoreau, Woodrow Wilson, Mark Twain, and Will Rogers. It was both humorous and stirring, and reminded the audience of the principles of democracy as an idea unto itself, not just the embodiment of perfection in one nation.

Vincent's fifth talk program was "Paradise Lost," the story of Paul Gauguin. Price — taking from the writings of this artist — told of the vicissitudes of his life and the tremendous longings that this great South Seas exile had kept to himself. Price had been the lucky buyer of the original manuscript version of *Paradise Lost,* Gauguin's anti-church tract, and hence derived the title of the evening. This program quickly joined "Dear Theo" and "Three American Voices" in audience popularity.

Added to Vincent's intricate day-to-day schedule was the completion of his visual autobiography, *I Like What I Know,* published by Doubleday and Company in the fall of 1959. Those who did not know Price were amazed that the movie actor and art historian could create a three-hundred-page volume, and earn good reviews at that. The august *New York Times* evaluated, "Vincent Price...is a dedicated, hard-working missionary for art. For years he has used his suave charm, his energy, his leisure, and his infectious enthusiasm to propagate the faith. Now he invites new disciples to an enrichment of life by making an absorbing first-person adventure story out of his lifelong love affair with art....He is bound by no accepted value judgments."

I Like What I Know sold over twenty thousand in its first three months in bookstores, completely selling out its first three printings, and going into a fourth. The volume stands today as the best example of Price's wide variety of tastes, and his summaries on different forms of art are clear, concise, and sometimes revolutionary. Note particularly his explanation of primitive art, "Understanding the appeal of primitive art has a great deal to do with understanding modern art, cubist art, abstract art. It was the 'discovery' of this art of simple people that helped bring about the modern Renaissance, just as the rediscovery of the art of Greece and Rome was a primal cause of the Italian Renaissance in the fourteenth or fifteenth century."

In the process of accumulating a great many honors for his art endeavors, Vincent was led into many new friendships, pursuits, and of course, hours of devoted effort. After he participated in the film *Revolution of the Eye,* he became friendly with Rene d'Harnoncourt, the director of the sponsoring Museum of Modern Art. The latter was also a specialist in primitive art and was then chairman of the United States Department of the Interior's Indian Arts and Crafts Board. When the two men discussed their cultural tastes at great length, they discovered a great breadth of similarity. The Indian Arts and Crafts Board chairman shrewdly invited Price to join the council, hoping the Price name would bring attention to the unheralded work of the organization. It was a wise move, for with the conscientiousness that was becoming his trademark, Price mentioned the board's work wherever he went, in all of his lectures, and in each of his newspaper and magazine interviews. Vincent was perhaps the first celebrity to attach himself to the American Indian's cause, and he did it apolitically, speaking out on the beauty and spirituality of the different culture. Vincent chose to speak to the hearts of the men and women of America, to the senses and emotions, rejecting as irrelevant the liberal-conservative party politics that had doomed such efforts before. Some said Price was the most effective Indian Board member; certainly he was the most active in proselytizing for the cause.

VINCENT PRICE UNMASKED

In 1959, Vincent was bestowed an honorary Doctorate of Fine Arts at the California College of Fine Arts and Crafts. At the same time, he was a member of the Board of Archives of American Art and was one of the Whitney Museum Friends of American Art. He was also quite active in his post as president of the University of California Art Council.

Price was also recording in that year. Like several other Hollywood figures (Paulette Goddard, Virginia Mayo, George Raft, Sir Cedric Hardwicke, Basil Rathbone, Don Ameche, and Cesar Romero), Price made an LP disc for the Co-Star label, reading one role of a redramatized play, and letting the listener fill in the missing role from a script at home. He also recorded a musical album for Dot records, called "The Vincent Price Gallery."

Vincent also appeared in print advertisements and television and radio commercials for a variety of products over the years. He only once found himself in difficulty for endorsing a product. In 1957, when he was scheduled to speak at Louisiana College, the lecture was picketed by some of the Fundamentalist students of this Baptist college. It seems that Price had recently been promoting a brand of liquor in national magazine advertisements, and hard liquor was strictly against the tenets of the Baptist faith. Nevertheless, a turnout of over one thousand heard him deliver his "Dear Theo" program at a special luncheon.

Price also expanded his multifarious activities into a new field. He began composing gourmet tips for national magazines, and often a newspaper interview with the celebrity would be accompanied by a favorite Price recipe. By now Americans were becoming accustomed to Price's expertise in many areas. The gourmet hints were accepted and used by many.

Vincent Price moved into the 1960s having already formed the wide base of his image as an American Renaissance man. He had been a zealous booster and patron of art; he was a popular actor in a genre of filmmaking, widely versatile in his television and radio appearances, and an occasional but generally accomplished stage performer; he was beginning to gain a solid reputation as a gourmet chef; he was the highest paid lecturer in the country; he had begun his recording career; he had composed a marvelous book on one man's adventure in the art world; and he remained a devoted husband and father.

Unlike many of the art and *haute* society crowd who decried his (debasing) appearances in the shock or horror films, Vincent accepted his role in them with pragmatic fatalism. "They all made money," he pointed out. "I'd prefer to make more artistic, important pictures. Who wouldn't? But in a period where few people go to the movies, it's good to be appearing in films that are well attended." Left unsaid was the obvious fact that it made Price a far more commercial property to be a man of such disparate interests: an art connoisseur who cavorted with the supernatural and the bloody on-screen; the macabre film player who was a sophisticated whiz in the kitchen; and an erudite raconteur in the parlor who kept company with celluloid ghouls. Little wonder that Price continued to pursue his path as a man of all seasons, all of which provided him with the funds, position, and publicity to foster his life's primary work — the study, explanation, and dissemination of knowledge about art.

The die was now cast for Vincent Price and all that remained for him was to paint the finishing touches to the self-portrait of this man now reaching his fiftieth year.

Chapter Six

"Vinnie is one of the best loved actors I know. He'll only sit with the crew....As a man of culture, you might think he'd be stand-offish, but he isn't. When our cookwagon didn't show up one day, he drove into town, bought groceries and made lunch from his own recipe for sixty people."

Louis Heyward

If Vincent Price had occasionally dipped into the vast reservoir of Hollywood "B" movies, young Roger Corman (born 1926) was absolutely drowning in both them and even lower-grade "C" films during the 1950s. Corman had directed and produced his first feature in 1955, called *Five Guns West*. This was quickly followed by such hastily assembled items as *The Intruder, Attack of the Crab Monsters, Not of This Earth, Teen-age Doll, Sorority Girl, War of the Satellites, A Bucket of Blood,* and *The Wasp Woman*. This somewhat depressing list of exploitation-style quickies would hardly qualify him, or so it seemed then, for a top-line feature, but Corman apparently did not seem to much care at that time. A lesson he had learned while churning out these "B to C" motion pictures was that it was not necessarily important to spend a great deal of money to produce a film with some very good moments. Later generations of moviegoers and critics were to agree and in the late 1960s Corman would evolve into a cult figure, with many of his early pictures praised for their free-wheeling, graphic qualities.

Along with the aforemenioned lesson, Corman had a dream — to create on film the entire body of work left to the world by Edgar Allan Poe. Corman shared his idea with James H. Nicholson and Samuel Z. Arkoff who had founded American International Pictures (AIP) and through whose facilities Corman had released the

102

bulk of his movies. Both Nicholson and Arkoff were former theater owners turned distributors, and their considerable talents were in the field of promotion, budgeting, and creating shrewd distribution patterns for the release of their films.

Nicholson and Arkoff were intrigued by Corman's Poe concept. They saw a chance to produce a series of exploitive Gothic horror films based on the works of a very prestigious American author, all of whose literature was in the public domain. Furthermore, the executives were well aware that Corman had a flair for turning out inexpensive pictures that looked better than they cost.

When AIP approved Corman's project, the director immediately signed Richard Matheson, a well-known writer of science-fiction novels, to adapt Poe's *The Fall of the House of Usher* into a film script. While Matheson worked, Corman searched for his cast.

Many people believed Corman chose Price for this venture strictly because of the actor's previous successes in horror-suspense films, but that was not the entire story. Just as important to Corman were Vincent's qualities as a human being. Price was intimate with the visual arts, he was a scholar particularly fond of Poe, and he was a man with an innate sense of good taste. He was also one of the few *known* American actors who could lend respectability to the effort, and who just might consent to appear in the low-budget film if the overall concept appealed to him. Corman explained the idea to Price, who listened receptively. The deal was closed and the film went into pre-production.

With Price headlining the cast, Corman was able to convince AIP to add additional money to the budget. When the executives read the script that Richard Matheson had devised, they set the budget ceiling at $750,000, including advertising and promotion. Although that represented an enormous outlay for AIP, it was very small by Hollywood standards then. Corman recruited high-class Hollywood production designer Daniel Haller to give the film's background a lush, vibrant look. Haller, Corman, and Price huddled together to find an artist capable of preparing the portraits of the Usher family, seven in number. Since Poe was basically an expressionist, Price believed the artist should reflect that style in the Usher gallery. Finally, Burt Shoenberg, a West Coast artist, was chosen to complement Poe's style with the portraits.

Even then, Corman leaned toward the school of "pure" cinema, meaning the director knew almost exactly what the final celluloid product would look like before it was even shot. This method had two great advantages: It cut costs and it usually protected the director from disastrous final editing cuts at the hands of the studio. Corman knew exactly what he wanted, and he put this across to the actors in a two-day rehearsal period during which he went over all the scenes and movements for the actors and crew.

House of Usher (1960) was shot in fifteen days, but Corman was experienced enough not to let that fast schedule indicate the quality of the film. For Corman, those were fifteen forty-hour days, and even Price, one of the most active men in Hollywood, admitted, "Corman is wonderful. His talent, energy, and drive amazes me at times."

When the color *House of Usher* was released, it was apparent that AIP had put every effort into the saturation promotional campaign. Huge advertisements highlighting the authorship of Poe and the appearance by Price heralded the opening of the film. The seventy-nine-minute feature garnered solid reviews. *The New York Daily News* gave it three and a half stars, saying, "...the genius of this tortured great is enhanced by the expert screen treatment of his century-old classic. Richard Matheson, scenarist, and Roger Corman, the producer-director, can and should get many a bow for the effort. Vincent Price is perfect as Roderick Usher....As a horror feature it's one of the best and certain to scare you silly."

The multi-hued photography and the entire atmosphere of the wide-screen film were cited by most critics as vital in transmitting Poe's eerie message. The Poe-Corman-Price-Matheson team scored a big hit, and a film that was made for well under a million dollars became one of the top box-office pictures of 1960. *House of Usher* managed to earn two million dollars in domestic rentals and scored an even greater success in Europe. Much of the ·picture's initial popularity impetus was due to Vincent promoting the film on an extensive publicity tour. (Journalist Joseph Morgenstern of the *New York Herald-Tribune* was only the first to notice that when interviewed about *House of Usher,* Price much preferred to talk about art rather than films.) Years later, when asked his reaction to the very first AIP Poe feature, Vincent judged, "I still think almost the best of all of them was *House of Usher.* I loved that. I loved the white-haired character I was playing because he is the most sensitive of all Poe's heroes — he's hypersensitive."

The film was so commercially (and artistically) successful that AIP and Corman made immediate plans for a second Poe film, *The Pit and the Pendulum* (1961). In an attempt to ensure the same type of box-office response *House of Usher* enjoyed, the same creative staff was employed by Corman: Richard Matheson as scripter,

Daniel Haller as art director, Floyd Crosby on camera, Les Baxter composing the music, and Anthony Carras editing the final film. Most importantly, Vincent Price was again contracted to star.

Made on the same budget as *House of Usher, The Pit and the Pendulum* scored an even greater success than its predecessor. In order to create a free-flowing plot line, the film necessarily veered from the Poe story more than the first effort had, thus irritating some Poe purists. However, critics in general agreed that Corman, Matheson, and Price had stayed within the spirit of Poe with their cinematic departure. Again, the atmospheric sets and the rich photography played an important role in the respect paid the film. Even if it was turned out on a low budget, it had the look of a film costing many times as much, and it was shot entirely in sixteen days.

For his efforts, Price was able to demand $125,000 plus a percentage of the box-office take. He was, by far, the costliest element in the picture, but also the most valuable. *Cut* magazine said of his histronics, "...with the lead *piece de resistance* by Vincent Price probably the best of his now classic maniac performances." To this day, people remember with fondness the particular wry quality with which Price's character says to John Kerr, who is being given a tour of the torture chamber, "Ah...yes...Torquemada spent many happy hours here, a few centuries ago." How many other performers could toss off such dialogue with the proper mixture of satanic glee and tongue-in-cheek?

With *The Pit and the Pendulum* already lensed, AIP requested Price to appear in another of their "classic" horror films. This was based not on Poe, but on Jules Verne, and it was to be scripted by Richard Matheson. It was *Master of the World* (1961), based on the novel of the same name with additions taken from *Robur, the Conqueror,* Verne's companion piece to the original.

Significantly, there were some vital personal changes. Roger Corman was busy editing *The Pit and the Pendulum,* while preparing for yet another Poe-based feature, so veteran director William Witney was brought in to handle the Matheson script. Daniel Haller was again art director, but he obviously did not have the same feeling for Verne that he did for the special ambiance of Poe. The chief prop of the new film was the *Albatross,* a giant, Goodyear-type dirigible that served as headquarters for Robur (Price's villain). It was vilified in many reviews. Indeed, made of impregnated paper, the *Albatross* looked like a cross between a blimp, a helicopter, a giant bat, and a nineteenth-century resort hotel — all in all, the type of warship to inspire laughs instead of terror.

The cast, though, was perhaps the best that had yet surrounded Price in an AIP feature. Charles Bronson, Vincent's silent cohort in *House of Wax,* was the Kirk Douglas-type hero, with Henry Hull bolstering the film with another of his irascible-old-men characterizations.

If anything, Vincent was even better as Robur than he had been as the Poe protagonists. Perhaps that was because he liked the character so much. As he later revealed, "I loved *Master of the World* because I thought it had a marvelous moralizing philosophy. I adored it. It was of a man who saw evil and wanted to destroy it. And if that meant the whole world, then it had to go." Obviously, Price had the enviable capacity to adapt to whatever project in which he was currently involved and to find some good within its substance, no matter what.

Audiences loved *Master of the World,* too, even while admitting it was not in the same fun class with the Poe "epics." *The New York Times* expostulated that the film deserved "a smattering of applause." The AIP promotional campaign was built around Price and Jules Verne, with the ad line "In the Tradition of *20,000 Leagues Under the Sea* and *Around the World in Eighty Days!,"* two other Verne novels that had scored great success in film versions for other producing companies. *Master of the World* became the third AIP-Price film to register over two million dollars in domestic film rentals, and Price's position as a sure-fire box-office draw was secure. He had reached beyond the position once held by Boris Karloff or Lon Chaney, Jr., and England's Christopher Lee and Peter Cushing had yet to reach their marquee peak, a point that still would not equal Price's now lofty status.

During the making of the AIP films, Vincent had spent his off-camera hours by writing a second book, *The Book of Joe.* Although the title portended some sort of religious tome, it was actually nothing more nor less than an endearing and charming story of a man (Price) and his faithful dog (Joe). Throughout almost two hundred pages, Price related humorous and touching anecdotes about Joe and various other animals Price had adopted through the years. The book established Price an an animal lover of the first rank, and though it did not enjoy the eventual sales of Jacqueline Susann's *Every Night, Josephine!,* Vincent's book revealed yet another major interest in the life of this incredibly active individual.

Because of the success of the AIP features, Vincent received an offer to appear, back to back, in three Italian-lensed movies. Vincent read the scripts provided, and thought two of them absolutely awful. It did not matter, however, for the prospect of spending an entire year in Rome was worth the career risk. Neither Vincent nor Mary had stayed very long in their previous visits to the ancient city, and they welcomed the chance to "dig around" the ruins and art troves.

Before they embarked for Europe, the Prices encouraged some of their friends to borrow one or more objects or paintings from their personal collection. The couple felt that someone should be able to enjoy the art during their absence. As Vincent explained this unique habit of lending, "Mary and I own between five hundred and six hundred items. We have so much, we couldn't possibly keep everything in our home all the time. As a result, much of our collection is on loan to friends. We feel if we're lucky enough to get nice pieces, we ought to share them. We run an informal picture-lending library. Works of art make us very happy and it's amazing how much happiness you bring to others by lending them out."

Once in Rome, Vincent and Mary had a few weeks to explore the crowded city before Price's presence was demanded on the sound stages. The first of these films was *Nefertiti,* later called *Nefertiti, Queen of the Nile* (1961). It was one of those dubbed, international co-ventures that made up so much of the European film production of the early 1960s, with a heady brew of spectacle, romance, intrigue, and bloodshed. Vincent was reunited with Jeanne Crain of *Leave Her to Heaven,* the latter still very attractive but unable to overcome the obstacles of such a helter-skelter production and its tattered script. The third box office "name" was Edmund Purdom, who, since his Hollywood career had faltered in the mid-1950s, had returned to Europe to ply the action-filmmaking market. The completed film had scant theatrical release in the United States, although it did finally put many people to sleep when shown on late night television.

From an Egyptian setting, Vincent switched to a swashbuckling pirate effort called *Gordon, The Black Pirate* (also known as *Rage of the Buccaneers* or *The Black Buccaneer)* (1962). Neither the presence of Price nor of ex-MGM "Latin Lover" star Ricardo Montalban did much to boost the artistic or commercial merits of this claptrap, and it was not until 1963 that the picture reached the United States.

Price's third Italian effort promised to be something very good. *The Last Man on Earth* was based on a solid novel by Richard Matheson called *I Am Legend*. The book had attracted a talent no less than Orson Welles, who had often said it was one of the most interesting ideas in the "horror" genre. Vincent was impressed with the book, too, and was flattered when producer Rober L. Lippert offered him the lead part. Matheson devised a screenplay for Lippert, but the producer did not care for it and brought in William Leicester to rewrite it. At this point Matheson disowned both the script and his participation in the production but was persuaded to allow his pen name, Logan Swanson, to be attached to the final screenplay. The direction of the picture, shot in Italy, was done by Sidney Salkow, and it emerged one grade below a low rating of abysmal. The final product was so trite that it forced many viewers to the opinion that Price was the only professional connected with the product. Not until 1964 was *The Last Man on Earth* distributed in the United States, and then because AIP acquired the picture to exploit the viable Price name.

Now that Vincent had completed his hack trio, the Prices returned to the United States in late 1961. They returned to a country much different from the one they had left. John F. Kennedy had been elected President during Vincent's Italian labors, and Kennedy urged Americans of all races, creeds, and economic backgrounds to involve themselves in the arts. Of course, Price had been exhorting his fellow countrymen to do the exact same thing for years.

Almost as soon as he was settled back in California, Price was asked to join the White House Fine Arts Committee. Vincent was eminently qualified for the post since one of his main focuses had always been the furthering of American art, and the White House job restricted him to dealing with the art of his native land. The prime task of the Fine Arts Committee was to replenish the art collection of the President's home. Sadly, many Presidents took certain works of art with them when they departed the White House, and by 1961, the art cupboard was practically bare. As Vincent described it, "The place had been allowed to go to ruin. Former Presidents simply pillaged it. Theodore Roosevelt even took out the lovely Georgian mantelpieces and replaced them with ones with buffalo heads. It wasn't until the Truman piano went through the floor one day that anybody started caring. Did you know Jackie once found a magnificent head of Washington in the men's room in the basement?"

As always, Vincent was extremely conscientious toward his duties on this job. He tried again and again to talk Jacqueline Kennedy out of her strong leanings toward the French Impressionists, trying instead to interest her in some of the young American artists. "But that's what I want," Mrs. Kennedy would insist, and French Impressionists were then what she got. Vincent remained on the job through the entire redecoration project, and up until the assassination of John F. Kennedy in November, 1963. Then, as it did for many Americans, a part of Vincent's contemporary world vanished. Almost immediately the White House Fine Arts Committee disbanded.

Of course, Vincent remained active in film work during his White House activities. He narrated Joseph Brenner's "documentary" of the African Zulu tribes and their customs called *Naked Terror* (1961). If that film was a depiction of native terror, Price's next AIP movie was literally filled with *Tales of Terror* (1962), again based on works of Edgar Allan Poe. James H. Nicholson and Samuel Z. Arkoff had once more brought together the creative team of Corman-Matheson-Price-Haller-Crosby-Carras, with the obvious assets of Peter Lorre, Basil Rathbone, and Debra Paget aiding the cause. Price was the only actor to appear in all three stories, with three widely divergent characterizations to portray. Of the role in the third tale, *The Facts in the Case of M. Valdemar,* Price explained, "I play an old man who is killed physically but kept alive in his mind. The question was: What would a man look like in this state? We settled for an old-fashioned mud pack — it dries and draws the skin up and then cracks open. It worked beautifully. But the hardest job was the part where the dead man actually comes back to life. They decided on a mixture of glue, glycerin, cornstarch, and make-up paint, which was boiled and poured all over my head. Hot, mind you. I could stand it for only one shot, then I'd have to run. It came out beautifully. It gave the impression of the old man's face melting away."

Richard Matheson utilized four different Poe stories in creating the three used on the screen. *Morella* was the first and *The Facts in the Case of M. Valdemar* was the third; the middle piece was a combination of *The Black Cat* and *The Cask of Amontillado.* Under the direction of Roger Corman, Matheson drew the three together into a semi-homogenous whole. *Tales of Terror* earned domestic gross rentals of approximately $1.5 million, a decline from past Corman-Poe-Price silver-screen efforts, but still making a tidy profit for all concerned.

Despite the dip in returns on *Tales of Terror,* AIP did not lose faith in the potency of the Price name on marquees. In fact, the studio executives released a press statement claiming that his name on a film meant more to the success of a film than such (once) hallowed spook names as Boris Karloff or Lon Chaney, Jr. Even *Newsweek* magazine credited Price with spurring a horror-film revival. In a full-page article concerning the return of horror pictures, *Newsweek* reported, "Vincent Price more than anyone else is responsible for leading the horror movie back from the grave. Price views his labors with amusement as well as enthusiasm. He is one of the most unassuming actors in Hollywood, and one of the most cultivated. It is the considered opinion of many that he makes movies in order to get money to spend on his art collection, unlike many actors who start an art collection to get rid of money they make from movies."

Price himself added, "Horror movies give me time and money to indulge my hobby. Besides, they are loads of fun to do and loads of fun to watch."

When Price completed filming *Tales of Terror* in January, 1962, he went on another lecture tour for the Leigh Bureau. This was the year he established his February rule, namely, for future years he would commit himself to doing a month and a half of lecturing, and he would always start on the first of February. The reason for implementing this rule was simply the need for organization. Vincent was active in so many areas, that it was sometimes difficult to schedule the lucrative lectures, a demanding activity that ranked among his favorites. By setting aside February and the first few weeks of March, Vincent could assure himself a steady place on the platform circuit. Since that time, he has been booked solid a year in advance. On this 1962 tour, he performed twenty-five dates in twenty-eight days with the "Three American Voices" program.

During these lectures, Vincent always saved time at the end of the program for questions from the audience. Surprisingly, hardly anyone ever questioned him about his movies, preferring to query him on the realm of art. One person did ask him what his nightmares were, and he answered that he always finds the Mona Lisa in a junk shop and somebody pokes a hole in it with an umbrella. "And that," he added, "is really terrifying."

He next did a cameo role in Allied Artists' *Convicts 4* (1962), originally titled *Reprieve,* playing, of all things, an author-critic. He played the part with restraint, on which the distributors capitalized by hinting that Price most likely was etching a celluloid characterization of himself.

Allied Artists executives thought they could perhaps emulate the success of AIP pictures with their own Price films, so after *Convicts 4,* they offered Price the lead in *Confessions of an Opium Eater,* based on the well-cherished novel by Thomas De Quincey. Unfortunately, producer-director Albert Zugsmith lacked the imaginative flair of Roger Corman, and the resultant picture hit the bottom of the 1962 feature-film barrel. It later turned up on television as *Souls for Sale,* a title that probably best described what the actors felt while making this dreary, low-budget film.

Price had completed yet another book during the filming of the two Allied Artists features, this time serving as editor and writing the foreword for *Drawings of Delacroix* for Borden Publishing Company. The book appeared simultaneously in hardcover and paperback, but was not a sales leader in its field.

AIP asked Price if he would be interested in doing a film based on *The Gold Bug,* once again in tandem with Corman and Matheson. Price said he would, so the project was put into pre-production, where it has stayed ever since.

Instead, Price went into another version of *Tower of London* (1962), a remake of the 1939 film in which he only had a featured role. This time, however, Vincent was palying the evil King Richard III. Although Roger Corman directed this vehicle, which was produced by his brother Gene, it had none of the satisfying ambiance of the Poe-AIP pictures, and its box office success was marginal.

With the completion of the unsatisfactory *Tower of London,* Vincent began what would probably be his most unapralleled endeavor in the world of art. In the summer of 1962, Sears Roebuck and Company, one of America's largest retail chain stores, decided to enter into the art world. Like most retail outlet stores, Sears had always merchandised the bathroom-kitchen-children's-room art consisting largely of unoriginal copies of wide-eyed kittens or teary-eyed orphans. Now, however, they proposed to sell art in a more proper fashion. In a press release, George Struthers, vice-president in charge of merchandising, announced, "We have found that good art is not readily available in all towns and cities throughout the country. While major metropolitan cities are supplied with fine art galleries, many medium- and small-sized cities have no such outlets or a limited number of them. This creates a need we plan to fill."

VINCENT PRICE UNMASKED

In a Sears board meeting, another vice-president of the company, Harry Sundheim, brought up the suggestion that perhaps Vincent Price would be interested in supervising the project. All agreed that it was a feasible idea, and that Price would give them both the publicity and the prestige the project warranted. No small consideration was that Price by this time was indelibly fixed in much of the public's mind as one of the country's leading art experts. Struthers flew to Los Angeles to meet with Price and his agent, Lester Salkow, about the proposed "Sears Art Gallery." Vincent responded with immediate enthusiasm, and the three reportedly made a deal on the spot.

As announced in September, 1962, Price was given *carte blanche* by the nationwide store to order some two thousand works of art at a variety of price ranges, not necessarily within the confines of the usual financial bracket of Sears shoppers. When ordered, these works were shipped to the Sears central depots in Los Angeles and Chicago. Price reportedly received a percentage of the sales fee of each work.

By November of 1972, Price had personally overseen the purchase of over twenty-seven hundred works that he had shipped to Sears' storage quarters. The store chain was then ready to unveil their unique effort. The plan was to premiere eleven different showcases in eleven different cities or towns. In this way, Sears could best analyze the regional factors determining the consumer purchase of art. As it turned out, they scarcely needed to analyze the market breakdown. In all eleven Sears outlets, the Vincent Price Collection of Fine Art was a smash hit. In Denver, five hundred people were waiting in line to view the exhibit before the store opened. In Oklahoma City, three thousand individuals showed up for the Sunday debut to buy over one hundred and twenty items. In Hayward, California, sixty items, ranging from $50 to $1,250 were sold in the first hour. In Sacramento, a crowd of four thousand jammed the store on opening day. In all, twelve hundred of the original twenty-seven hundred pieces were retailed in the eleven stores within the first three days of customer promotion. Sears had its own smash hit.

Not only did Vincent purchase all the art, but each item so acquired bore a small critique on the back written by Price, explaining why he liked it. The work also had the Sears gallery label, a French idea Vincent borrowed so that Sears' art could establish a pedigree. Even Mary Price got into the Sears project, designing all the mats and moldings, so the customer bought an already sensibly framed work of art, ready for immediate hanging.

That first collection included some twenty-seven Rembrandt etchings, plus examples of Dürer, Goya, Whistler, Millet, and Reginald Pollack. No one learned more about art quicker than the Sears personnel suddenly thrust into a new *haute mode*. For example, Charles Pearson, former supervisor of household furnishings for Sears, was placed in charge of the art warehouse in Chicago. After several batches of Price's selections arrived, he told one reporter on the scene, "I didn't know a Hogarth from a Goya, but I'm learning fast."

There were numerous reasons why the expansive Sears program appealed to Vincent. First and foremost was the concept of the average family being able to purchase fine works of art on the down-payment plan, just as young Vincent had done at the age of twelve through the auspices of a kindly dealer. "To me, it's a thrill, an indescribable thrill, to see working people buying good art at $5 down and $10 a month." (This down-payment plan accounted for about eighty percent of all the works sold in the Vincent Price Collection of Fine Art.)

Price also rebelled against the stuffiness of certain galleries, knowing full well how intimidating some of the finer establishments were to the average person who walked in off the street. "You know how it is at the galleries," he said. "You go in and they immediately make you feel ignorant with their big talk. Well, our salesmen don't know a bloody thing about the paintings they're selling — except for the critiques I've written to go with the works." Vincent had planned it that way, believing that if the salesmen were novices like the customers, they would not be able to unduly influence anyone in their purchases.

In the nine months between November, 1962 and August 1963, Price bought nearly fifteen thousand works of art for Sears, keeping in mind that the top retail price for a work would be about $3,500. By that time a dozen different exhibits were touring the Sears stores. In addition to buying the art, Vincent attended about fifteen openings during the first year of the program.

By late 1963, Vincent admitted that even he was exhausted from his constant search for worthwhile buys for Sears. "It keeps me so busy," he said, "I sometimes employ agents to buy up stuff for me. The other day I went into a gallery here (London) and asked to see the works of one particular artist. 'I'm sorry, Mr. Price,' they told me, 'but some nut in California has been buying it all up.' The nut, of course, was myself."

Vincent would continue his job with the Sears organization throughout the 1960s, always with great success. In these years, he bought over fifty-five thousand works of art and supervised the buying of even more. The experiment had been so successful that other stores began installing art galleries, but none proved as viable as the Sears plan, largely because these other companies lacked a man of Price's calibre at the center of their programs.

* * *

During the filming of *Tower of London,* Vincent signed a contract with American International, guaranteeing them one picture per year. For his part, Price received a cash payment in the area of $125,000 per picture plus a percentage of the proceeds. Of course, if he made cameo or supporting appearances in other AIP films, his salary was negotiable. But once a year, under this nonexclusive agreement, he had to star in a "horror"-related film.

After his daughter, Mary Victoria Price, was born in late 1962, Price took time away from filmmaking and his Sears venture to remain at home with the mother and child. During that period, he began work on yet another book, *The Villain Still Pursues Me.* About halfway through the project, Vincent realized its chatty, informal style would serve the lecture circuit far better than it would literary circles, so it joined his platform repertory.

The Villain Still Pursues Me concerned the history of movie heavies, and more specifically, how Price got himself trapped into the stereotype of the movie bad guy. It was in this talk that Vincent offered one of his wittier observations of the spook-movie cycle, "You know, a great many scientists and college professors are fans of horror pictures. It isn't true that you make such entertainments to appeal to twelve-year-old minds. It's just that a lot of fine minds revert to twelve years old for relaxation."

At the start of 1963, Vincent began work on *The Raven* (1963). This entry was a bit different from the previous AIP Poe pictures. Whereas the others were noted for pure terror, *The Raven* was as funny as it was terrifying, and this change of ambiance was intentional. Backed by the same production team, save for Ronald Sinclair replacing Anthony Carras as editor, Price, Peter Lorre, and the once grand master himself, Boris Karloff, romped in sumptuous color settings.

Obviously, an eighteen-stanza poem, no matter how classic, hardly serves as a scenario for an eighty-six-minute feature. Thus Richard Matheson took the famed raven premise, fleshed out the character of a girl named Lenore, and invented a screenplay that followed the Poe style, though in a tongue-in-cheek manner. Matheson was roundly criticized in some quarters for giving the dialogue too contemporary a sound, such as the bit where Lorre peers around a filthy, cobweb-ridden cellar and muses aloud, "Gee, hard place to keep clean, huh?" But Matheson did not create that jocular line; in fact, he did not create many of the actual lines in the final product. As Vincent explains, "Peter knew every line of the script perfectly, but loved to invent his own, and sometimes his ad libs were so humorous Corman let them stay in."

Further regarding *The Raven,* Price recollects, "Boris, Peter, and I got together and read the script and decided it didn't make any sense at all. So then we sort of dreamed up the broader laughs. I told the director, 'Roger, we must tip them off right away that there's something very different about this picture.' So every time I walked across my study, I hit myself on the end of the telescope. Of course, this immediately set the mood."

The final results of *The Raven* earned critical favor. *Time* magazine admitted, "You'll scream with terror!," while *Newsweek* said, "Of all the horror pictures, *The Raven* flaps the wildest wings." Even Walter Winchell got into the act and called the film "A Chiller-Palooza!" As for the performances, The Hollywood *Reporter* printed, "Price, Lorre and Karloff perform singly and in tandem like what they are, three seasoned pros who can take a gentle burlesque and play it to the end of its value without stretching it past the entertainment point. They are performances, in their own way, that are virtuoso." *The Raven* grossed approximately $1.4 million in distributors' domestic rentals. It also served to introduce Jack Nicholson to moviegoers. It would be another five years before he would emerge as a major screen talent, but for the present he would continue to appear in friend Roger Corman's features and even to co-script some of the ventures.

A more serious film assignment for Vincent in 1963 was *Chagall,* a twenty-six-minute documentary about the famed French painter. Vincent was engaged to narrate the film, which won an Academy Award as Best Documentary Short Subject. In his acceptance speech at the Oscar ceremonies, director Lauro Venturi personally thanked Vincent for his contributions to the project.

All of Vincent's hectic activities caught up with him in the spring of 1963, when he suffered repercussions from a fresh ulcer condition. He recovered rapidly after minor surgery. While he was recuperating, AIP approached him with the idea of starring in a picturization of H. G. Wells' *When the Sleeper Awakes.* Roger Corman was to direct the science-fiction fantasy about a man in suspended animation waking up to a world many years in his future. The project never materialized at AIP. As Price explained, "The trouble is, it was written so long ago that science has caught up with many of the 'wonders' in it, and we're waiting for someone to concoct a whole new set of marvels." A decade later, that man would be Woody Allen who shaped the Wells' work into the comedy vehicle *Sleeper,* a successful starring picture made for *himself.*

In place of the Wells' project, Price went into *Diary of a Madman* (1963), a United Artists adaptation of Guy de Maupassant's *The Horla* and other stories. Daniel Haller was hired as art director, in the hopes that he could add spice to the modestly budgeted film with some striking visual production values. However, Reginald Le Borg provided very pedestrian direction, and the feature emerged as an undistinguished thriller entry. As for Price's performance in this lackluster venture, *Variety* observed, "Price, that master of the wickedly arched eyebrow, handles his role with the ease acquired through a career of myriad villainous personifications, although there are times when he seems like a man more in need of an aspirin than a psychiatrist."

As a favor to his AIP bosses, Price provided a campy cameo in the studio's *Beach Party* (1963), the first of a series of very successful teenage-set capers starring Frankie Avalon and Annette Funicello. Price was briefly spotted in the musical lowjinks as Big Daddy.

Vincent consented to another United Artists entry, also produced by Robert E. Kent. This one was *Twice-Told Tales* (1963). Using the canon of Nathaniel Hawthorne, director Sidney Salkow whipped the three-storied feature into a workable production. In the third segment, *The House of the Seven Gables,* Price enjoyed the occasion to play the George Sanders' role in this truncated version of the 1939 edition, and he made the most of it. (Price's original role was nonexistent in this new version.) *The New York Daily News* gave *Twice-Told Tales* three stars, opening the review with, "Vincent Price puts on three shows for the price of one....removing tongue from cheek, temporarily, in homage to Nathaniel Hawthorne."

By this time, Price had done four films in a row without much of a rest. His fifth was *The Comedy of Terrors* (1963), written for AIP by Richard Matheson, the latter also serving as co-producer. The film, done in a humorous tenor, was notable mostly because it was the first and only time that four senior members of the Hollywood "spook" brigade appeared together in one film: Price, Boris Karloff, Peter Lorre, and Basil Rathbone. The *Comedy* had the normal first-line AIP crew, except for Roger Corman, who was then preparing yet another filmic assault on Edgar Allan Poe. In his place was Jacques Tourneur, who was, unfortunately, too heavy-handed in his directorial style to handle such a venture in the proper spirit.

Because of its line-up of horror veterans and the heavy AIP promotional campaign, *The Comedy of Terrors* was a box-office success before it was even released, but the results provided only marginal profits. It was an indication that horror film devotees preferred to have their terror movies done in straight motif, without the self-spoofing elements present. It was an attitude AIP did not always care to appreciate.

Price emerged with the lion's share of the reviews on *The Comedy of Terrors*. Bob Salmaggi of the New York *Herald-Tribune* was of the opinion that "...the film unearths a few laughs...largely due to Mr. Price's delicious boozy hamminess as a shiftless, drunken funeral parlor director."

As would be expected, Price very much enjoyed the filming of *The Comedy*. Karloff and Lorre were real friends of his, and Rathbone was as cordial with Price as he was with anyone else in the film industry. Significantly, only Rathbone bridled at his image of an actor in "horror" pictures. The other three accepted their fates philosophically, if not artistically.

Almost to prove this acceptance, Price rejected a stage offer by Katharine Hepburn to play Prospero in William Shakespeare's *The Tempest*. The reason for such an astounding refusal? "I'd have gotten five hundred dollars for eight weeks work, and though I'd like to have done it, I just couldn't afford it." Price further explained, "I've got ex-wives and present wives and mothers-in-laws to support. So has everyone, I guess, save Katie Hepburn. She's smart. She walks alone."

As 1964 began, Price was represented on American movie screens by the imported *The Last Man on Earth*. In February, he took off on his annual, grueling lecture-tour schedule, after making his first appearance on the Red Skelton television hour. Eventually Price would be a guest over thirty times on the comedian's show.

Also in release at this time was *The Haunted Palace* (1964), another AIP Poe picture. This one was based on a story by H.P. Lovecraft and was done without the aid of a Richard Matheson scenario. Instead it had a screenplay by Charles Beaumont, which bordered on the literal and pedantic, rather than the subjectively fanciful and symbolic. The picture did gross a respectable $1.3

million in distributors' domestic rental. However, its most surprising success came a few years later when the picture became the highest grossing feature ever released in Australia. One of the most popular authors in Australia is Lovecraft, a fact that guaranteed immediate success for this film in that country.

Because production costs had soared in Hollywood to the point where it was practically impossible to film a low-budget feature of any quality, AIP and producer-director Roger Corman agreed to lense *The Masque of the Red Death* (1964) at Elstree Studios in England. The picture, starring Price, was shot on the sound stage adjacent to where Roger Moore was toiling in the television series of "The Saint," another Price role of long ago.

The Masque of the Red Death was based on the story of the same name by Poe, but one of the film's gory highlights, depicting the dwarf's revenge, was borrowed from another Poe tale, *Hop Frog.* Charles Beaumont's scripting on this production was far more in keeping with the Corman-Price canon, and the picture abounded in opportunities for the viewer to undergo free and controlled verbal and visual associations. A major asset to this landmark film was the absolutely fantastic photography of Nicholas Roeg, who a few years later would emerge as a high-caliber director with such films as *Performance, Walkabout,* and *Don't Look Now.*

The team of Corman and Price scored one of their greatest artistic hits with this film. Although the picture made the usual North American distributors' rental gross of over $1.4 million, it was censored in the very country of its birth, England. Apparently, the "Black Mass" sequences involving Hazel Court were thought a bit too religiously and sexually convoluted for the British theater patrons to endure. Only after these sequences were deleted was the film allowed to be shown in British theaters.

With their creative partnership so successful, it was inevitable that Price would be called upon to explain his rationale for the workability of his professional union with Corman. "Where Roger and I have worked very well together has been in the fact that I am a terrible stickler for explanations. Why does a man do something? What should the audience know, see, feel or hear, to know what makes the character do something preposterous? In almost every case, the character I play is not a villain, not a monster; he is someone who is put upon by fate."

Vernon Fell was one of those individuals who were "put upon by fate." He was the hero of Poe's *The Tomb of Ligeia* (also known as

The House at the End of the World) (1965). Another AIP-Corman-Price film, it was to prove the last of the series, and many feel that it is the best. Certainly it was the one with the highest degree of critical acclaim. The London *Times* said, "Here at last Mr. Corman has done what it always seemed he might be able some time to do: make a film which could without absurdity be spoken of in the same breath as Cocteau's *Orphee*." In New York, the Museum of Modern Art held a special four-day screening of the movie, hailing it as one of the contemporary masterpieces of the cinema.

on *Murders in the Rue Morgue* and *A Descent into the Maelstrom,* two other Poe tales. The latter was never done, but the former was produced by AIP in 1971 with Jason Robards starring under Gordon Hessler's direction. From this point onward, both Price's and Corman's careers* would move in different directions. Both remained under the AIP aegis for the present, Corman later to form New World Pictures, a film-distribution company that would handle multi-level properties, including among them the films of the Swedish director, Ingmar Bergman.

By 1965, Vincent was settling into a fairly steady routine: a few films each year; perhaps a book every two years or so; fifty or so lectures; constant committee meetings with the various art councils on which he served; traveling the globe seeking materials for Sears; television and radio shows; as well as dinner parties at the Price home involving any one of a number of Price gourmet treats.

The Library of Congress was one of the institutions that was cognizant of Price's incredible array of activities, and it gave him special recognition as a man with "widely varied interests and accomplishments that give him special status." They requested that he donate his writings, correspondence, movie and TV scripts, and other documents to the library's permanent collection as national mementos.

When a coterie of Sears executives approached Vincent to supervise the redesigning of an edition of the Bible for broader contemporary identification, Price agreed to oversee the project, and thus the *Michelangelo Bible* was produced. Relying on the King James version of both the Old and New Testaments, this Bible featured 121 plates by the great Renaissance artists, fifty-six of

---

* *Recently Roger Corman enunciated his perceptions on the Vincent Price mystique. "The keynote of his art lies, I believe, in his uncanny ability to embody and project the effects of mental aberration. He is rightly noted for his fine speaking voice and suave, polished presence through which he can convey eerie graduations of a sinister motivating force."*

which were in color. While distinctive in its tooled-leather binding and with its retail price of thirty dollars, this volume did little better than any other edition of the Bible. Moderate sales seem to be inherent in this part of the book-publishing world.

Another book sold through the Sears outlets, though not exclusively by them, was the Bernard Geis publication, *A Treasury of Great Recipes* (1965) by Vincent and Mary Price. The elaborate volume was a combination of recipes, comments, and reviews of some of the finer eating establishments the Prices had visited. For the Prices finer food meant superior in taste, not just delicate and expensive in cuisine. As Vincent explained, "Mary and I are collectors of everything, all the arts, decorative art, folk art, and the menus from the finest restaurants in the world. Enjoying and preparing fine food is an art. Looking over old menus, remembering the mouth-watering delicacies of various cafes, Mary and I decided to share these dishes with other gourmets by way of a book. The recipes are not too difficult for the average housewife to tackle and the results are sure to win ecstatic compliments from family and dinner guests." Included in the *Treasury* are recipes from such eating establishments as Tour D'Argent in Paris, The Jockey Club in Madrid, Antoine's in New Orleans, and Le Pavillon in New York. To prove the book's democratic scheme, there even was the recipe for hot dogs sold in Chavez Ravine, baseball home of the Los Angeles Dodgers. The twenty-dollar *Treasury* book, still in print, has thus far sold over three hundred thousand copies.

Also in 1965, Vincent received the George Washington Carver Institute annual award for outstanding contributions to art, science, education, and betterment of race relations. Price was a popular choice, and the dinner that accompanied his acceptance of the tribute was overflowing with Hollywood and art-world associates.

Although Corman had abandoned the Poe genre, AIP was not willing to relinquish its foothold on such a gold mine. Vincent was signed to do *War Gods of the Deep* (1965), based on the Poe poem, *City under the Sea*. It was produced in England under the direction of Jacques Tourneur and emerged more a science-fiction entry than a horror picture. The box-office gimmick of combining Price on-screen with aging teen-age-idol Tab Hunter did not work. Daniel Haller, art director for many of the Poe-Corman-AIP films, was the producer of this color venture.

After completing his annual February lecture tour, Vincent expanded his talk itinerary to include overseas dates. He had always felt that America was a land as steeped in history as almost any other country. He included in that history all the events that took place before the landing of the white man on his country's shores. When lecturing in England and on the Continent, he boosted American Indian art and modern American art alike. Everywhere he went, he was one of the most ardent good-will ambassadors that America has ever had. Significantly, and as a testament to his diplomacy abroad, when England's Princess Margaret and Lord Snowden visited the United States in November, 1965, the first public visit they made was to the Price home, where they dined on one of Vincent's gourmet meals.

Price was hired by Italian producer Romolo Marcellini to supply the narration for *Taboos of the World* (1965), a pseudo *Mondo Cane* documentary, which AIP distributed in the United States and Canada. AIP then approached Vincent to play another mad doctor in *Dr. Goldfoot and the Bikini Machine* (1965) to be directed by Norman Taurog. *Bikini Machine* was a loosely conceived comedy designed to capitalize on the science fiction-horror market (via Price), the teen-age crowd (via Frankie Avalon and Dwayne Hickman), and the James Bond movie craze. Because it made $1.9 million in distributors' domestic rentals, AIP sanctioned a follow-up, which was filmed inexpensively in Italy by usually in-control director, Mario Bava. Even Price who could out-mug the best of scene-stealers, found himself relegated to the background as the lowbrow comedy team of Franco Franchi and Ciccio Ingrassia wove their distinctly unimaginative spell over the skimpy production.

In the midst of his heavily saturated workaday schedule in 1966, Vincent found time for two particularly intriguing activities. One was his marvelously funny characterization of the Egghead on ABC-TV's "Batman" series, proving anew what a fine comedian he could be when given the proper chance. The other enterprise was the start of a new career.

Stephen Booke, financial public-relations executive, had returned to New York from Australia where he had just discovered the marvels of aborigine primitive art. Booke was astonished to learn that there were very few outlets in the United States, beyond expensive art volumes, for the average person to acquire useful knowledge about art. Booke was an ex-journalist, one who had accumulated many friends in the reporting field. One of these associates was Arthur Laro, executive vice-president of the *Chicago Tribune-New York News* syndicate. Booke approached Laro with the idea of a weekly syndicated art column that would deal with the basics of the entire art world.

It was natural that both Booke and Laro agreed that someone of Vincent Price's caliber was the proper individual to write such a column. Booke contacted Price, and the two discussed the concept. From the start Price was enthusiastic about the project. After Price prepared a few sample columns, a deal was concluded and was sanctioned by Vincent's superiors at Sears who reasoned that their organization could only benefit from the additional publicity. In explaining the column, which made its official debut in the spring of 1967, Price offered, "It's great to have an outlet to describe all the things I see around the world when I travel for film locations, lecture tours, or business. I know that without a new job, I wouldn't have the motivation to sit down and record my feelings. In my eight hundred words, I try to cover all the arts. To my mind, this includes cooking, decor, the theater, and architecture as well as painting, sculpture, and music. I may write about a Mexican recipe or a Spanish cathedral or the Australian art exhibit. Usually, I try to be a reporter rather than a critic, telling people how it is rather than how it should be. But that doesn't mean I won't praise or condemn a particular work or artist when this is warranted. It's a wonderful format which gives me wide freedom of expression." The column was soon appearing in over eighty newspapers across North America, and lasted for a period of over two and a half years, when Price decided to call it quits. Basically, he felt that it was no longer profitable for him to continue such time-consuming labors.

While Vincent was in Europe making *Dr. Goldfoot and the Girl Bombs,* he also filmed *House of 1000 Dolls* (1967) for producer Louis Heyward. The picture had the rancid smell of failure, despite a cast that included Price, Martha Hyer, and George Nader. AIP released it on the bottom half of double bills with the marijuana exploitation feature, *Maryjane.* Price then jaunted to South Africa to make *The Jackals* (1967) for Robert D. Webb's production unit. It was a remake of 20th Century-Fox's *Yellow Sky* (1948), with Price in the grandfather role once played by James Barton.

As a change from his usual run of activities, Price played Captain Hook in a West Coast revival of *Peter Pan.* He also narrated and guided the CBS-TV art special *Eye on Art: the St. Louis Scene.* Revisiting his home town with the video camera crew gave him a special thrill, even though the city had changed its look in the thirty-five years since he had left St. Louis permanently. The ultra-modern St. Louis Archway edifice, the gateway to the West, was typical of the metropolis' new look. Other TV assignments that year included a return engagement as the Egghead in "Batman" and the beginning of his long association with the celebrity game show, "The Hollywood Squares." Vincent appeared on over twenty-five segments of the television tic-tac-toe game during 1967 alone.

With the overwhelming success of their first cookbook, Vincent and Mary Price compiled *The National Treasury of Cooking* (1967), a five-volume paperback edition published by the Stravon Educational Press. It was just another illustration of how Vincent always managed to keep his name in the public's mind, while at the same time having the personal enjoyment of creative satisfaction.

After nine years of service as a member of the U.S. Department of the Interior's Indian Arts and Crafts Board, on August 30, 1967, Vincent was made chairman of that group. Through this new post, Price began to spend many hours at the Indian reservations, helping to inaugurate school programs offering guidance in the preparation of new arts programs. He took special interest in the Institute of American Art in Santa Fe, New Mexico, a museum under the directorship of Lloyd New.

In early November, 1967, Vincent began rehearsals for his first Broadway musical (and his first Broadway show in thirteen years). A musical version of Arnold Bennett's turn-of-the-century novel, *Buried Alive,* which had been filmed several times, it was retitled *Darling of the Day.* The musical concerns the life of a British painter who pretends he is dead and causes great problems when he assumes the identity of the late man's butler. Patricia Routledge was chosen as Price's co-star on the strength of her performance in *How's The World Treating You?* the season before. With music by Jules Styne, lyrics by E. Y. Harburg, and choreography by Lee Theodore, *Darling of the Day* was directed by Noel Willman. It was capitalized by producers Joel Schenker and the Theater Guild at $500,000, with RCA Records supplying $150,000 of the budget in return for the recording rights.

The period piece opened at the Shubert Theater in Boston for a four-week trial run on December 20, 1967. It received better-than-average reviews, particularly for its charming score. The production then debuted on Broadway at the George Abbott Theater (January 27, 1968), where audiences heard Price sing forth in his baritone voice for nine solo and joint numbers. Some of the reviews were very laudatory, "...thoroughly delightful. It has charm, tunefulness, humor, imagination, a good book, impeccable taste and a handsome production. Mr. Price is convincing and charming as the artist in hiding...a superior musical comedy!" (Richard Watts, *The New York Post*). However, Dan Sullivan of *The New York Times,* whose regular beat was the night-club scene and not the theater and who had to substitute for the otherwise busy Clive Barnes, hated the play, stating that "Blandness and staleness are the problems...." As for Price, Sullivan observed, "Mr. Price, who used to be a movie baddie, goes to special pains here to convince us that he is really a nice guy: lots of frank smiles and coy lecture-circuit twinkles. He sings too, and not badly. But he is not a man to make bricks with straw, and straw is just what his part is made of." Walter Kerr in a Sunday *New York Times* write-up of the show noted, "It is also necessary to put up with certain of Mr. Price's performing habits. His gestures seem to indicate that he is scattering dinner near the chicken coop, his self-congratulatory chuckles could be sold as candy in the lobby."

Darling of the Day struggled on for thirty-two performances and then folded, at a loss of almost $700,000. Ironically, the RCA cast album of the show was "posthumously" released and has now become something of a collector's item.

After his stage debacle, Price left for England to do another film for co-producer Louis Heyward, confident that at least in the movie horror market he had a responsive audience. Based on Ronald Bassett's novel, *Witchfinder General,* the film was to be the most violent and the most controversial vehicle Price has made to date. Although it utilized the novel's title for its English release, AIP switched it to *The Conqueror Worm* (1968) for American distribution, a title derived from one phrase in a poem by Edgar Allan Poe. In fact, AIP "cheated" even more by dubbing in the voice of Price reading this short Poe verse at the film's conclusion, a procedure which then allowed the company to advertise the motion picture as Edgar Allan Poe's *The Conqueror Worm.*

The director of this color shock film was Michael Reeves, a twenty-five-year-old Englishman. In the course of relating the story of Matthew Hopkins, a real-life "witch finder," torturer, and executioner of mid-seventeenth-century England, Reeves littered the screen with gore and violence in every form: graphic, psychological, political, and dramatic. The humor, the campy and anachronistic fun that was becoming a staple of most AIP terror films, was completely missing. Reeves intended *The Conqueror Worm* to be a boldly stated exercise in unrelieved terror and he amply succeeded. Within the picture, witch finder Price had a marvelous chance to stretch his characterization of Hopkins to the peaks of villainy, since the figure was a complete scoundrel, one with no redeeming qualities and one who was more evil than the devil himself. On-camera, Price had never been so mad, or vicious, or serious in intent.

When *The Conqueror Worm* debuted in America, it was roundly scored by critics as being excessively violent, truly sickening, and an exercise in bad taste. These anti-reviews served to whet the appetites of action-hungry film fans, leading the picture to gross $1.5 million in distributors' domestic rentals. Ironically, although audiences reveled in the blood and gore of *The Conqueror Worm,* it was regarded at the time by most as just another of the Price-Poe-AIP series, one that was increasing its depiction of violence in relation to the times. However, in more recent years the picture has built its own cult following. That director Michael Reeves committed suicide shortly after the film premiered only deepens the mysteries attached to the picture.

While in Britain shooting *The Conqueror Worm,* Vincent was signed to make a cameo appearance in *The Magic Christian* (1970) along with Christopher Lee, Yul Brynner, Raquel Welch, Laurence Harvey, et al. Sadly, *Worm's* production schedule went overtime, and Vincent was unable to perform in *The Magic Christian.* Price also accepted a role in the Tigon-American International project, *Curse of the Crimson Alter* (also known as *The Crimson Cult*) (1968), a movie that would reteam him with Boris Karloff once again. Barbara Steele, sex queen of the spooky movies, was also set for the Louis M. Heyward project to be directed by Vernon Sewell. The Mervyn Haisman-Henry Lincoln script was not up to Karloff's standards, and while Gerry Levy was adding additional materials to this modern witchcraft tale, Vincent had to go on to other professional commitments. He was replaced by Christopher Lee in the role of J.D. Morley, master of Craxted Lodge, Greymarsh, where strange happenings were the order of the day and night.

Vincent did make another show-business appearance with Karloff, in September of 1968, a few months before Karloff's death (February 2, 1969). It was on the "Red Skelton Comedy Hour" on NBC-TV. Price and Karloff did a sketch entitled "Who Steals My Robot Steals Trash." In it, Vincent and his scientist father (Karloff) attempt to use Skelton's brain for their robot. The two masters of menace also sang a parody of the song, "The Two of Us," with new lyrics spoofing the horror flicks.

Vincent continued his popular association with "The Hollywood Squares," taping over forty segments in 1969. Also for NBC he appeared on two episodes of "Laugh-In" and was a guest contestant on the network's "Name Dropper" program.

While in Hollywood, Vincent did a picture for United Artists, one totally out of his recent line of screen work — a Western. Starring Clint Walker and Anne Francis, *More Dead Than Alive* (1969) was a low-key, quasi-successful study of a gunman who, because of his killer reputation, is unable to hang up his six-shooters and live peaceably. Unfortunately this Robert Sparr-directed feature was tossed away on a double bill. Price was the indelicate showman who exploits Walker's gunslinger stock-in-trade. In a later excruciating slow-motion sequence, the viewer watches five bullets tear through Vincent's body, thus eliminating the latter from the plot-line.

A deal was consummated for Price to co-star with Christopher Lee in *Taste the Blood of Dracula* (1971), another in the popular British-made vampire series filmed by Hammer Film Productions. But when the production budget was later slashed — even stock-market recessions take their toll on celluloid blood baths — Price was released from his obligation. Lee as Dracula was essential to the plot, but Vincent's major role could be divided up among other supporting players. Then it was announced that producer Francos Rodriquez had signed Price to portray Dr. Von Helsing to Christopher Lee's Count Dracula in a Spanish-lensed *El Conde Dracula* (*Dracula '71*) (1971), but once again by the time this project actually got under way Price had dropped out, to be replaced on-camera by Herbert Lom.

If European production companies could not meet Price's salary and script demands, there were always the annual lecture tours in the States, and in 1969, Price performed thirty-seven dates in forty days of cross-country plane-hopping. By this time, there was no doubt that Vincent was one of the most popular platform speakers available. He was dubbed by the press "the lecturer *extraordinaire!*" And this was just what he played in a two-day cameo role in *The Chautauqua,* a nonmusical Elvis Presley film, although in the movie Vincent expounds on the beauty of Shakespeare and not art classics. When the 1920s-set movie was finally released as *The Trouble with Girls* (1969), it was generally ignored, as were the guest spots by Price and John Carradine.

Apparently Vincent could seldom say no to a commercially sound offer. Stravon Educational Press asked the Prices to prepare a follow-up cookbook, which they did with *The Come into the Kitchen Cookbook* (1969), a more modest gourmet sampler, designed with a more homey overtone. AIP then negotiated with Vincent to bail them out of a financial pinch. They had become involved with an arty tri-part European production based on Edgar Allan Poe stories entitled *Histoires Extraordinaires,* directed by Roger Vadim, Federico Fellini, and Louis Malle. Despite the presence of such box-office "names" as Brigitte Bardot, Alain Delon, Jane and Peter Fonda, and Terence Stamp, the picture seemed a gloomy prospect for the American release market. After redubbing the film, retitling it *Spirits of the Dead* (1969) and adding a Ray Charles song, Price was utilized to speak an off-camera prologue and epilogue narration. Thus AIP could promote the film in the mold of past AIP-Poe-Price pictures. However, all their efforts were in vain. The picture was still a bust on the American film market.

While in England negotiating for further pictures, Vincent could not resist the opportunity to play the domineering Dr. Sloper in a BBC-TV production of *The Heiress,* based on Henry James' *Washington Square.* Basil Rathbone had played the role on Broadway and Sir Ralph Richardson on the screen. After the successful airing of the Price rendition, there was talk of the American National Educational Television network optioning the program for U.S. telecasting, but nothing developed.

More important to Vincent's career, AIP's welfare, and Price's legion of film fans, he signed a three-film agreement with producer Louis Heyward. The three movies were to be backed by AIP. The first was *The Oblong Box* (1969), loosely conceived from yet another Edgar Allan Poe story. At last Price was paired on-screen with Christopher Lee. If terror-film addicts expected terrific dramatic impacts from the two sovereigns of the sinister, they were sorely disappointed. Most of this brooding, Gothic celluloid study focused on the morose Julian Markham (Price) and his strangely ill brother (Alastair Williamson). Lee was given relatively little on-camera time as Dr. Neuhartt, a victim within the story. While there was gore in abudance, the film contained a disquieting mixture of voodoo, monsterism, and brutality, resulting only in unsatisfactory entertainment. *The Oblong Box* grossed a rather modest $1.02 million in U.S. and Canadian distributors' rentals.

Gordon Hessler, who had directed *The Oblong Box,* was also in charge of *Scream and Scream Again* (1970). It was based on Peter Saxon's contemporary novel, *The Disoriented Man.* In an effort to boost the box-office take, Price was teamed with both Christopher Lee and Peter Cushing, a leading triumvirate of horror-film stars.

Sadly, the results were a mishmash. As if to justify the presence of Lee and Cushing, a vampirism theme was inserted in the tale, while Price seemed overly detached, at least plotwise, playing the menacing creator of a race of supermen.

No one was particularly happy with *Scream and Scream Again,* and for the next Price-Heyward-Hessler-AIP feature, *Cry of the Banshee* (1970), the creative forces returned to a more classical horror mode. The setting was the sixteenth century, and director Hessler painted the screen with more gore, no humor, and an increased reliance on heavy atmosphere. The film marked the screen return of one-time Continental stage-and-screen star Elizabeth Bergner, but in the role of an old crone named Ona she looked as decrepit and depressing as the film itself. As if in desperation, AIP featured a tombstone in the advertisements for this picture, bearing the legend "Edgar Allan Poe Probes New Depths of Horror!" What Poe had to do with the origins of this film still remains a mystery.

When Price returned to Hollywood, there was an overtone of staleness to his film career that his last several movie ventures had not eradicated. He and AIP were well aware that their future joint pictures must take a new turn, if they were to compete financially in the changing movie market. Real-life horrors — the Charles Manson murder case, assassinations of political figures, skyjacking, etc. — were making anything on-screen seem very tame.

While AIP was exploring new approaches to Vincent's screen future, the actor kept busy on television. He was a guest on more than fifty "Hollywood Squares" shows and was seen four times on "Dinah's Place" where he demonstrated to Miss Shore and the home viewers some amazingly simple dining recipes. He acted on the "Here's Lucy" video show and on dramatic series like "Mod Squad."

When asked why he did not take a breather from public appearances, Price responded, "I'm an old ham. I go nuts when I'm not working and I'll do almost anything. I love acting, even in nonsense. For me, acting is an expression of joy."

With the end of the 1960s, another chapter in Price's life closed. Sears decided to dismantle its art-sale program. It had served its purpose, so much so that the many independent store chains who had copied the idea were now making it much more difficult for Sears to locate the quality items it had acquired throughout the past decade. Price fully understood the reasoning. "It was wonderful," he said of his buying sprees on Sears' behalf. "I was like a secondhand millionaire."

But as the 1970s developed, observant people at large knew that Vincent Price was not a secondhand anything.

Chapter Seven

"Turquoise for my body.
Silver for my soul.
I was united with beauty all around me."
　　　　— from a poem by Charles C. Long,
　　　　　a Navaho.

Just as *House of Wax* indelibly altered Vincent Price's film career, in its own way *The Abominable Dr. Phibes* (1971) was as influential. On one hand, American International Pictures proudly publicized the film as Price's one hundredth motion picture, a claim that was difficult either to prove or dispute. With all the documentaries, short and long, in which Vincent had either performed or narrated, besides his TV work, the total was very likely near or even above the AIP figure. Aside from the centenarian milestone, what *Phibes* represented was an element of deeper meaning.

For many viewers and critics *Phibes* personified the perfect Vincent Price film. It was wrapped in an art-deco style; it had an insane, yet misunderstood, hero; it contained ingenious and bloody murder; and the whole package underscored a high camp atmosphere that constantly highlighted and reenforced the comedy elements. Moreover, it finally gave Price an originally devised screen character that could be totally associated with him. For a change, Price was not portraying a figure from Edgar Allan Poe literature, but fleshing out a characterization devised especially for him. Thus the film created a special audience identification that long had been part of Christopher Lee's career as the screen's newest *Dracula* but had been missing from Price's assorted movie forays into the Grand Guignol.

130

RIGHT: As Prince Prospero in *The Masque of the Red Death* (American International, 1964). BELOW: With Lon Chaney, Jr. in *The Haunted Palace* (American International, 1964).

TOP LEFT: With Martha Hyer in *House of 1000 Dolls* (American International, 1967). TOP RIGHT: With Elizabeth Shepherd in *The Tomb of Ligeia* (American International, 1965). ABOVE: With Jack Mullaney, Frankie Avalon, and Dwayne Hickman in *Dr. Goldfoot and the Bikini Machine* (American International, 1965). RIGHT: As The Captain in *War Gods of the Deep* (American International, 1965).

C.

David

Pickup By:
10/14/2021

.

.

.

.

.

.

ABOVE: As Matthew Hopkins in *The Conqueror Worm* (American International, 1968). TOP RIGHT: With Anthony Newlands in *Scream and Scream Again* (American International, 1970). RIGHT: With Clint Walker in *More Dead Than Alive* (United Artists, 1969). FAR RIGHT: With Diana Ivarson in *The Jackals* (Twentieth Century-Fox, 1967).

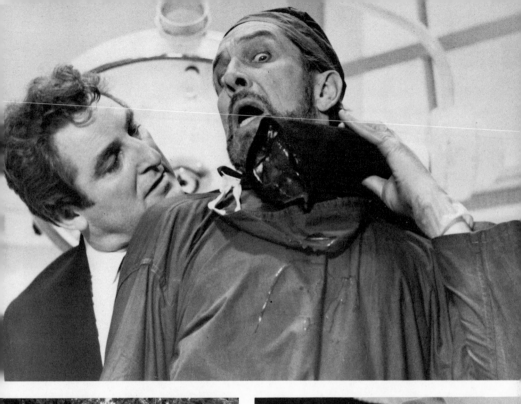

ABOVE: With Robert Morley, Dennis Price, Robert Coote, and Ian Hendry in *Theater of Blood* (United Artists, 1973). TOP RIGHT: At the recording session for *Darling of the Day* cast album (1968). CENTER RIGHT: With Hugh Griffith in *Cry of the Banshee* (American International, 1970). BOTTOM RIGHT: With Joseph Cotten in *The Abominable Dr. Phibes* (American International, 1971).

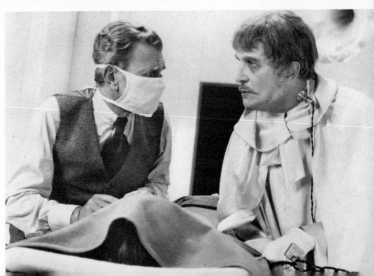

RIGHT: On the set of *Madhouse* (American International, 1974) with Peter Cushing. BELOW. In *Madhouse* as "Dr. Death".

Louis Heyward produced this British-made feature directed by Robert Fuest. Since the inflationary rates of the Hollywood unions continued to be prohibitive, a permanent fact of Vincent's moviemaking life was that all his AIP pictures were being done in England. Not only did this cut costs, but British actors seemed much less reluctant about appearing in a "horror" film than their Hollywood counterparts. The *Phibes* supporting cast was excellent: Hugh Griffith and Terry-Thomas were among the British players, while Joseph Cotten, an ex-Mercury Theater chum of Vincent's, held up the American end.

When asked why his revengeful protagonist in this picture was a doctor, Price answered, "If all the mad doctors were extracted from crime, horror, and science fiction, you wouldn't have much left. Think of Dr. Jekyll, Dr. Fu Manchu, Dr. Cyclops, Dr. Caligari, Dr. No, Dr. Strangelove, etc. People are wary of doctors, anyway, and mystified by the paraphernalia of surgery and medical research. It's always been a rich field for horror stories." Price himself might well have been scared by a few doctors in his youth, for his performance as Dr. Anton Phibes was the epitome of the mad doctor.

The critics went almost as mad as Phibes in praising the film. The Chicago *Sun-Times* proclaimed, "*The Abominable Dr. Phibes* has taken over the Chicago Theater, after the lengthy hegemony of *Love Story,* like a fresh whiff of formaldehyde, with a witty ad display ('Love means never having to say you're ugly') and a name cast...Price is marvelous." The Philadelphia *Inquirer* enthused, "The camp horror movie reaches a pinnacle of absurd glory...they should strike off a magenta Oscar for this one." The Fort Lauderdale *News* offered its very perceptive observations, "John Wayne recently won an Academy Award for putting himself on in *True Grit.* Price's portrayal here makes Wayne look like a beginner at the art. For Price is doing the same thing — laughing at films which have made him famous." *The New York Daily News* shouted, "Dr. Phibes is just what a horror movie should be..." The film seemed to receive acclaim from every corner of the country. Willard Van Dyke, then director of films at the Museum of Modern Art in New York, requested the movie screened at that venerable institution, and *Newsweek* magazine reported it received "unexpected cultural kudos" at the museum.

Financially, *Dr. Phibes* drew in $1.5 million in distributors' domestic grosses, and AIP immediately planned a sequel, to be lensed as soon as Price could find the time. More than anything, the movie served to bridge Price's screen image from the Poe-sian figure of the 1960s to the mock-horror figure of the 1970s, with the on-camera character generally as much to be pitied as to be abhorred. Price brought his own charisma to the role, giving the deranged celluloid physician as much heart as blood and bitters.

While *Phibes* was rejuvenating Price's box-office standing, the actor was busy with his many other projects. So many were they that his income was reported between $300,000 and $400,000 with only a third of the annual take coming from theatrical motion pictures. He did a cameo in a mystery spoof for "ABC Movie of the Week" called *What's a Nice Girl Like You . . .* (December 18, 1971) that starred Brenda Vaccaro. He also did more than sixty segments of "The Hollywood Squares," and about twenty other television shows.

He also made his second contribution to the Library of Congress, sorting and delivering twenty-one manuscript containers of material. The behest was divided into three categories: 1) miscellaneous correspondence, twelve boxes; 2) personal, including some family papers, five boxes; and 3) requests and invitations, four boxes. The documents covered the years 1961-1967.

He narrated a Canadian documentary, *The Beginning of the End of the World,* a film with a revolutionary concept. It was designed to be shown simultaneously by thirty-eight projectors in special theaters and planetariums. With a Skitch Henderson score to complement the visuals and Price's narration, the film premiered on August 25, 1971, at the Omnitheatre in Winnipeg. Vincent was so enthused about this cinema project that he attended this premiere. Although it received its critical dues, it has not been shown widely for the obvious reason of its expense and special cinematic needs.

Vincent also made a pilot film for a projected television series entitled "Boo!" It found no network sponsors.

Price continued his frenetic work pace, insisting "I've always believed it was much more important to work than to be rich."

Almost as if to establish the truth of that statement, he gave more lectures than ever before, even creating a new program spoofing American eating habits. It was entitled "What the Hell Do You Do with the Parsley?" It was a lesser talk, delivered only at occasions that warranted an irreverent approach.

He remained active in all the art councils and committees, and even had time to prepare another art book, *The Vincent Price Treasury of American Art.* Done in conjunction with *Country Beautiful,* it proved to be much more than just another coffee-table-type volume. He also wrote background pieces on art for various art journals and some weekly family-oriented magazines.

Price made no secret about his disenchantment with President Richard Nixon's attitude toward the arts. Price saw the spark of cultural interest that surrounded the Kennedy years fall into decline with the Nixon Administration. Despite or because of this, Vincent felt he should remain on the Indian Arts and Crafts Board. He did, however, take occasional verbal punches at some of the official indifference he encountered. "We are responsible to the Secretary of the Interior," he told a Washington reporter one afternoon. "We've had a rough time, sometimes, finding out who the Secretary of the Interior is."

Vincent expanded his activities in proselytizing the cultural contributions of the American Indins. He urged Doubleday and Company to publish *The Whispering Winds,* a volume of poetry by Indian children. Price took occasion upon publication to publicize the volume whenever and wherever possible.

Since the early days of his association with the Indian Arts and Crafts Board, Price had pushed the members to elect an Indian to their board. He believed that the board ruled without representation by not having an Indian member, and brought his resolution to the table year after year. After a few years as chairman, he was able finally to force the issue. A Cherokee Indian was elected to membership, and when no board vacancy occurred, Vincent gave up his own seat. It was the type of gesture that showed how sincerely he felt about the Indian cause. A few months later, when Marlon Brando refused the Oscar in protest over Hollywood's treatment of the American Indian, Vincent was asked what he thought of the Indian uprising at Wounded Knee. "I think they are going about it in the wrong way," he replied, "*but* everything the Indians say is true. You have never seen such poverty." Price had no public comment on Brando's actions.

Back in the film fold, Robert Fuest again guided Vincent through the *Phibes* paces with *Dr. Phibes Rises Again* (1972). AIP teamed Price with Robert Quarry, who had gained his own special reputation with his entries, *Count Yorga, Vampire* (1970) and *The Return of Count Yorga* (1971). The setting this time was England and Egypt, but the picture was shot largely in London. Once more the ambiance of camp-art deco permeated the production, giving a special timeliness to the *Ten Little Indians* homicide premise of the plot.

Of the indulgent self-mockery contained in the two *Phibes* motion pictures, Price has said, "I find almost anything funny, and myself funniest of all. I don't mean that I'm a comedian, but I find that the minute I take myself seriously I've got to laugh because it's so ridiculous. It's what gets me through an awful lot of films, this sense of the ridiculous." *Phibes* was one of his favorite roles, and although the film was very funny and broad in its spoofing, he approached it differently. "*Phibes* was something I had to take very seriously when I was doing it so it would come out funny. All the same, it was agony for me because my face was covered with plastic, and I giggled and laughed the whole time, day and night, and the make-up man and I were practically married because the make-up kept dissolving and he had to patch me up every five minutes."

The critics were not as enthusiastic about the follow-up entry in the *Phibes* canon, and for that matter neither was the public. *Dr. Phibes Rises Again* had diminished box-office receipts. It caused AIP to drop plans to continue the series in future installments.

During the filming of the second *Phibes,* Price did a television series on London's BBC network called "Cooking: Price-Wise." This show featured Vincent in the studio kitchen, helping Britons prepare good food on limited budgets. The show was telecast in six installments.

Since the *Phibes* screen duet had revenge as its central motif, Price was looking for just that special quality in the many scripts submitted to him thereafter. As he explained, "There's a big revival of interest in the Jacobean theater of revenge. Revenge is really the only evil human emotion that is not dated, and it is in everyone. Our motives of mayhem today are so senseless. You mug someone on the street for $1.98 and then shoot him for the fun of it. Revenge is one of these great ballsy things. You killed my wife and now I'm going to kill you." Luckily, he found the right script, written by Anthony Greville-Bell, called *Theater of Blood* (1973).

Instead of the eye-for-an-eye revenge motive of *Phibes,* United Artists' *Theater of Blood* offered a man seeking revenge for having been so long ignored. The plot concerned a Shakespearean actor killing a group of pompous London critics who refused to admit he possessed any talent. About the character of Edward Lionheart, Price said, "*Theater of Blood* was a dream to make, and very real to me. I really understand the man who is doing his very best and yet is unrecognized."

In this color, British-made feature, Price's Lionheart kills all of his victims in variations on great scenes from the plays of the bard. It allowed the filmmakers the opportunity to use many guest stars as the ten victims, and to focus on the black-comedy elements of the killings. Most critics appreciated the gallows-humor approach, while complimenting Price on his athletic performance in which he donned several disguises, gaits, and dialects. Whether rolling his eyes in oversized double takes or chuckling diabolically, Price offered his own *tour de force* performance.

United Artists was so pleased with the film, Price, and the cast (which included Diana Rigg, Jack Hawkins, Coral Browne, Robert Morley, Dennis Price, Diana Dors, Milo O'Shea) that they mounted an expensive saturation publicity campaign that highlighted the picture's black comedy and, of course, the pivotal performance by Price. "Vincent Price has reserved a seat for you in *Theater of Blood*," the ad announced, beneath which was a collage showing six very dead movie critics. The film was taken seriously in most quarters, and a few critics even noticed how neglected Price had been in some circles over the many years. Many film critics now began to review Vincent's career with positive reflection. He was beginning now to emerge as an elder statesman in the film industry, not just the kingpin of the "horror" flicks.

Despite the popularity of *Theater of Blood* and the studio's attempt to see the film as an "A" production, it could not and did not compete with the box-office pull of the newer type of "B" productions, the black action and the Kung Fu films. *Theater of Blood* earned only a little over one million dollars in U.S. and Canadian gross rentals.

Vincent did not slacken his participation on television in the new decade. In the 1970s alone, he appeared on more than 250 segments of "The Hollywood Squares," three of "The Carol Burnett Show," several guest appearances on late-night talk shows, and turned up on a score of variety and game programs. As for dramatic appearances, he did one that almost ranked with the best of his motion-picture performances, as Michael Bastion in *Black Day for Bluebeard* (NBC, March 19, 1974) on a monthly segment of the ninety-minute outing, "The Snoop Sisters." The sleuthing sisters were portrayed by two of Vincent's old friends, Helen Hayes and Mildred Natwick. In this episode, Price's Michael Bastion was a gourmet and "horror" movie star, one accused of killing his wife. Through the entire show, Price provided a performance remarkable for its self-deprecating humor and charm.

For his next theatrical film, Vincent picked another revenge piece, though this time he was on the receiving end. In *Madhouse* (1974) he played another horror film actor, a sad, beleaguered man known to the world for his portrayal of "Dr. Death," and accounted one of the most successful screen villains in movie history. Brought back after a long retirement to reincarnate his famous role, he is mentally tortured by and accused of many killings that villain

Peter Cushing actually committed in his guise. Cushing's on-camera motive is one any actor could understand and appreciate — years before *he* had wanted the part of Dr. Death. Several clips from Price's old movies were highlighted during this London-shot film, honoring his career as well as defining his on-camera character.

Instead of resting on the weekends during the shooting of *Madhouse,* Vincent commuted by train to Manchester to do the BBC-TV show, "The Movie Quiz," which featured celebrity guests in a contest of memories concerning the film world. Each Sunday night for many weeks, Vincent would complete the video quiz show in the late evening, then jump on a train for the overnight trip to London, arriving at the film studio for his 6:30 A.M. call. In addition to all this activity, many weekday nights were filled with a stint as a disc jockey on Radio One broadcasts throughout the London environs.

Unfortunately and perhaps understandably such work output on Price's part during these years were bound to have its toll on his private life. On August 17, 1973, Mary Price filed for divorce in a Santa Monica court, after twenty-four years of marriage. The split was termed friendly, and the unofficial reason given was the enormous workload Vincent insisted upon maintaining. Mary asked for, and received, custody of their eleven-year-old daughter, Mary Victoria.

Back in England, Vincent and actress Coral Browne, the latter more famous for her sexually offbeat role in the motion picture *The Killing of Sister George* (1969) than for all the years of her multi-media activities put together, continued their friendship, which had begun on the *Theater of Blood* sound stages. While the press blazened headlines linking the two performers in the most unexpected match of the decade, sources close to Price insisted that the rapport was based on mutual cultural interests rather than romantic notions that might lead to marriage.

The beginning of 1974 saw Vincent performing in *Percy's Progress,* a cinematic follow-up to *Percy* (1971), which had also featured Elke Sommer. For his six-day cameo work — playing an Onassis-like figure, Price joined the crew on location in Cyprus and back at the London studios. Vincent was scheduled to start work on *The Naked Eye,* a new terror yarn to be financed by AIP, but the script, which had already gone through several drafts, proved to be still untenable to Price. With the collapse of this venture, Price is wont to admitting that in the mid-1970s it has become more and more difficult to package the proper production elements of his type of movie; and that if current economic trends, strikes, depressions, etc., continue, the day of the American-filmed entry in England might well be over. In its wake, all but the omnibus type of Gothic fright film, like *Tales from The Crypt* (1972), *Asylum* (1973), and *Tales that Witness Madness* (1973) would be curtailed.

Vincent returned to the United States in February, 1974, to once again appear on the lecture circuit. It provided the usual comforting sort of revenue and, more important for Price, a willing audience who thrived on his assorted topics and his distinctive manner of presentation. It is estimated that in a one-month period he appeared in front of nearly a quarter of a million people on those tours.

He then traveled to Warsaw, Poland, where the Polish government was staging an exhibition of early American art. As the pre-eminent expert in that field, Vincent was selected to lecture on the development of that art. One of his own paintings, *The Death of Sitting Bull,* was on exhibit, and Vincent quite naturally took that opportunity to plug Indian art. Noticed during his appearance in Warsaw were the Indian jewelry he usually wears in public, including a beautifully crafted turquoise watchband and many Indian rings. "The jewelry is good luck," Price told the Polish onlookers. He proceeded to explain that according to Indian folklore, Turquoise wards off the eternal negativism of the evil eye.

While in Warsaw, Price learned he had been voted Best Actor by the International Festival of Science Fiction and Fantasy Films. This *Grand Prix* award confirmed that Price is just now receiving the acclaim due him.

As for Price's future, plans are being made for a movie version of Shakespeare's *Troilus and Cressida.* He found a summer 1974 midwest music-tent tour of *Oliver* (he played the role of Fagin) pleasant and remunerative and plans other such ventures. He is also hoping to star in a television special based on the life of Bram Stoker (1847-1912), the Dublin-born writer who originated *Dracula.* Also, Price will be heard as the voice of Anwar, the grand vizier of Persia, in *The Cobbler and the Thief,* a feature-length animated version of Indries Shah's *Nasruddin.*

Obviously the side of Price that reflects his love of the art world will continue to flourish. He is contemplating more art and cookbooks. He will continue to participate on art juries. His lecture-circuit play-dates for upcoming years are already filled. He has been appointed to the Arts Advisory Council for the National Bicentennial Celebration. Concomitant with this, he is preparing a special new lecture to celebrate America's two hundredth birthday.

As another performing advertisement, he has inaugurated still another type of his special evening in which he mixes theater, lectures, and music — a program in which he performs selections from the works of Edgar Allan Poe, accompanied by a full orchestral background. On play-dates thus far, he has joined with the St. Louis Orchestra and, on a later occasion, with the Denver Philharmonic.

Regarding his personal life, for which he deliberately leaves little time, Vincent is adamant in maintaining that his son Barrett is his best friend. The two have much in common, and the son appears to have acquired all of the father's cultural sensitivities. Barrett is a practicing poet, has taught anthropology at the University of New Mexico, worked for the Westinghouse Institute, has a great interest in the American Indian lore, and writes a weekly scatter-shooting column in a New Mexico newspaper.

Price continues his recording career, reading stories aimed particularly at children. He received a Grammy nomination for *Ghosts, Witches, and Goblins* in 1974, and followed it with the equally successful *A Graveyard of Ghost Tales*.

For Vincent Price, now in his sixties, retirement is not only unlikely, but probably impossible. He insists he has too much he wants to accomplish, and too many new vistas to explore. As he has said, "They will have to bury me before I retire, and even then, my tombstone will read, 'I'll be back!' "

* * *

The professional success of Vincent Price stands as an intriguing example of an actor adjusting his life to accommodate an extremely commercialized artistic structure. The artist in America is on his own and, in general, he alone shapes the course of his life and career, creating his own career breaks and developing his own exploitable talent. This grueling process often takes place in an atmosphere of total, and therefore brutalizing, indifference.

But, if anything, Vincent Price has been a survivor. Lacking the destructive inner negativism of some past show-business victims (from Everett Sloane to Montgomery Clift and Marilyn Monroe), Price has fortunately perceived the alternatives of life. Most often he has known exactly what he is capable of doing as a performer, and what he could not successfully carry off at the box-office. More important, he has understood what compromises he must make to remain true to own sense of dignity. Through his various performing-career levels (on Broadway, as a 20th Century-Fox contractee, a free-lancing featured player, and more recently, as a horror-film great) he has striven to remain sensitive and open to his love for the higher reaches of art.

VINCENT PRICE UNMASKED

It is ironic, then, that to maintain his special standard of total life, many people insist he has sacrificed his integrity as an actor. Whether or not this debatable point is true may be beside the point, for Vincent Price has come to terms with his own life, and it is a life that he seems to enjoy thoroughly. On the face of the mask, the public sees him as a flamboyantly baroque actor of horror films, a performer who just now may be approaching the acclaim he so often has deserved in the past. Behind the mask, Price is a cultured, sensitive, and gentle man, both enjoying and living his brand of life to the very fullest while sharing a lion's portion of this enjoyment with a wide, varied, and enthusiastic public.

To some, this two-sided nature would seem schizophrenic. For Price, it highlights the duality an American actor must sometimes acquire. With the state of the creative arts as it is today, the choice Price has made must be accepted as a singularly pragmatic individual solution to the actor's never-ending dilemma of survival.

A philosopher once wrote that the purpose of life was trifold — to learn, to grow, and to experience. Vincent Price has obviously fulfilled this definition. The adventurous spirit and curious nature that has taken him to the four corners of the world has taught him a respect for life in all its forms. His sharp and open mind has forced growth by constantly asking the impossible questions. His sensitivity and great love of live have given him the capacity to experience all the wonders he confronts. In the future he will remain on this path. For Vincent Price, Renaissance man, it is the only way.

Vincent Price On Broadway

VICTORIA REGINA
Broadhurst Theater:

December 26, 1935 - 204 performances
August 21, 1936 - 311 performances

Producer-director, Gilbert Miller; drama by Laurence Housman; set designer, Rex Whistler.

Harry Plimmer (Lord Conygham); Mary Austin (Maid Servant); Babette Feist (Duchess of Kent); Helen Hayes (Victoria); Lewis Casson (Lord Melbourne); Vincent Price (Prince Albert); George Macready (Prince Ernest); Mary Heberden (Lady Muriel); Renee Macready (Lady Grace); James Bedford (Mr. Oakley); Cherry Hardy (Duchess of Sutherland); Helen Trenhoime (Lady Jane); Tom Woods (General Grey); James Woodburn (John Brown); George Zucco (Lord Beaconsfield); Herschel Martin (Sir Arthur Bigge); Felix Brown (Imperial Highness); Gilbert McKay (His Royal Highness).

THE LADY HAS A HEART
Longacre Theater:

September 25, 1937 - 90 performances

Producers-directors, Rufus Phillips, Watson Barratt; drama by Ladislaus Bus-Fekete; adaptor, Edward Roberts.

Judith Alden (Klari); Vincent Price (Jean); Hilda Spong (Countess Mariassy); Elissa Landi (Countess Katinka); Lumsden Hare (Count Albert Mariassy); Royal Beal (Count Gyorgy); Derek Fairman (Radio Announcer); Katherine Standing (Ilonka); Tom Bate (Ferenez); Richard Bowler (Electrician).

THE SHOEMAKER'S HOLIDAY
Mercury Theater:

January 1, 1938 - 69 performances

Director, Orson Welles; comedy by Thomas Dekker; music, Lehman Engel; costumes, Millia Davenport.

George Coulouris (King); Frederic Tozere (Sir Hugh Lacy); Joseph Cotten (Rowland Lacy); William Mowry (Askew); John Hoysradt (Sir Roger Oteley); Vincent Price (Master Hammon); John A. Willard (Master Warner); George Duthie (Master Scott); Whitford Kane (Simon Eyre); Norman Lloyd (Roger); Hiram Sherman (Firk); Elliott Reid (Ralph); Francis Carpenter (Dodger); Stefan Schnabel (Dutch Skipper); Arthur Anderson (Boy); William Alland (Serving Man); Alice Frost (Rose); Edith Barrett (Sybil); Marian Warring-Manley (Margery); Ruth Ford (Jane); William Howell, Charles Baker (Attendants); Charles Baker, Tillston Perry, George Lloyd, Frederick Ross, Frederick Thompson, John Berry (Soldiers); Richard Wilson, William Herz, James O'Rear, Frank Westbrook (Shoemakers).

HEARTBREAK HOUSE

Mercury Theater:

April 29, 1938 - 48 performances

Stager, Orson Welles; comedy by George Bernard Shaw; settings, John Koenig; costumes, Millia Davenport.

Geraldine Fitzgerald (Ellie Dunn); Brenda Forbes (Nurse Guinness); Orson Welles (Captain Shotover); Phyllis Joyce (Lady Utterword); Mady Christians (Heslone Hushabye); Erskine Sanford (Mazzini Dunn); Vincent Price (Hector Hushabye); George Coulouris (Boss Mangan); John Hoysradt (Randall Utterword); Eustace Wyatt (Burglar).

OUTWARD BOUND

Playhouse Theater:

December 22, 1938 - 255 performances

Producers, Robinson Smith, Bramwell Fletcher, William A. Brady; Stager, Otto Preminger; drama by Sutton Vane; settings, Watson Barratt.

Morgan Farley (Scrubby); Helen Chandler (Ann); Alexander Kirkland (Henry); Bramwell Fletcher (Mr. Prior); Florence Reed

(Mrs. Clivedon-Banks); Vincent Price (Reverend William Duke); Laurette Taylor (Mrs. Midget); Louis Hector (Mr. Lingley); Thomas Chalmers (Reverend Frank Thomson).

ANGEL STREET
John Golden Theater:
December 5, 1941 - 1,292 performances

Presenter-director, Shepard Traube; drama by Patrick Hamilton; scenery-costumes, Lemuel Ayres.

Judith Evelyn (Mrs. Manningham); Vincent Price (Mr. Manningham); Elizabeth Eustic (Nancy); Florence Edney (Elizabeth); Leo G. Carroll (Rough).

RICHARD III
New York City Center Theater:
December 9, 1953 - 15 performances

Producer, Jean Dalrymple; director, Margaret Webster; drama by William Shakespeare; music, Alex North; costumes, Emerline Roche; production designer, Richard Whorf.

Jose Ferrer (Richard, Duke of Gloucester); Staats Cotsworth (George, Duke of Clarence); Paul Ballantyne (Brackenbury); William Post, Jr. (Lord Hastings); Maureen Stapleton (Anne); Tom Tryon (Tressel); Benedict MacQuarrie (Berkeley); G. Wood (Priest); Jessie Royce Landis (Queen Elizabeth); Philip Huston (Earl Rivers); Bert Whitley (Lord Grey); Vincent Price (Duke of Buckingham); John Straub (Marquis of Dorset); Florence Reed (Queen Margaret); Eugene Stuckmann, Jack Bittner (Murderers); Norman Roland (Edward IV); John Glennon (young Clarence); Margaret Wycherly (Dowager Duchess of York); Stanley Carlson, Jack Fletcher, Will Davis (Citizens); John Connoughton (Edward, Prince of Wales); Charles Taylor (Richard, Duke of York); Leopold Badia (Lord Mayor of London); James Arenton (Bishop of Ely); Wallace Widdencombe (Bishop); Dehl Berti (Messenger); Charles Summers (Duke of Norfolk); Jay Barney (Sir Richard Ratcliff); Robinson Stone (Lord Lovel); Bill Butler (Scrivener);

Sandy Campbell (Page); Kendall Clark (Sir James Tyrell); Peter Harris, Richard Cowdery, Robert Ludlum (Messengers); Douglas Watson (Henry, Earl of Richmond); Bill Butler (Sir James Blunt); Vincent Donahue (Sir William Brandon); John Glennon (Earl of Oxford).

BLACK-EYED SUSAN
Playhouse Theater:
December 23, 1954 - 4 performances

Presenter, Gordon W. Pollock, Hart and Goodman; director, Gregory Ratoff; drama by A. B. Shiffrin; settings-costumes, William Molyneux.

Vincent Price (Dr. Nicholas Marsh); Kay Medford (Dr. Zelda Barry); Everett Sloane (Dr. Louis Beaumont); Dana Wynter (Susan Gillespie); Charles Boaz (Peter Gillespie).

DARLING OF THE DAY
George Abbott Theater:
January 27, 1968 - 32 performances

Presenters, Theater Guild, Joel Schenker; director, Noel Willman; based on the novel *Buried Alive* by Arnold Bennett; music, Jules Styne; lyrics, E. Y. Harburg; choreography, Lee Theodore, scenery, Oliver Smith; costumes, Raoul Pene duBois; lighting, Peggy Clark; musical director-vocal arranger, Buster Davis; dance music, Trude Rittman; orchestrator, Ralph Burns. Original cast album — RCA Victor.

Peter Woodthorpe (Oxford); Vincent Price (Priam Farll); Charles Welch (Henry Leek); Carl Nicholas (Old Gentleman); Brenda Forbes (Lady Vale); Ross Miles (Cabby); Leo Leyden (Doctor); Patricia Routledge (Alice Challice); Joy Nichols (Daphne); Teddy Green (Alif); Marc Jordan (Bert); Beth Howland (Rosalind); Reid Klein (Sydney); Larry Brucker (Attendant); Paul Eichel (Frame Maker); Mitchell Jason (Duncan); John Aman (Equerry); Charles Gerald (King); John Aman (Constable); Camila Ashland (Mrs.

Leek); Herb Wilson, Fred Siretta (Curates); Michael Lewis (Pennington); Leo Leyden (Judge); Marian Haradlson, Kay Oslin, Jeannette Seibert, Maggie Task, Maggie Worth, John Aman, Larry Brucker, Paul Eichel, Reid Klein, Carl Nicholas, Albert Zimmerman (Singers); Bonnie Ano, Reby Howells, Beth Howland, Georgianne Thon, Phylis Wallach, Denise Winston, Christopher Chadman, George Lee, Jim May, Ross Miles, Fred Siretta, Herb Wilson (Dancers).

Musical Numbers: "Mad for Art," "He's A Genius," "To Get out of This World Alive," "It's Enough to Make a Lady Fall in Love," "A Gentleman's Gentleman," "Double Soliloquy," "Let's See What Happens," "Panache," "I've Got a Rainbow Working for Me," "Money, Money, Money," "That Something Extra Special," "What Makes a Marriage Merry," "Not on Your Nellie," "Sunset Tree," "Butler in the Abbey."

The Feature Films Of Vincent Price

SERVICE DE LUXE *(Universal, 1938) 85 min.*

Associate producer, Edmund Grainger; director, Rowland V. Lee; story, Bruce Manning, Vera Caspary; screenplay, Gertrude Purcell, Leonard Spigelgass; costumes, Irene; art directors, Jack Otterson, Jack Ottering; camera, George Robinson; editor, Ted J. Kent.

Constance Bennett (Helen Murphy); Vincent Price (Robert Wade); Charles Ruggles (Robinson); Helen Broderick (Pearl); Mischa Auer (Serge Bibenko); Joy Hughes (Audrey); Frances Robinson (Secretary); Halliwell Hobbes (Butler); Raymond Parker, Frank Coghlan, Jr. (Bellhops); Nina Guilbert (Mrs. Devereaux).

By the time of *Service De Luxe,* Hollywood filmmakers had exhausted nearly every conceivable variation of the screwball comedy genre that once seemed so fresh in *Three-Cornered Moon* (1933) and *My Man Godfrey* (1936). Critics were so saturated with wacky film premises that this release was labeled a "pathetically unfunny farce" (Brooklyn *Daily Eagle)*.

In *Topper* (1937), Constance Bennett had shown she could almost match Carole Lombard, the queen of screwball pictures, but in *Service de Luxe,* thin-waisted Bennett was uninspired. She mechanically breezed through her role as the slick co-owner (with Helen Broderick) of an elaborate luxury service bureau geared to pamper every eccentric need of New York's ultra rich. In pre-Production Code vehicles of the early 1930s, the plot would have called for Bennett to have an illicit love affair and mother an irresistible tike. Here, however, the formula script offered her as an overcompetent career gal who wilts at the no-nonsense charms of a hayseed tractor inventor (Vincent Price) and marries him, no less, at the climax.

For on-camera comedy diversion there were the smooth antics of Charles Ruggles as a wealthy engineer and cook, Broderick as Bennett's flip business partner and confidant, Joy Hodges as a willful debutante, Mischa Auer as a deposed Russian nobleman turned chef, and Halliwell Hobbes as an harrassed butler.

Considering the production obstacles and cast competition, Price fared all right as the young hero who vows to be a manly male in the

151

big city. Whether tinkering with a tailor over prices or combating determined Bennett and Hodges, he held his own as the attractive straight man. The critics were properly impressed. "He's a lean, lanky young man of the Joel McCrea type and he has all the assurance and charm necessary for a click on the screen." (*The New York Daily News*) "Though a bit hard to get into the camera vertically, seems a likely hero." (*The New York Times*) "He is personable, with not too slick a manner even in a brittle comedy." (New York *Sun*)

THE PRIVATE LIVES OF ELIZABETH AND ESSEX *(Warner Bros., 1939) about 106 min.*

Executive producer, Hal B. Wallis; associate producer, Robert Lord; director, Michael Curtiz; based on the play *Elizabeth the Queen* by Maxwell Anderson; screenplay, Norman Reilly Raine, Aeneas MacKenzie; music, Erich Wolfgang Korngold; art director, Anton Grot; sound C. A. Riggs; costumes, Orray-Kelly; assistant director, Sherry Shourds; special effects, Byron Haskin, H. F. Koenekamp; dialogue director, Stanley Logan; camera, Sol Polito; editor, Owen Marks.

Bette Davis (Queen Elizabeth); Errol Flynn (Earl of Essex); Olivia de Havilland (Lady Penelope Gray); Donald Crisp (Francis Bacon); Alan Hale (Earl of Tyrone); Vincent Price (Sir Walter Raleigh); Henry Stephenson (Lord Burghley); Henry Daniell (Sir Robert Cecil); James Stephenson (Sir Thomas Egerton); Nanette Fabray (Miss Margaret Radcliffe); Ralph Forbes (Lord Knollys); Robert Warwick (Lord Mountjoy); Leo G. Carroll (Sir Edward Coke); Guy Bellis (Lord Charles Howard); and Rosella Towne, Maris Wrixon, John Sutton, Doris Lloyd, Forrester Harvey.

In 1939, playwright Maxwell Anderson had created a Broadway success with his lyrical period drama, *Elizabeth the Queen*. The distorted screen version opted instead for grandiloquent and swashbuckling historical pageantry. The overstated emotion-charged encounters between Elizabeth I (1553-1603) and the earl of Essex (1556-1601) became a professional battle royale between Warner Brothers' studio nobility, Bette Davis and Errol Flynn, a bout that threatened to obscure the import of the lush screenfare. However, thanks to some reliance on historical fact, Davis' monarch emerged supreme at the drama's turgid finale, which found Flynn's lord

152

literally losing his head for valuing political superiority over romantic coupling.

Vincent Price was thrust among the Warners' stock company to portray the haughtily polite Sir Walter Raleigh, the part played by Percy Waram onstage and by Richard Todd in Davis' later screen return to *The Virgin Queen* (1955). Price's near-cameo part was stately but unmemorable.

TOWER OF LONDON *(Universal, 1939) 93 min.*

Producer-director, Rowland V. Lee; screenplay, Robert N. Lee; music director, Charles Previn; orchestrator, Frank Skinner; make-up, Jack Pierce; art director, Jack Otterson; set decorator, Russell Gausman; costumes, Vera West; camera, George Robinson; editor, Ed Curtiss.

Basil Rathbone (Richard, Duke of Gloucester); Barbara O'Neil (Queen Elizabeth); Nan Grey (Lady Alice Barton); Miles Mander (King Henry VI); John Sutton (John Wyatt); Vincent Price (Duke of Clarence); Leo G. Carroll (Lord Hastings); Lionel Belmore (Beacon Chiruegeon); Rose Hobart (Anne Neville); Boris Karloff (Mord); Ian Hunter (King Edward IV); Ronald Sinclair (boy King Edward); John Herbert-Bond (young Prince Richard); Ernest Cossart (Tom Clink); Ralph Forbes (Henry Tudor); Frances Robinson (Duchess Isobel); John Rodion (Lord DeVere); Walter Tetley (Chimney Sweep); Georgia Caine (Dowager Duchess); Ivan Simpson (Retainer); G. P. Huntley (Prince of Wales); Nigel De Brulier (Archbishop, St. John's Chapel); Holmes Herbert, Charles Miller (Councilmen); Venecia Severn, Yvonne Severn (Princesses); Louise Brien, Jean Fenwick (Ladies in Waiting); Michael Mark (Servant to Henry VI); C. Montague Shaw (Major Domo); Don Stewart (Bunch); Reginald Barlow (Sheriff at Execution); Robert Greig (Father Olmstead); Ivo Henderson (Haberdeer); Charles Peck (Page Boy); Harry Cording (Tyrell-Assassin); Jack C. Smith (Forrest-Assassin); Colin Kenny, Arthur Stenning (Soldiers); Evelyn Selbie (Beggar Woman); Denis Tankard, Dave Thursby (Beggars); Claire Whitney (Civilian Woman); Ernie Adams (Prisoner Begging for Water); Russ Powell (Sexton-Bell Ringer); Ann Todd (Queen Elizabeth's Daughter).

By Universal standards this film was a lavish retelling of the gory events surrounding the reign of terror of Richard III (Basil Rath-

bone) in fifteenth-century England, with popular historical myths*
serving as the excuse for an excess of fiendish horror. The macabre
film continually ripens with age, but at the time it was considered
just a gruesome variation of the shock film. The New York Post
reported, "Somehow the picture manages to be neither history nor
horror, each apparently having a bad effect on the other."

Leering and sneering his way to the coveted throne, Rathbone
methodically eliminates all his royal competitors. One of his many
victims is the bon vivant Duke of Clarence (Vincent Price) the
unlucky brother of King Edward IV (Ian Hunter). After a macabre
drinking contest with Rathbone, Price finds himself drowning in a
tank of Malmsey wine.

Boris Karloff earned the heartiest audience response as the
club-footed, bald high-executioner Mord, but Price did not go
unnoticed as the hedonistic nobleman. Twenty-three years later,
Price would have the opportunity to emote as the diabolical
scoundrel Richard III in the unfortunately pallid remake of Tower
of London. By then he would have replaced Karloff as king of the
horror flicks.

THE INVISIBLE MAN RETURNS *(Universal, 1940) 81 min.*

Associate producer, Kenneth Goldsmith; director, Joe May;
based on the character created by H. G. Wells; Curt Siodmak, May;
screenplay, Siodmak, Lester Cole; music, Charles Previn; special
effects, John P. Fulton; camera, Milton Krasner.

Vincent Price (Geoffrey Radcliffe); Sir Cedric Hardwicke (Rich-
ard Cobb); Nan Grey (Helen Manson); John Sutton (Dr. Frank
Griffin); Forrester Harvey (Ben Jenkins); Cecil Napier (Willis
Spears); Harry Stubbs, Matthew Boulton (Policemen); Edward
Fielding (Prison Governor); Ivan Simpson (Cotton); Bruce Lester
(Chaplain); Paul England (Detective); Mary Gordon (Cook); Ellis
Irving (Miner); Mary Field (Woman); Eric Wilton (Fingerprint
Man); Leyland Hodgson (Chauffeur); Dave Thursby (Bob, a War-
den); Jimmy Aubrey (Plainclothesman); Dennis Tankard, George

*For some thoughtful reflections on the much-maligned British monarch, there are,
among other factual and fictional studies: "Richard Third: His Life and Character
Reviewed in the Light of Recent Research" (1906) by Clements R. Markham;
"Daughter of Time" (1952) by Josephine Tey; "Richard the Third" (1956) by
Paul Murray Kendall; "To Prove a Villain: The Case of King Richard the
Third" (1964) by Taylor D. Littleton, Robert R. Rea; "Richard Third and the
Princess in the Tower" (1965) by John Langdon-Davies.

Lloyd, George Kirby, Harry Cording, George Hyde (Miners); Louise Brien (Griffith's Secretary); Ernie Adams (Man); Frank Hagney (Bill, a Policeman); Frances Robinson (Nurse); Frank O'Connor (Policeman at Colliery); Frank Hill (Policeman Attending Cobb); Photograph of Claude Rains (John Griffin).

When his brother is mysteriously murdered and he is wrongfully accused, Geoffrey Radcliffe (Vincent Price) utilizes Dr. Frank Griffin's (John Sutton) remarkable serum to become invisible, avoid the gallows, and track down the real culprit.

Briskly directed by Joe May, this entry made much of the visual gimmick that had been so macabrely exciting in the 1933 *The Invisible Man* starring Claude Rains. Peculiarly, Vincent Price's unrelenting seriousness contributed little to the intended atmosphere of eerie entertainment. Rather, it was jovial Inspector Sampson (Cecil Kellaway) and villainous Richard Cobb (Sir Cedric Hardwicke) who provided the modest production with its character.

Price's first major entry in the cinema blood-curdling field led the new York *Herald Tribune* to judge, "I think he is better in the disembodied section than in the final sequence (where he reappears)."

Having mocked the series in *The Invisible Woman* (1940), Universal herein provided a serious approach, which continued through the "follow-ups," *The Invisible Agent* (1942) and *The Invisible Man's Revenge* (1944).

THE HOUSE OF SEVEN GABLES *(Universal, 1940)* 89 min.

Associate producer, Burt Kelly; director, Joe May; based on the novel by Nathaniel Hawthorne; screenplay, Lester Cole; art director, Jack Otterson; set decorator, Russell Gausman; camera, Milton Krasner; editor, Frank Gross.

George Sanders (Jaffrey Pyncheon); Margaret Lindsay (Hepzibah Pyncheon); Vincent Price (Clifford Pyncheon); Dick Foran (Matthew Holgrave); Nan Grey (Phoebe Pyncheon); Cecil Kellaway (Philip Barton); Miles Mander (Deacon Arnold Foster); Alan Napier (Fuller); Harry Woods (Wainwright); Margaret Fealy, Caroline Cooke, John K. Loofbourrow, Marty Faust, Murdock MacQuarrie (Town Gossips); Gilbert Emery (Gerald Pyncheon);

Charles Trowbridge (Judge); Hugh Sothern (Reverend Smith); Edgar Norton (Weed); Mira McKinney (Mrs. Reynold); Ellia Irving (Man); Harry Stubbs (Printer); Harry Cording (Blacksmith); Kernan Cripps (Workman); Colin Kenny (Foreman); Robert Dudley (Bailiff); Etta McDaniel (Black Woman); Nelson McDowell (Courtroom Spectator); Hal Budlong (Driver); Ed Brady (Man with Blacksmith); Margaret Fenly (Woman Customer); Russ Powell (Grocer); Leigh De Lacy (Laundress); Claire Whitney (Woman).

The New York World-Telegram snapped of this film, "(the) results suggest that it would have been wiser for all concerned if it had never been removed from the library shelves..." but other less demanding sources admitted, "It is splendidly cast and just as splendidly directed." (New York Herald-Tribune)

Following relatively closely a major portion of Nathaniel Hawthorne's 1851 novel of mid-nineteenth-century Massachusetts life, the film has George Sanders appear as the black-hearted Jaffrey Pyncheon, who willingly sacrifices his older brother (Vincent Price) in a vengeful bid to locate for himself the family riches alledgedly burried in the ancestral home. Price served a long prison sentence for his supposed murder of Gerald Pyncheon (Gilbert Emery). When he is released later, the near-broken man finds that his long-ago sweetheart (Margaret Lindsay) had remained true through the many years.

The New York Times recorded, "As the soully oppressed lovers, Vincent Price and Margaret Lindsay perform in the perfect lavender-and-old lace tradition, with much sighing and misting of eyes." The screen efforts of Price and Lindsay did much to compensate for the lack of grimness of the house or the tragedy of the blighted romance, elements so crucial to Hawthorne's work. As the good brother, Price exuded sterling on-camera humaneness, and physically he was at his most handsome in his period trappings.

GREEN HELL *(Universal, 1940)* *87 min.*

Producer, Harry Edington; director, James Whale; screenplay, Frances Marion; camera, Karl Freund; editor, Ted J. Kent.

Douglas Fairbanks, Jr. (Keith Brandon); Joan Bennett (Stephanie Richardson); George Sanders (Forrester); Vincent Price (David Richardson); Alan Hale (Doctor Nils Loren); Gene Garrick (Graham); George Bancroft (Jim "Tex" Morgan); John Howard

(Hal Scott); Francis McDonald (Gracco); Ray Mala (Mala); Peter Bronte (Santos); Kay Linaker (Woman); Bob Fischer (Explorer); Noble Johnson (Indian Chief); Franco Corsaro (Man); Julian Rivero (Proprietor); Yola d'Avril, Nena Quartaro, Anita Camargo, Lupita Tovar (Native Girls); Tony Paton (Bartender); Wilson Benge (Butler); Iron Eyes Cody (Indian); Eumenio Blanco (Well-Dressed Native).

This tacky feature "...apparently was filmed for that particular brand of blood and thunder addict who doesn't care much about plot credibility if he can have his thrills, actions, excitement and hullabaloo." (New York Daily Mirror) In trying to provide some form of entertainment for every genre lover, the movie neutralized itself into a silly romantic-adventure outing. In fact, many considered this British imperialism-style melodrama the outstanding worst film of the year.

Athletic Douglas Fairbanks, Jr., heads an archeological expedition into the "green hell" of the Brazilian jungle, becoming involved with headhunting cannibals, lost Inca temples, and unfriendly whites. Group member Vincent Price soon dies (his deathbed speech is a paragon of incongruities) from a native's poison dart, and his widow (Joan Bennett) finds consolation with dashing Fairbanks.

BRIGHAM YOUNG-FRONTIERSMAN
(20th Century-Fox, 1940) 114 min.

Producer, Darryl F. Zanuck; associate producer, Kenneth Macgowan; director, Henry Hathaway; based on the book by Louis Bromfield; screenplay. Lamar Trotti; art directors, William Darling, Maurice Hansford; music, Alfred Newman; camera, Arthur Miller; editor, Robert Bischoff.

Tyrone Power (Jonathan); Linda Darnell (Zena); Dean Jagger (Brigham Young); Brian Donlevy (Angus Duncan); Jane Darwell (Eliza); John Carradine (Port Rockwell); Mary Astor (Mary Ann Young); Vincent Price (Joseph Smith); Jean Rogers (Clara Young); Ann Todd (Mary Kent); William Robertson (Hebar Kimball); Moroni Olsen (Doctor Richards); Marc Lawrence (Prosecutor); Stanley Andrews (Hyrum Smith); Frank Thomas (Hubert Crum); Fuzzy Knight (Pete); Dickie Jones (Henry Kent); Selmer Jackson

(Caleb Kent); Russell Simpson (Major); Arthur Aylsworth (Jim Bridges); Chief Big Tree (Big Elk); Claire Du Brey (Emma Smith); Tully Marshall (Judge); Ralph Dunn (Jury Foreman); George Melford (John Taylor); Frederick Burton (Mr. Webb); Davison Clark (Johnson); Dick Rich (Mob Leader); Edwin Maxwell (Leader of Mob); Edmund MacDonald, David Kirkland (Elders); Charles Halton (Prosecutor); Lee Shumway, Charles Middleton, Philip Morris (Members of Mob); Frank LaRue (Sheriff); Cecil Weston, Ruth Robinson (Women).

In 1846 America, members of the Church of Jesus Christ of the Latterday Saints (better known as the Mormons) made a fifteen-hundred-mile westward trek to Salt Lake City, Utah. On-camera, the chronicle began as a sturdy testament to a courageous group who combated religious intolerance, winter storms, and plagues of locusts and critics. However, the film ended up as a thin showcase for the romantic entanglements of the too-beautiful Tyrone Power and Linda Darnell.

Vincent Price was well cast as Joseph Smith (1805-1844), the founder of the Mormon religion, its visionary and prophet. He is the one who is tried for treason in Carthage, Illinois, and later becomes the victim of mob violence. When the masses break into the local jail, his body is riddled with bullets and the dying man falls through a shattered window. Thereafter, his sturdy disciple, Brigham Young (Dean Jagger) assumes command of the flock and leads them to a new homeland out west.

Price's far-reaching performance, within the confines of his small part, was a foreshadowing of his stellar work in *The Baron of Arizona* (1950).

HUDSON'S BAY *(20th Century-Fox, 1940)* 95 min.

Producer, Darryl F. Zanuck; associate producer, Kenneth Macgowan; director, Irving Pichel; screenplay, Lamar Trotti; art directors, Richard Day, Wiard B. Ihnen; camera, Peverell Marley, George Barnes; editor, Robert Simpson.

Paul Muni (Pierre Esprit Radisson); Gene Tierney (Barbara); Laird Cregar (Gooseberry); John Sutton (Lord Edward Crewe); Virginia Field (Nell Gwyn); Vincent Price (King Charles); Nigel Bruce (Prince Rupert); Morton Lowry (Gerald Hall); Robert Greig

(Sir Robert); Chief Thundercloud (Orimha); Frederic Warlock (English Governor); Montagu Love (Governor); Ian Wolfe (Mayor); Chief John Big Tree (Chief); Jody Gilbert (Germaine); Jean Del Val (Captain); Eugene Borden, Constant Franke (Sentries); Lilyan Irene (Maid);Keith Hitchcock (Footman); Dorothy Dearing (Girl); John Rogers (Sailor); Reginald Sheffield (Clerk); Robert Cory (Orderly); Denis d'Auburn, Eric Wilton (Concillors).

This sprawling film represented more distorted history from the aegis of studio mogul Darryl F. Zanuck. The ambitious frontier epic cost over eight hundred thousand dollars (a very tidy sum in the 1940s), but it failed to evolve as the splendid outdoor drama intended. For the most part, it was just too conversational and conventional for its own good. Moreover, it was badly hampered by Paul Muni's unjustified over-emoting as the folksy French-Canadian Pierre Esprit Radisson, who created one of the world's greatest trading company in 1667 northern America, aided by a sedate banished English nobleman (John Sutton) and by a rotund, zesty fellow-Canadian (Laird Cregar).

In the tantalizingly few English court sequences, Vincent Price promenaded as the natty, snobbished, bewigged King Charles II (1661-1700) who initially opposes the charter for the Hudson Bay Fur Trading Company. Price's royal caricature was indeed superficial theatrics, but a very welcome relief from the overly romantic liaison of Sutton and his British nobelwoman (Gene Tierney). Virginia Field was on-camera all too briefly as Price's practical mistress, the (in)famous Nell Gwyn.

THE SONG OF BERNADETTE *(20th Century-Fox, 1943) 156 min.*

Producer, William Perlberg; director, Henry King; based on the novel by Franz Werfel; screenplay, George Seaton; art directors, James Basevi, William Darling; set decorators, Thomas Little, Frank E. Hughes; music, Alfred Newman; orchestrator, Edward Powell; assistant director, Joseph Behm; sound, Rogert Heman; special camera effects, Fred Sersen; camera, Arthur Miller; editor, Barbara McLean.

Jennifer Jones (Bernadette); William Eythe (Antoine); Charles Bickford (Peyremale); Vincent Price (Dutour); Lee J. Cobb (Dr.

Dozous); Gladys Cooper (Sister Vauzous); Anne Revere (Louise Soubirous); Mary Anderson (Jeanne Abadie); Patricia Morison (Empress Eugenie); Aubrey Mather (Lacade); Charles Dingle (Jacomet); Edith Barrett (Croisine); Sig Ruman (Louis Bouriette); Blanche Yurka (Bernarde Casterot); Ermadean Walters (Marie Soubirous); Marcel Dalio (Callet); Pedro de Cordoba (Le Crampe); Jerome Cowan (Emperor Louis Napoleon); Charles Waldron (Bishop of Tarbes); Moroni Olsen (Chaplain); Nana Bryant (Convent Mother Superior); Manart Kippen (Charles Bouhouhorts); Merrill Rodin (Jean Soubirous); John Maxwell Hayes (Father Pomian); Jean Del Val (Estrade); Tala Birell (Mme. Bruat); Eula Morgan (Mme. Nicolau); Frank Reicher (Dr. St. Cyr); Charles La Torre (Duran); Linda Darnell (Blessed Virgin); Nestor Paiva (Baker); Dorothy Shearer (Mother Superior); Nino Pipitone, Sr. (Mayor's Secretary); Edwin Stanley (Mr. Jones); Lionel Braham (Baron Massey); Ian Wolfe (Minister of the Interior); Andre Charlot (Bishop); Cecil Weston, Maria Pape, Marjorie Cooley (Women); Ruth Robinson (Nun); Alan Napier (Psychiatrist); Frank Leigh (Cleric); Harry Denny (Priest); Ernest Gohn, Hans Herbert (Scientists); George Gleboff, Mayo Newhall, Edward Van Sloan, Tom Stevenson (Doctors); Dickie Moore (Adolar); Arthur Hohl, Fritz Leiber (Monks); Curt Furberg, Armand Cortez, Louis Arco, George Sorel (Franciscan Monks); Jean De Briac, Davison Clark, Antonio Filauri, Julian Rivero (Dominican Monks); Edward Keane, Hooper Atchley (Policemen).

A meticulously executed and very tasteful tribute to the simple French peasant girl (Jennifer Jones) who beholds visions of the Virgin Mary (Linda Darnell) in the countryside grotto in 1858, thus beginning a religious controversy that shook France for decades.

Director Henry King, a stalwart on the Fox lot, helmed a fine supporting cast to backstop relative newcomer Jones (who won an Oscar); Anne Revere as her plain, devout mother, Charles Bickford as Cure Peyremaie, pastor of the Lourdes church, who at first opposes Bernadette as an obvious, willful storyteller; regal nun Gladys Cooper who is envious of Bernadette's unique privilege of being the recipient of visits from Heaven; godmother Blanche Yurka; and Vincent Price as the viperish imperial prosecutor who attempts to consign Bernadette to a sanatorium.

In Price's final scene at the grotto his thoughts are spoken on the sound track, for he is now suffering from a cancerous growth in his throat. His dialogue ends with "Bernadette, pray for me." Midst all

160

the hosannas showered on the extravagantly pious, but non-proselytizing feature, Price was cited by the New York *Herald-Tribune*, among others, for his "excellent job."

THE EVE OF ST. MARK *(20th Century-Fox)* *96 min.*

Producer, William Perlberg; director John M. Stah; based on the play by Maxwell Anderson; screenplay, George Seaton; art directors, James Basevi, Russell Spencer; set decorators, Thomas Little, Frank E. Hughes; music, Cyril J. Mockridge; music director, Emil Newman; sound, Eugene Grossman; assistant director, S.E. Johnson; special camera effects, Fred Sersen; camera, Joseph La Shelle; editor, Louis Sacking.

Anne Baxter (Janet Feller); William Eythe (Quizz West); Michael O'Shea (Sergeant Mulveroy); Vincent Price (Marion); Ruth Nelson (Nell West); Bob Bailey (Corporal Tate); Joann Dolan (Lill Bird); Toni Favor (Sal Bird); George Mathews (Sergeant Ruby); John Archer (Carter); Murray Alper (Sergeant Kriven); Dickie Moore (Zip West); Joven E. Rola (Pepita); Harry Shannon (Chaplain); Roger Clark (Captain); Jimmy Clark (Neil West); Harry Carter (Medical Officer); Harry Strang (Military Police); Rod Bacon, Michael Owen, Blake Edwards, John Whitney (Soldiers); Milton Kibbee (Pete Feller); Matt McHugh (Cabdriver); Buddy Yarus (Polinski).

The Eve of St. Mark had been an outstanding offering of the 1942 Broadway season. Much praise had been heaped on Maxwell Anderson's sensitive blank-verse paean to a typical American farm boy, one of the first to become an active part of America's fighting army in World War II. Twentieth Century-Fox paid a whopping three hundred thousand dollars for the screen rights to this 306-performance success. However, by the time the drama could reach the silver screen in 1944, world events had altered so greatly that the script seemed badly dated, with other already released war films making this patriotic effort appear excessively derivative. Morever, the bite of Anderson's sober work was compromised by a newly constructed upbeat ending that found the surviving group of GIs escaping the Japanese onslaught at Corregidor. This turn of events obscured the play's basic moral dilemma: Should American soldiers hold onto untenable positions in order to kill more Axis enemies before dying, or should they be more concerned with their own safety and escape to fight another day?

Balancing the scenes of service training and combat action in the Philippines were the Americana sequences, with handsome but bland William Eythe carrying out his idyllic midwestern romance with glossy-eyed ingenue Anne Baxter. By inheriting James Monks' stage part, Vincent Price played one of his few on-camera all-American good-guy roles. Many viewers found him "uncommonly good" in capturing the "ridiculous aplomb" of his Dixie-bred character, a luxury lover who has spent most of his pampered life waiting to inherit a family fortune that must first pass to a grandfather, three aunts, two uncles, and seven cousins. Price was the soft soldier always in debt to service buddies Michael O'Shea, Stanley Prager, and Bob Bailey, and the sort of erudite comrade who answers bewildered Eythe's query as to what is happening by ruminating, "I shall look for the answer tonight in the bottom of a large rum and coke."

Because Price's scenes were of a filler nature, *PM's* critic could justifiably sound off, "...despite his great voice and diction, (he) seems a mere poetry machine, to be turned on and off at will."

WILSON *(20th Century-Fox, 1944) C:-154 min.*

Producer, Darryl F. Zanuck; director, Henry King; screenplay, Lamar Trotti; music, Alfred Newman; orchestrator, Edward Powell; art directors, Wiard Ihnen, James Basevi; set decorators, Thomas Little, Paul S. Fox; assistant director, Joseph Behm' sound, E. C. Ward; special camera effects, Fred Sersen; camera, Leon Shamroy; editor, Barbara McLean.

Alexander Knox (Woodrow Wilson); Charles Coburn (Professor Henry Holmes); Geraldine Fitzgerald (Edith Wilson); Thomas Mitchell (Joseph Tumulty); Ruth Nelson (Ellen Wilson); Sir Cedric Hardwicke (Senator Henry Cabot Lodge); Vincent Price (William Gibbs McAdoo); William Eythe (George Felton); Mary Anderson (Eleanor Wilson); Ruth Ford (Margaret Wilson); Sidney Blackmer (Josephus Daniels); Madeleine Forbes (Jessie Wilson); Stanley Ridges (Admiral Grayson); Eddie Foy, Jr. (Eddie Foy); Charles Halton (Colonel House); Thurston Hall (Senator E. H. Jones); James Rennie (Jim Becker); Katherine Locke (Helen Jones); Stanley Logan (Secretary Lansing); Marcel Dalio (Clemenceau); Edwin

VINCENT PRICE UNMASKED

Maxwell (William Jennings Bryan); Clifford Brooke (Lloyd George); Tonio Selwart (Von Bernstorff); John Ince (Senator Watson); Charles Miller (Senator Bromfield); Anne O'Neal (Jennie the Maid); Arthur Loft (Secretary Lane); Russell Gaige (Secretary Colby); Jameson Shade (Secretary Payne); Reginald Moore (Secretary Burleson); George Anderson (Secretary Houston); Robert Barrat (Secretary Meredith); George Macready (McCoombs); Frank Orth (Smith); Francis X. Bushman (Barney Baruch); Cy Kendall (Charles F. Murphy); Emory Parnell (Chairman of Democratic Committee); Isabel Randolph (Housekeeper); Emmett King, Gibson Gowland, Scott Seaton, George Carleton (Senators); Jeffrey Sayre (Specialty Dancer); Jack Stoney, Ben Erway, Earle Dewey, Grandon Rhodes, Edward Earle, Carroll Nye, Griff Barnett, Ian Wolfe, John Forrest, Paul McVey (Reporters); William Yetter, Otto Reichow (German Delegates); Phyllis Brooks (Granddaughter); Sidney Blackmer (Dockstader); Forrest Taylor (Orator) ; Major Sam Harris (General Bliss); Montague Shaw (Harry L. White); Larry McGrath (Secretary Wilson); David Cavendish, Ray Cooper (Secretaries).

"Pictures like *Wilson* have little if anything to do with mature serious cinema as such, and those who think of *Wilson* as a mature film are not in the least concerned with its liveliness or deadness as a work of art; they are excited because serious ideas are being used on the screen. Something well worth excitement, I'll grant; but how much?" (James Agee *(The Nation)*

Determined patriot Darryl F. Zanuck allocated over three million dollars of this studio's funds for this zealous, overblown 154-minute history lesson. Surely there could have been less expensive means of communicating Zanuck's acknowledgement that a viable world organization was necessary to stabilize global peace. Many sources branded this noble gesture as out-and-out propaganda for Franklin D. Roosevelt's fourth Presidential term.

In the course of this no-expenses-spared chronicle, viewers were "treated" to episodes in the political and domestic life of Woodrow Wilson (Alexander Knox), the twenty-eighth president of the United States. The handsomely mounted production focused on the years from 1909-1920, climaxing with Wilson's failure to persuade America to accept the League of Nations.

In the midst of this blow-by-blow continuity, which utilized over 143 speaking parts, Vincent Price was authoritative as William Gibbs McAdoo (1863-1941), the Secretary of the Treasury who, upon wedding Eleanor Wilson (Mary Anderson) became the President's son-in-law. Much of Price's on-camera time was spent in arguing with Wilson against hasty action after the torpedoing of Allied ships in 1915.

LAURA *(20th Century-Fox, 1944) 88 min.*

Producer-director, Otto Preminger; based on the novel by Vera Caspary; screenplay, Jay Dratier, Samuel Hoffenstein, Betty Reinhardt; art directors, Lyle Wheeler, Leland Fuller; set decorators, Thomas Little, Paul S. Fox; assistant director, Tom Dudley; music, David Raskin; music director, Emil Newman; sound, E. C. Ward; special camera effects, Fred Sersen; camera, Joseph La Shelle; editor, Louis Loeffler.

Gene Tierney (Laura); Dana Andrews (Mark McPherson); Clifton Webb (Waldo Lydecker); Vincent Price (Shelby Carpenter); Judith Anderson (Ann Treadwell); Dorothy Adams (Bessie Clary); James Flavin (McAvity); Clyde Filmore (Bullitt); Ralph Dunn (Fred Callahan); Grant Mitchell (Corey); Kathleen Howard (Louise); Harold Schlickenmayer, Harry Strang, Lane Chandler (Detectives); Frank La Rue (Hairdresser); Alexander Sacha, Dorothy Christy, Aileen Pringle, Terry Adames, Jean Fenwick, Yolanda Lacca, Forbes Murray, Cyril Ring, Nester Eristoff, Kay Linaker, Cara Williams, Gloria Marlin, Beatrice Gray, Kay Connors, Frances Gladwin (Bits); Buster Miles (Office Boy); Jane Nigh (Secretary); William Forrest (Man); John Dexter (Jacoby).

Ironically no Hollywood executive seriously considered producing Vera Caspary's neat thriller until European-born Otto Preminger read the work. The celluloid results were "A smart murder-mystery, expertly tailored in script, casting, and direction..." (*Variety)*

The ambience of this surprise drama is created gy scenes in such Gotham watering spas as El Morocco, Sardi's, the Stork Club, and the Algonquin bar, but the action essentially revolves around the alluring but very wholesome ex-office worker Laura Hunt (Gene Tierney) who allegedly has been murdered. Solid detective Mark McPherson (Dana Andrews) enters the scene, only to find himself falling in love with the ghostly vision of loveliness of the murdered woman. He is pitted in this sophisticated caper against a trio of tainted suspects: waspish newspaper critic Waldo Lydecker (Clifton Webb), who engineered Laura's (Gene Tierney) rise into the society art world; parasitic playboy Shelby Carpenter (Vincent Price), who thrives on flattery and fondness; and determined blue-blooded matron Ann Treadwell (Judith Anderson), who proves to be Price's mistress.

When the inbred characters square off into a deadly contest, debonair Webb and reticient Andrews take the limelight, leaving a few crumbs of artistic spoils for Price's weak-willed ne'er do-well. As Tierney's former fiance, elegant Price must compete in lofty word battles with Webb concerning the all-desirable girl. Movie critics noted that Price, in this George Sanders-type portrayal, played the cad most effectively.

THE KEYS OF THE KINGDOM *(20th Century-Fox, 1944) 137 min.*

Producer, Joseph L. Mankiewicz; director, John M. Stahl; based on the novel by A. J. Cronin; screenplay, Mankiewicz, Nunnally Johnson; music, Alfred Newman; orchestrator, Edward Powell; art directors, James Basevi, William Darling; set decorators, Thomas Little, Frank E. Hughes; assistant director, F. E. Johnston; sound, Eugene Grossman; special camera effects, Fred Sersen; camera, Arthur Miller; editor, James B. Clark.

Gregory Peck (Father Francis Chisholm); Thomas Mitchell (Dr. Willie Tullock); Vincent Price (Reverend Angus Mealy); Rose Stradner (Mother Maria Veronica); Roddy McDowall (Francis as a Boy); Edmund Gwenn (Reverend Hamish MacNabb); Sir Cedric Hardwicke (Monsignor Sleeth); Peggy Ann Garner (Nora as a Child); Jane Ball (Nora); James Gleason (Dr. Wilbur Fiske); Anne Revere (Agnes Fiske); Ruth Nelson (Lisbeth Chisholm); Benson Fong (Joseph); Leonard Strong (Mr. Chin); Philip Ahn (Mr. Pao); Arthur Shields (Father Tarrant); Edith Barratt (Aunt Polly); Sara Allgood (Sister Martha); Richard Loo (Lieutenant Shon); Ruth Ford (Sister Clotilde); Kevin O'Shea (Father Craig); M. H. T. Tsiang (Hosannah Wong); Si-Len Chen (Philomena Wang); Eunice Soo Hoo (Anna); Dennis Hoey (Alex Chisholm); Abner Biberman (Bandit Captain); J. Anthony Hughes (Ned Bannon); George Nokes (Andrew); Hayward Soo Hoo (Chia-Yu); Joseph Kim Richard Wang (Chinese Servants); James Leong (Taoist Priest);

Moy Ming (Chinese Physician); Frank Eng (Father Chou); Oie Chan (Grandmother); Clarence Lung (She Wing Soo Hoo (Orderlies); Ruth Clifford (Sister Mercy Mary).

In a richly leisurely fashion, this refined and faithful film representation of the A. J. Cronin novel examines the career merits of an aging Catholic missionary priest (Gregory Peck) who is to be relegated to a charity retirement home in Scotland. Monsignor Sleeth (Sir Cedric Hardwicke) is sent to examine Peck's case to make a determination. As the haughty, bored Hardwicke reviews Peck's clerical career, he changes his initial opinion, realizing this simple man has accomplished amazing victories for the Church. Within flashbacks, one sees Peck as a child (played by Roddy McDowall) who witnesses the murder of his father because he was a Roman Catholic. In later life Peck becomes a humble disciple of God serving in strife-ridden China where, from his base in the village of Pai Tan, he amasses a strong religious following. Interwoven in this overly detailed account is the growing relationship of understanding between Peck and a German mother superior (Rose Stradner), in which the latter aristocrat learns humility from Peck's examples.

Contrasted with the benevolent Reverent Hamish MacNabb (Edmund Gwenn) and the methodist missionary Dr. Wilbur Fiske (James Gleason) is the worldly Church politician, Reverend Angus Mealy (Vincent Price), a one-time boyhood chum of Peck. On one occasion Price comes to visit Peck's simple parish and is distressed that bombs have destroyed the church, thus preventing his sermonizing there and reporting the event to his superiors at home. Price essayed his snobbish role rather broadly leading *The New York Times* to carp, "An oddly distasteful impersonation of a worldly canon—aside from the unattractiveness of the role—is given by Vincent Price."

A ROYAL SCANDAL *(20th Century-Fox, 1945)* *94 min.*

Producer, Ernst Lubitsch; director, Otto Preminger; based on the play *The Czarina* by Lajos Biro, Melchoir Langyel; screenplay, Edwin Justis Mayer; art directors, Lyle Wheeler, Mark Lee Kirk; set decorators, Thomas Little, Paul S. Fix; assistant director, Tom

VINCENT PRICE UNMASKED

Dudley; sound, Alfred Bruzlin; music, Alfred Newman; orchestrator, Edward Powell; special effects, Fred Sersen; camera, Arthur Miller; editor, Dorothy Spencer.

Tallulah Bankhead (Czarina); Charles Coburn (Chancellor); Anne Baxter (Anna); William Eythe (Alexei); Vincent Price (Marquis de Fleury); Mischa Auer (Captain Sukov); Sig Ruman (General Ronsky); Vladimir Sokoloff (Malakoff); Mikhail Rasumny (Drunken General); Grady Sutton (Boris); Don Douglas (Variatinsky); Egon Brecher (Wassilikow); Eva Gabor (Countess Demidow); Frederick Ledebur, Paul Baratoff, George A. Gleboff, Fred Nurney, Leonid Snegoff, Henry Victor, Wilton Graff, Michael Visaroff, General Sam Savitsky, Eugene Beday, Nestor Eristoff, Richard Ryan, Eugene Sigaloff (Russian Generals); Virginia Walker, Renee Carson, Sandra Foloway, Roxanne Hiltron, Dina Smirnova, Martha Jewett, Ann Hunter (Ladies in Waiting); John Russell (Guard); Fred Essler, Marek Windheim, Torben Meyer, Victor Delinsky (Stooges); Arno Frey (Captain); Harry Carter (Footman); Feodor Chaliapin, Mario Gang, George Shdanoff (Lackeys).

Assorted actresses had played Catherine the Great (1729-1796) onstage and on the screen, including Mae West, Pola Negri, Marlene Dietrich, and Elisabeth Bergner, leaving scant room for any fresh revelation from Tallulah Bankhead in this pedestrian costume account. *The New York Times* analyzed, "The fault is quite obviously in the writing....where satire in large and splendid movement would seem the most promising attack, they (the scripts) have hewed to a style of cautious hinting, with only vague glints of wit and travesty."

In the course of ponderously relating the political intrigue and catastrophic love-making at the royal court in St. Petersburg, even the mighty individualist Bankhead was overshadowed in a welter of hooped skirts and powdered wigs. Resourceful Charles Coburn was on hand as the czarina's chancellor, with Mikhail Rasumny and Sig Ruman as two conspiring generals, Anne Baxter as a virginal lady-in-waiting, and William Eythe as a moralist soldier whom the ruler chases about her boudoir. When not eying Eythe, Bankhead's empress found momentary diversion in bantering with the Marquis de Fleury (Vincent Price), the French ambassador. In the course of the plodding story, Price is seduced by the queen.

LEAVE HER TO HEAVEN *(20th Century-Fox, 1945) C-111 min.*

Producer, William A. Bacher; director, John M. Stahl; based on the novel by Ben Ames Williams; screenplay, Jo Swerling, music, Alfred Newman; orchestrator, Edward B. Powell; art directors, Lyle Wheeler, Maurice Ransford; set decorators, Thomas Little, Ernest Lansing; assistant director, Joseph Behm; sound, E. Clayton Ward; special camera effects, Fred Sersen; camera, Leon Shamroy; editor, James B. Clark.

Gene Tierney (Ellen Berent); Cornel Wilde (Richard Harland); Jeanne Crain (Ruth Berent); Vincent Price (Russell Quinton); Mary Phillips (Mrs. Berent); Ray Collins (Glen Robie); Gene Lockhart (Dr. Saunders); Reed Hadley (Dr. Mason); Chill Wills (Leick Thorne); Darryl Hickman (Danny Harland); Paul Everton (Judge); Olive Blakeney (Mrs. Robie); Addison Richards (Bedford); Harry Depp (Catterson); Grant Mitchell (Carlson the Bank Vice-President); Milton Parsons (Medcraft the Mortician); Earl Schenck (Norton); Hugh Maguire (Lin Robie); Betz (Cook at Robie's Ranch); Jim Farley (Conductor); Charles Tannen (Man); Mae Marsh (Fisherwoman).

"Sumptuous Technicolor mounting and a highly exploitable story lend considerable importance...." *Variety)* in the picturization of Ben Ames Williams' best-seller novel. The combination of a well-honed chiller plot and Gene Tierney's petulant depiction of a cold-blooded murderess gave this film prominence beyond its worth.

Whether in the New Mexico desert or the north-wood lake country, super-possessive Ellen Berent (Tierney) will do anything to avoid sharing her novelist spouse (Cornel Wilde) with others: including letting his crippled younger brother (Darryl Hickman) drown, forcing her own miscarriage by tumbling down a flight of stairs, or by finally poisoning herself and casting suspicion on Wilde when she believes he is attracting the attention of her sister (Jeanne Crain).

Vincent Price appears late in the story (told in flashback) as Tierney's former flame, Russell Quinton. Within the menacing tale he is the theatrical prosecuting district attorney at the climatic murder trial, who delights in gaining "revenge" on his lost love, by persecuting Ellen's on-trial sister (Crain). Rather unfairly, *The New York Times* decided that Price, among others, played his part too "mechanically." On the contrary, his venomous portrayal of a man thriving on pettiness and nastiness—hidden under the cloak of lawyerlike diligence—was a rich acting exercise, which had the solid foundation of creditable character motivation (something many of his later horror pictures lacked).

SHOCK *(20th Century-Fox, 1946) 70 min.*

Producer, Aubrey Schenck; director, Alfred Werker; based on the story by Albert DeMond; screenplay,Eugene Ling; additional dialogue, Martin Berkeley; art directors, Lyle Wheeler, Boris Leven; set decorators, Thomas Little, O. Clement Halverson; music, David Buttolph; music director, Emil Newman; orchestrator, Arthur Morton; assistant director, E. Dunn; sound, Alfred Bruzlin, Harry M. Leonard; special effects, Fred Sersen; camera, Glen MacWilliams, Joe MacDonald; editor, Harmon Jones.

Vincent Price (Dr. Corss); Lynn Bari (Elaine Jordan); Frank Latimore (Lieutenant Paul Stewart); Anabel Shaw (Janet Stewart); Michael Dunne (Stevens); Reed Hadley (O'Neil); Renee Carson (Mrs. Hatfield); Charles Trowbridge (Dr. Harvey); John Davidson (Mr. Edwards); Selmer Jackson (Dr. Blair); Pierre Watkin (Hotel Manager); Mary Young (Miss Penny); Charles Tannen (Hotel Clerk); Margaret Brayton, Claire Richards (Nurses); Bob Adler (Male Nurse); George E. Stone (Cabdriver).

"The disturbing thing is that this picture strives for emotional effect by presenting the villainous psychiatrist in the most fearsome and horrifying light." *(The New York Times)*

Eminent psychiatrist Dr. Cross (Vincent Price), adied by a friendly nurse (Lynn Bari), slays his wife. Instead of solving his problems, this feat creates new chaos for Cross, since the crime was witnessed by one Janet Stewart (Anabel Shaw). Luckily for Cross, the woman was already in a semi-hysterical state awaiting the delayed release of her army-aviator husband from a Japanese prison camp. Therefore, it is easy for him to convince the late-arriving spouse (Frank Latimore) that she must be incarcerated at the local sanitarium. Fortunately Latimore has second thoughts abut his wife's sanity and, aided by district attorney-investigator O'Neil (Reed Hadley), the real culprit is apprehended.

This plot gimmick of disbelief that the claimant has observed a murder would be more effectively used in *The Window* (1949), *Rear Window* (1954), *Witness to Murder* (1954), and *Night Watch* (1973). However, this modest talky programmer has its own champions, largely because of Price's unrelentingly sinister performance. As *Variety* evaluated, he "...makes a sufficiently deadly menace..."

DRAGONWYCK *(20th Century-Fox, 1946) 103 min.*

Producer, Darryl F. Zanuck; director, Joseph L. Mankiewicz; based on the novel by Anya Seton; screenplay, Mankiewicz; art directors, Lyle Wheeler, J. Russell Spencer; set decorator, Paul S. Fox; music, Alfred Newman; orchestrator, Edward B. Powell; choreography, Arthur Appel; assistant director, Johnny Johnston; sound, W. D. Flick, Roger Heman; special camera effects, Fred Sersen; camera, Arthur Miller; editor, Dorothy Spencer.

Gene Tierney (Miranda); Walter Huston (Ephraim Wells); Vincent Price (Nicholas Van Ryn); Glenn Langan (Dr. Jeff Turner); Anne Revere (Abigail); Spring Byington (Magda); Connie Marshall (Katrine); Henry Morgan (Bleecker); Vivienne Osborne (Johanna); Jessica Tandy (Peggy O'Malley); Trudy Marshall (Elizabeth Van Bordon); Reinhold Schunzel (Count De Granier); Jane Nigh (Tabitha); Ruth Ford (Cornelia Van Borden); Scott Elliott (Tom Wells); Boyd Irwin (Tompkins); Keith Hitchcock (Mr. McNab); Maya Van Horn (Countess De Grenier); Francis Pierlot (Dr. Brown); Arthur Thompson, Al Winter, Larry Steers, Wallace Dean, Tom Martin (Servants); Edwin Davis, Selby Bacon (Black Boy Dancers on Boat Deck); Ruth Cherrington, Elizabeth Williams (Dowagers); John Chollot (French Count); Virginia Lindley (Helena); Nanette Vallon (French Countess); George Ford, Alexander Sacha, Nestor Eristoff, Ted Jordan, William Carter (Men); Mickey Roth (Nathaniel); Jamie Dana (Seth); Robert Walter Baldwin, Harry Humphrey, Robert Malcolm, Trevor Bardette, Arthur Ayleworth, Tom Fadden, Clancy Cooper, Addison Richards (Farmers); Betty Fairfax (Mrs. NcNab); Douglas Wood (Mayor); Steve Olsen (Vendor); Gertrude Astor (Nurse); Charles Waldron (Minister); Grady Sutton (Hotel Clerk).

After Charlotte Bronte's ultimate Gothic thriller *Jane Eyre* was published in 1847, a good many subsequent novelists tried to duplicate that tale's eerie qualities. Among them was Daphne du Maurier's *Rebecca* and more recently Anya Seton's *Dragonwyck,* which also became a best seller and a popular film. The screen version of the Seton piece relied on heavy picturesque scenes to recapture some of the flavor of upstate New York in the 1840s, where brooding Nicholas Van Ryn (Vincent Price), as the tyrannical patroon of the Dragonwyck estate, is levying a heavy tax on the tenant farmers and a higher fee on his oppressed, obese wife (Vivienne Osborne).

No such genre piece would be complete without a wide-eyed heroine. Here Miranda (Gene Tierney), product of a God-fearing Greenwich, Connecticut family, is brought to the foreboding Dragonwyck house where she is to be companion to Price's six-year-old daughter (Connie Marshall). It is not long before Miranda surmises that Price, her distant cousin and later husband, is a killer. By this point she has given birth to a son, who soon dies. She is about to be killed by the deranged Nicholas, but is saved at the last minute by friendly Dr. Jeff Turner (Glenn Langan).

For the first time in a full-bodied characterization, which he did with the part of the hissable, avaricious husband. "It is one of his best roles to date, and he handles it for all its worth." *(Variety)* There is a well-delineated, if sometimes unsubtle, transformation as Price brings about his first wife's death through poisoned flowers, weds the innocent Miranda, and then goes berserk when his long-desired male heir suddenly dies. Whether playing the harpsichord or succumbing to the influence of drugs in his red tower room, he fully conveys a proud, cultured man tormented by haunting visions and drugs. "Clean-shaven and elegantly tailored, he...makes a formidable Bluebeard, and his movements of suave diabolism are about the best in the film." It is a tribute to Price's emoting that one can feel a tinge of sympathy for him as he lies dying and mumbles, "That's right. Take off your hats in the presence of the patroon."

THE WEB *(Universal, 1947) 91 min.*

Producer, Jerry Bresler; director, Michael Gordon; based on the story by Harry Kurnitz; screenplay, William Bowers, Bertram Milhauser; art directors, Bernard Herzbrun, James Sullivan; set decorators, Russell A. Gausman, William L. Stevens; music, Hans J. Salter; orchestrator, David Tamkin; assistant director, F. O.

Collings; sound, Charles Felstead, Charles Carroll; camera, Irving Glassberg; editor, Russell Schoengarth.

Edmond O'Brien (Bob Regan); Ella Raines (Noel Faraday); William Bendix (Lieutenant Damico); Vincent Price (Andrew Colby); John Abbott (Charles Murdock); Maria Palmer (Martha Kroner); Fritz Leiber (Leopold Korner); Howland Chamberlain (James Nolan); Joe Kirk, William Haade, Ethan Laidlaw (Plainclothesmen); Tito Vuolo (Emilio Canepa); Patricia Alphin (Secretary); Robin Raymond (Girl in Paper Morgue); Wilton Graff (District Attorney); Pierre Watkin (Mr. Porter); Alex Frazer (Medical Examiner); Jack G. Lee (Maintenance Man); Lorin Baker (Assistant); Lee Phelps (Policeman); Ted Stanhope (Clerk); Russell Conway (Mike the Fingerprint Man); Bob Allen (Office Boy); Jack Gargan (Ticket Man); Gino Corrado (Waiter); Lee Shumway (Cop); Ralph Montgomery (Photographer).

Hollywood filmmakers would have viewers believe that in a crime picture, the police are so dumb that they are always the last to suspect the actual villains. However, in this meandering Grade B feature, Lieutenant Damico (William Bendix) of the New York police force is an unobtrusive but persistent investigator. He is convinced that defendant Bob Regan (Edmond O'Brien), a struggling young lawyer turned bodyguard, is being framed on a justifiable homicide charge. The real killer seems to be Regan's employer, Andrew Colby (Vincent Price), a wily industrialist who has a grudge against his ex-partner and a yen for is attractive secretary (Ella Raines).

As the employer who is attempting to cover up a five-year-old embezzlement caper, Price exuded an "oily elegance" that gave a fitting patina to his characterization.

MOSS ROSE *(20th Century-Fox, 1947) 82 min.*

Producer, Gene Markey; director, Gregory Ratoff; based on the novel by Joseph Shearing; screenplay, Jules Furthman, Tom Reed; adaptator, Niven Busch; art directors, Richard Day, Mark Lee Kirk; set decorators, Edwin B. Willis, Paul S. Fox; music, David Buttolph; orchestrators, Edward Powell, Maurice de Packh; music director, Alfred Newman; assistant director, Ad Schaumer; sound, George Leverett, Roger Heman; special camera effects, Fred Sersen; camera, Joe MacDonald; editor, James B. Clark.

VINCENT PRICE UNMASKED

Peggy Cummins (Belle Adair); Victor Mature (Sir Alexander Sterling); Ethel Barrymore (Lady Sterling); Vincent Price (Inspector Clinner); Margo Woode (Daisy Arrow); George Zucco (Craxton); Patricia Medina (Audrey); Rhys Williams (Deputy Inspector Evans); Felippa Rock (Liza); Carol Savage (Harriett); Victor Wood (Wilson); Patrick O'Moore (George Gilby); Billy Bevan (White Horse Cabby); Michael Dyne (Assistant Hotel Manager); John Rogers (Fothergill); Charles McNaughton (Alf); Alex Frazer (Mr. Bulke); Gilbert Wilson, Stanley Mann (Footmen); Alex Harford (Cassian); John Goldsworthy (Minister); Sally Sheppard (Maid); Paul England (Pub Owner); Al Ferguson (Constable); Colin Campbell (Art Gallery Attendant); Leonard Carey (Coroner); Norman Ainsley (Deputy Coroner); Tom Moore (Foreman in Coroner's Court); Phil Sudano (Stevans); Basil Walker (Thompson); Wallace Scott, Colin Kenny (Cabdrivers); Frank Baker (Man Lodger); Doreen Munroe (Woman Lodger); Gerald Oliver Smith (Hotel Desk Clerk); Russ Clark (Constable); Francis Pierlot (Train Conductor).

By its very nature a period drama or comedy is at the mercy of its art director, set decorator, and the costumer. In this visually well-conceived production, the staid flavor of turn-of-the-century England was constantly present and effective, establishing a proper framework for the thriller. However, as a suspense story it had failings that director Gregory Ratoff was unable to overcome. "After the first few reels, *Moss Rose* is not very mysterious, but it is sometimes exciting, even when it doesn't puzzle." *Time* magazine)

At the core of this film is Peggy Cummins' Belle Adair, a sweet, but very ambitious, cockney showgirl who is determined to use her blonde beauty and charm to better her social position. Her life's desire is to reside among the gentry. Opportunity comes her way when her rooming-house neighbor is murdered and she realizes that her well-bred caller, Sir Alexander Sterling (Victor Mature), may be involved in the homicide. Before long she has blackmailed Sir Alexander into inviting her to his Devonshire manse presided over by his stately mater (Ethel Barrymore). Through dint of perseverance Belle deals successfully with his jealous financee (Patricia Medina), but the combination of deranged son and protective mother nearly cost her her life. Fortuitously, Scotland Yard Inspector Clinner (Vincent Price) is on the case and arrives in the nick of time to insure that Belle does not fall victim to the moss rose-Bible murderer.

173

VINCENT PRICE UNMASKED

On the right side of the law again, Price was decorous, but not unctuous, as the lawman who pierces through Barrymore's matronly reserve and Mature's facetious quietness to solve the case. Despite the briefness of his role, Price's full-bodied characterization ("does very nicely" said *The New York Times)* made the proceedings and the finale more than adequately creditable.

THE LONG NIGHT *(RKO, 1947) 101 min.*

Producers, Robert Hakim, Raymond Hakim, Anatole Litvak; director, Litvak; based on the story by Jacques Viot; screenplay, John Wexley; music director, Dmitri Tiomkin; art director, Eugene Lourie; set decorator, Darrell Silvera; assistant director, Aaron Rosenberg; sound, Richard Van Hessen, Clem Portman; special effects, Russell A. Culley; camera, Sol Polito; editor, Robert Swink.

Henry Fonda (Joe); Barbara Bel Geddes (Jo Ann); Vincent Price (Maximilian); Ann Dvorak (Charlene); Howard Freeman (Sheriff); Moroni Olsen (Chief of Police); Elisha Cook, Jr. (Frank); Queenie Smith (Janitor's Wife); David Clarke (Bill); Charles McGraw (Policeman); Patty King (Peggy); Robert A. Davis (Freddie); Will Wright (Janitor); Ray Teal (Hudson); Pat Flaherty (Sergeant); Dick Reeves (Cop); Jack Overman (Man); Byron Foulger (Man with Bike); Murray Alper (Bartender); Mary Gordon (Old Lady).

This unmemorable Hollywood remake of Marcel Carne's well-received *Le Jour se Leve (Daybreak)* (1939) caused critics to comment, "If atmosphere and mood could alone sustain a motion picture...(this film) would rank among the most effective of the ear." (New York *Herald Tribune)*

The action of this black-and-white melodrama was now set in a grimy mill town on the Pennsylvania-Ohio border, where middle-aged Maximilian (Vincent Price), the glib honky-tonk magician, ignores his loyal show assistant (Ann Dvorak) and, instead seduces dreamy, inexperienced Jo Ann (Barbara Bel Geddes). This thoughtless, immoral act causes a fatal confrontation between the braggart and Jo Ann's hard-working ex-GI sweetheart (Henry Fonda). The end result finds Maximilian shot and a bewildered Joe barricading himself in his room against the unpitying police. As a curiosity-aroused crowd gathers, Joe ponders just how and why he has to come to this unfortunate and deadly situation.

Price's emoting as the second-rate vaudeville artist left a great deal to be desired, especially in contrast to screen newcomer Bel Geddes and veteran Dvorak. *The New York Times* claimed he was "too utterly precious" and the New York *Herald-Tribune* reasoned that his "...grotesque figure is not as real as the rest of the picture."

UP IN CENTRAL PARK *(Universal, 1948)* 88 min.

Producer, Karl Tunberg; director, William A. Seiter; based on the play by Dorothy Fields, Herbert Fields, Sigmund Romberg; screenplay, Tunberg; production designer, Howard Bay; set decorators, Russell A. Gausman, Ted Offenbecker; music, Romberg; orchestrator, Johnny Green; songs, Dorothy Fields and Romberg; assistant director, William Holland; make-up, Bud Westmore; costumes, Mary Grant; sound, Leslie I. Carey, Joe Lapis; special effects, David S. Horsley; camera, Milton Krasner; editor, Otto Ludwig.

Deanna Durbin (Rosie Moore); Dick Haymes (John Matthews); Vincent Price (Boss Tweed); Albert Sharpe (Timothy Moore); Tom Powers (Regan); Hobart Cavanaugh (Mayor Oakley); Thurston Hall (Governor Motley); Howard Freeman (Myron Schultz); Mary Field (Miss Murch); Tom Pedi (O'Toole); Moroni Olsen (Big Jim Pitts); William Skipper, Nelle Fisher (Dancers); Patricia Alphin, Nina Lunn, Bunny Waters (Guests); Wayne Tredway, Frank McFarland, Harry Denny, Hal Taggart, Ed Peil, Sr. (Politicians); G. Pat Collins (Ward Heeler); Curt Bois (Maitre d'); George Spaulding (Barton); Billy Newell (Stage Manager); Martin Garralaga (Bertolli); Thomas Jackson, Tom P. Dillon (Officials); Richard Kipling (Waiter with Trick Tray); Alice Backes (Swedish Immigrant Girl); Charles Miller (Jones); Tudor Owen (Footman); Bert Moorhouse (Democrat); Carol Dawn Pierson (Little Girl Dancing); Eve Pearson (Ticket Seller); Carl Sepulveda (Carriage Driver); Charles Weskin (Alderman); Stuart Holmes, Art Thompson (Judges); Rod de Medici (Immigrant); Boyd Ackerman, Leslie Sketchley (Policemen).

As a 1945 Broadway outing, this period musical featured Wilbur Evans, Maureen Cannon, Noah Beery, and Betty Bruce. Thanks largely to the sentimental Sigmund Romberg-Herbert and Dorothy

175

Fields songs ("The Big Back Yard," "It doesn't Cost You Anything to Dream," etc.) and the extravagant publicity gimmicks of producer Michael Todd, the show lasted for a 504-performance run.

Universal acquired the property as a Deanna Durbin vehicle, but then stripped the script of most of the score and the 1880s New York flavor. One can only wonder what dancer Fred Astaire would have accomplished if he had directed the film as planned. William A. Seiter who did helm the musical was at his best in handling a stunning Currier and Ives skating sequence, but for the most part the proceedings were lugubrious and centered in overstuffed parlors instead of in Central Park.

Plumpish Durbin offered a monochromatic portrayal of colleen immigrant Rosie Moore and sang "Oh Say Do You See What I See?" "Carousel in the Park," and the Pace, Pace Mio Dio" aria from Verdi's opera *La Forza del Destino*. Smiley Dick Haymes appeared as the energetic (!) *New York Times* reporter out to expose corruption and woo Durbin. (His solo vocal interlude was "When She Walks in the Room.") Then there was Vincent Price as politician William Marcy Tweed (1823-1878), known as Boss Tweed, who was later indicted for this corrupt political practices. The physical, intellectual, and emotional disparities between the actor and the real-life grafter were astounding. Said *The New York Times*"... a more inappropriate choice could hardly be imagined. This is not meant to reflect on Mr. Price's acting ability; it's merely a case of the actor not fitting the character."

Needless to say, *Up in Central Park* was a harbinger of Durbin's cinema washout, which occurred after her next feature.

ABBOTT AND COSTELLO MEET FRANK-ENSTEIN *(Universal, 1948) 92 min.*

Producer, Robert Arthur; director, Charles T. Barton; screenplay, Robert Lees, Frederic I. Rinaldo, John Grant; art directors, Bernard Herzbrun, Hilyard Brown; set decorators, Russell A. Gausman, Oliver Emert; music, Frank Skinner; orchestrator, David Tamkin; costumes, Grace Houston; make-up, Bud Westmore; assistant director, Joseph E. Kenny; sound, Leslie I. Carey, Robert Pritchard; special effects, David S. Horsley, Jerome H. Ash; camera, Charles Van Enger; editor, Frank Gross.

Bud Abbott (Chick); Lou Costello (Wilbur); Lon Chaney (Lawrence Talbot); Bela Lugosi (Dracula); Glenn Strange (Monster);

Lenore Aubert (Sandra Mornay); Jane Randolph (Joan Raymond); Frank Ferguson (Mr. McDougal); Charles Bradstreet (Dr. Stevens); Howard Negley (Mr. Harris); Joe Kirk, George Barton, Carl Sklover, Joe Walls (Men); Helen Spring (Woman at Baggage Counter); Clarence Straight (Man in Armor); Harry Brown (Photographer); Paul Stader (Sergeant); Voice of Vincent Price (Invisible Man).

In the World War II period, Universal had a tremendous box-office success with two established formulas—zany Bud Abbott and Lou Costello slapstick features and horror-monster capers. Both genres suffered a postwar slump and it was decided to combine the two. The gambit worked with filmgoers, even if purists objected to having the likes of Dracula (Bela Lugosi), the Wolfman (Lon Chaney), the Frankenstein monster (Glenn Strange), and the Invisible Man (voice of Vincent Price) made the butt of the vaudeville team's lowbrow jokes.

Imagine rotund Wilbur's (Costello) dismay when he learns that Sandra Mornay (Lenore Aubert) and her medical cronies intend to donate his brain to their electrically charged monster. For most of the ninety-two-minute running time, Costello and straight man-pal Chick (Abbott) endeavor to elude their captors on a tight little island. Just when they think they have escaped their demented hosts, who should "appear" in their rowboat? None other than the translucent form of the Invisible Man (Price).

THE THREE MUSKETEERS *(MGM, 1948)*
C-125 min.

Producer, Pandro S. Berman; director, George Sidney; based on the novel by Alexandre Dumas; screenplay, Robert Ardrey; art directors, Cedric Gibbons, Malcolm Brown; set decorators, Edwin B. Willis, Henry W. Grace; music, Herbert Stothart, with themes by Tchaikovsky; orchestrator, Albert Sendrey; music director, Charles Previn; assistant director, George Rhein; make-up, Jack Dawn; costumes, Walter Plunkett; sound, Douglas Shearer, Conrad Kahn; montages, Peter Ballbusch; special effects, Warren Newcombe; camera, Robert Planck; editors, Robert J. Kern, George Boemler.

Lana Turner (Milady Countess DeWinter); Gene Kelly (D'Artagnan); June Allyson (Constance Bonacieux); Van Heflin (Athos); Angela Lansbury (Queen Anne); Frank Morgan (Louis

XIII); Vincent Price (Richelieu); Keenan Wynn (Planchet); John Sutton (Duke of Buckingham); Gig Young (Porthos); Robert Coote (Aramis); Reginald Owen (Treville); Ian Keith (Rochefort); Patricia Medina (Kitty); Richard Stapley (Albert); Byron Foulger (Bonacieux); Sol Gross (Jussac); Richard Simmons (Count De-Wardes); Robert Warwick (D'Artagnan Sr.); William 'Bill' Phillips (Grimaud); Albert Morin (Bazin); Norman Leavitt (Mousqueton); Marie Windsor (Spy); Ruth Robinson (Mother); Tom Tyler (Traveler); Kirk Alyn, John Holland (Friends); Reginald Sheffield (Subaltern); William Edmunds (Landlord); Irene Seidner (Landlord's Wife); Francis McDonald (Fisherman); Paul Maxey (Major Domo); Arthur Hohl (Dragon Rouge Host); Gil Perkins (Guard); Mickey Simpson (Executioner).

When Alexandre Dumas penned *Les Trois Mousquetaires* in 1844 it seemed he had devised the ultimate swashbuckling novel. In the twentieth century, filmmakers around the globe seized upon the adventure yarn, now in the public domain, as the basis for several sword-and-cloak renditions, the most famous being Douglas Fairbank's 1921 silent feature. Metro-Goldwyn-Mayer produced their own glorious Technicolor edition in 1948. The Robert Ardrey screenplay may have had "...more ups and down than the Berlin airlift." (*Time* magazine) but the lushly mounted proceedings "...are richly designed, lavishly costumed, impeccable to its last elaborate detail." (*Cue* magazine)

Within the familiar chronicle set in 1626 France, carefree D'Artagnan (Gene Kelly) merrily joins forces with three of King Louis XIII's most adventurous musketeers (Van Heflin, Gig Young, Robert Coote), each pledging "One for all and all for one." They are soon embarked on a mission to reclaim two diamond studs that Queen Anne (Angela Lansbury) has imprudently bestowed on her lover (John Sutton). The bumpy trail leads D'Artagnan to England, with luscious Milady Countess DeWinter (Lana Turner) ordered by Richelieu (Vincent Price) to waylay him. For her unsuccessful efforts, Turner is beheaded in the finale, with Richelieu finding himself in disfavor with the pacified monarch.

Many performers had portrayed Cardinal Richelieu (1585-1642) on-camera, including Nigel De Brulier in the 1921 *The Three Musketeers,* George Arliss in *Cardinal Richelieu* (1935), and Raymond Massey in *Under the Red Robe* (1936). These performances were in the grand manner, whereas Price's interpretation lacked the asp's bit. (Vincent Price's Richelieu almost comes to life, but not

178

quite." *(New York Herald-Tribune)* One problem was that Metro decided to disguise the fact that Price's character was indeed a cardinal. In fact, the actor was garbed in cavalier costume and plumed hat, giving little indication that he was actually His Eminence.

Whatever misgivings one may have had about Price's "Hollywood *haute"* interpretation of the role, it at least had zest and life, something Charlton Heston's robed performance lacked in the 1974 movie spoof of *The Three Musketeers.*

ROGUE'S REGIMENT *(Universal, 1948) 86 min.*

Producer, Robert Buckner; director, Robert Florey; story, Buckner, Florey; screenplay, Buckner; art directors, Bernard Herzbrun, Gabriel Scognamillo; set decorators, Russell A. Gausman, Oliver Emert; music, Daniele Amfitheatrof; orchestrator, David Tamkin; music director, Milton Schwarzwald; songs, Jack Brooks, Serge Walter, Walter Jurmann; assistant director, Horace Hough; make-up, Bud Westmore; choreography, Billy Daniels; costumes, Orry Kelly; sound, Leslie I. Carey, Richard De Wesse; camera, Maury Gertsman; editor, Ralph Dawson.

Dick Powell (Whit Corbett); Marta Toren (lili Maubert); Vincent Price (Mark Van Ratten); Stephen McNally (Carl Reicher); Edgar Barrier (Colonel Mauclaire); Henry Rowland (Erich Heindorf); Carol Thurston (Li-Ho-Kay); James Millican (Cobb); Richard Loo (kao Pang); Philip Ahn (Tran Duy Gian); Richard Fraser (Rycroft); Otto Reichow (Stein); Kenny Washington (Sam Latch); Dennis Dengate (O'Hara); Frank Conroy (Colonel Lemercier); Martin Garralaga (Hazarat); James F. Nolan (American Colonel); Paul Bryar (Chief of Police); Gordon Clark (Lieutenant Verdier); Harry Meller, Robert Verdaine, Kell Nordenshield, Willy Wickerhauser, John Royce (Legionnaires); Lester Sharpe (Kavenko); Eugene Borden (Doctor); Maurice Marsac (Lieutenant); Victor Sen Yung (Rickshaw Boy); Charles J. Flynn (Dispatch Rider); John Doucette (German); Artarne Wong (Chinese Vendor); Leo Schlesinger (Soldier); Kei Thing Chung (Viet Guard); Paul Coze (Commander); John Peters (Lutheran Priest); Albert Pollett (Frenchman); Jerry Mills (Soldier on Train).

At this juncture of his career ex-crooner Dick Powell was still immersed in his tough-guy image-building. Here he was cast as the army intelligence officer who enlists in the French Foreign Legion to track down one-time Nazi officer Carl Reicher (Stephen McNally). Universal publicized the lackluster feature with the tag line, "Adventure flames...in the world's hot-spot of danger and intrigue!" At best, the ordinary drama was "reasonably active" *(The New York Times)* in action, but decidedly deficient in general entertainment.

Powell was properly resolute, McNally efficiently dastardly as the Martin Bormann figure, and Marta Toren ("the temptatious hit of *Casbah*" was exotic as the night-club chanteuse and French operative. As for Vincent Price's Mark Van Ratten, he bounded in and out of the scenes as a local antique dealer and double-dealing gunrunner who threatens McNally with exposure. Perhaps most distressing about Price's performance was his embarrassingly labored German accent, making his appearance more amateurish than necessary.

THE BRIBE *(MGM, 1949) 98 min.*

Producer, Pandro S. Berman; director, Robert Z. Leonard; based on the story by Frederick Nebel; screenplay, Marguerite Roberts; art directors, Cedric Gibbons, Malcolm Brown; set decorators, Edwin B. Willis, Hugh Hunt; music, Mikos Rozsa; song, Nacio Herb Brown and William Katz; assistant director, Ben Glazer; make-up, Jack Dawn; Ava Gardner's costumes by Irene; sound, Douglas Shearer, Fred MacAlpin; special effects, Warren Newcombe, A. Arnold Gillespie; camera, Joseph Ruttenberg; editor, Gene Ruggiero.

Robert Taylor (Rigby); Ava Gardner (Elizabeth Hintten); Charles Laughton (A. J. Bealer); Vincent Price (Carwood); John Hodiak (Tug Hintten); Samuel S. Hinds (Dr. Warren); John Hoyt (Gibbs); Tito Renaldo (Emilio Gomez); Martin Garralaga (Pablo Gomez); Pepe Hernandez (Bellboy); Nacho Galindo (Clerk); Marcel de la Brosse, Albert Pollet (Frenchman); Walter A. Merrill, Frank Mayo (Americans); Robert Cabal, David Cota, Richard Lopez (Bellboys); Fernando Alvarado (Flute Player); Peter Cusanelli (Rhumba Dancer); Jerry Pina (Stunt Juggler); Harry Vejar (Indian); Felipe Turich (Clerk); William Haade (Walker); Joe Dominguez (Waiter); Julian Rivero (Boatman); Ernesto Morelli (Bartender); Albert Morin (Jose the Waiter).

The publicity campaign for co-star Ava Gardner ("Her Lips Were a Bribe...Her Kiss a Betrayal") was as fatuous and outmoded as the picture itself. As for this film starting any new cinema love teaming between Gardner and Robert Taylor ("Together for the First Time and We Do Mean Together"), forget it.

Rigby (Taylor) of the U.S. Justice Department arrives in a seedy Caribbean port where at the local cafe he encounters tantalizing Elizabeth Hintten (Gardner), she of the ruby-red lips, blank eyes, and undulating hips. It soon develops that Rigby has been assigned to break up a war-surplus racket, and that Elizabeth (who "sings" "Situation Wanted") is the bait supplied by syndicate-boss Carwood (Vincent Price) to lure the law enforcer off the case. As an added inducement to Operation: Corrupt Taylor, sniveling beachcomber A. J. Bealer (Charles Laughton), also part of the gang, offers stiff-lipped Rigby a ten-thousand-dollar bribe. When the long overdue finale occurs, Carwood and his cronies are subdued, Elizabeth is separated from her drunken, ill ex-Air Force husband (John Hodiak), and rugged Rigby has salvaged his job, pride, and his new-found romance.

Price, who "leers with diabolic glee" *(The New York Times)* as the organization's mastermind, has a touching sequence in which he dumps Taylor in the sea during their marlin fishing trip. For the sake of the continuity, Taylor just misses becoming shark food.

BAGDAD *(Universal, 1949) C-82 min.*

Producer, Robert Arthur; assistant producer, Morgan Cox; director, Charles Lamont; story, Tamara Hovey; screenplay, Robert Hardy Andrews; art directors, Bernard Herzbrun, Alexander Golitzen; set decorators, Russell A. Gausman, John Austin; songs, Jack Brooks, Frank Skinner; assistant director, Jesse Hibbs; make-up, Bud Westmore, Emil LeVigne; choreography, Lester Horton, Bella Lewitsky; costumes, Yvonne Wood; sound, Leslie I. Carey, Glenn E. Anderson; camera, Russell Metty; editor, Russell Schoengarth.

Maureen O'Hara (Princess Marjan); Paul Christian (Hassan); Vincent Price (Pascha Ali Nadim); John Sutton (Raijul); Jeff Corey (Mohammed Jad); Frank Puglia (Saleel); David Wolfe (Mahmud); Fritz Leiber (Emir); Otto Waldis (Morengo); Leon Belasco (Beggar); Ann Pearce (Tirza).

In a fluffy way, this childish cloak-and-sandal yarn pokes fun at "burning-sands" movies, but in itself it fails to provide those necessary touches to make it either a substantial satire or even the real McCoy.

English-educated Princess Marjan (Maureen O'Hara) returns to Bagdad, the capital of her Bedouin country to learn that her father has been assassinated by the mysterious bandits known as the Black Robes. She unwisely turns to Pasha Ali Nadim (Vincent Price), the Turkish military governor, for council, not realizing the dastard is in cahoots with the desert marauders and their leader Raijul (John Sutton). Hassan, whom flaming redhead Marjan had initially suspected, actually proves to be the hero of the piece.

As the confounding culprit, Price was "friendly as a cobra" *(The New York Times)*, but certainly no match for athletic Christian nor the captivating O'Hara, who not only performs assorted native dances but also sings three songs.

CHAMPAGNE FOR CAESAR *(United Artists, 1950) 99 min.*

Executive producer, Harry M. Popkin; producer, George Moskov; director, Richard Whorf; story-screenplay, Hans Jacoby, Fred Brady; music, Dmitri Tiomkin; art director, George Van Marter; assistant director, Ralph Stosser, Leon Chooluck; camera, Paul Ivano; editor, Hugh Bennett.

Ronald Colman (Beauregard Bottomly); Celeste Holm (Flame O'Neil); Vincent Price (Burnbridge Waters); Barbara Britton (Gwenn Bottomley); Art Linkletter (Happy Hogan); Gabriel Heatter, George Fisher (Announcers); Byron Foulger (Gerald); Eleye Marshall (Frosty); Vici Raaf (Waters' Secretary); Douglas Evans (Radio Announcer); John Eldredge, Lyle Talbot, George Leigh, John Hart (Executives); Mel Blanc (Caesar's Voice); Peter Brocco (Fortunegeller); Brian O'Hara (Buck-T Man); Jack Daly (Scratch-T Man); Gordon Nelson (Lecturer); Herbert Lytton (Chuck Johnson); George Meader (Mr. Brown).

James Stewart's *The Hackpot* (1950) was a subdued exaggeration of the financial-emotional repercussions of being a radio game-show winner. On the other hand, *Champagne for Caesar* is a broad lampoon of the radio quiz-show craze that soon loses credibility in its wide sideswipes at the radio industry.

Encyclopedic Beauregard Bottomly (Ronald Colman) plans on escalating his winnings on the "Masquerade for Money" game show in the hope of wiping out this threat to America's intellect. As head of the program's sponsoring company (Milady Soaps, "the soap that sanctifies") Burnbridge Waters (Vincent Price) hires comely Flame O'Neil (Celeste Holm) to vamp urbane Colman and prevent him from reaping too much financial gain. Meanwhile Colman's sweet sister (Barbara Britton) falls in love with the show's cloying master of ceremonies (Art Linkletter). A rushed, cop-out ending—Bottomly cannot recall his own Social Security number—leaves a rancid taste to the proceedings.

One of the winker links in this picture is Price's burlesque portrait of a soap tycoon. "Some of his broad aberrations offer faintly satirical thrusts at advertising genius, but most of them are duds." *(The New York Times)*

THE BARON OF ARIZONA *(Lippert, 1950)* 97 min.

Producer, Carl K. Hittleman; director, Samuel Fuller; based on article in *The American Weekly;* screenplay, Fuller; assistant director, Frank Fox; art director, P. Frank Sylos; set decorators, Otto Siegel, Ray Robinson; music, Paul Dunlap; make-up, Vernon Murdock; sound, Garry Harris; sound effects, Harry Coswick; special effects, Ray Mercer; camera, James Wong Howe; editor, Arthur Hilton.

Vincent Price (James Addison Reavis), Ellen Drew (Sofia de Peralta Reavis); Beulah Bondi (Loma Morales); Vladimir Sokoloff (Pepito Alvarez); Reed Hadley (John Griff); Robert Barrat) Judge Adams); Robin Short (Lansing); Barbara Woodell (Carry Lansing); Tina Rome (Rita); Margia Dean (Marquesa); Edward Keane (Surveyor General Miller); Gene Roth (Father Guardian); Karen Kester (Sofia as a Child); Joseph Green (Gunter); Fred Kohler, Jr. (Demming); Tristam Coffin (McCleary); I. Stanford Jolley (Secretary of the Interior); Terry Frost (Morelle); Angelo Rosito (Augie); Zachary Yaconelli (Greco); Adolfo Ornelas (Martinez); Wheaton Chambers (Brother Gregory); Robert O'Neil (Brother

Paul); Stephen Harrison (Assistant Surveyor); Stuart Holmes (Senator); Jonathan Hale (Governor); Stanley Price (Senator Reynolds); Sam Flin (Senator); George Meader (Hank); Ed East (Bit); Dick Cramer, Al Haskel (Phoenix Men).

Perhaps one of the most colossal swindles in American history was nearly perpetrated by James Addison Reavis (Vincent Price), who in the 1870s almost convinced Congress that he was indeed the baron of Arizona and that the 113,000 square miles of prime territory was his lawful domain. Had the feature's budget been more flexible or director Samuel Fuller—then at the beginning of his cinema career—been more agile in manipulating his professional cast, this ninety-seven-minute chronicle of greed versus love would have been memorable rather than merely competent.

In 1872 a minor clerk (Price) in the booming Arizona land office realizes how *easy* it would be to concoct evidence of his "legitimate" claim to a stretch of valuable property. Part of his hoax requires promoting farm girl Sofia de Peralta (Karen Kester as the child; Ellen Drew as the adult) as the alleged heir to this Spanish land grant. Just as he methodically forges documents both in America and in Spain to substantiate his claim, he patiently instructs the girl in the ways of aristocratic living. Subsequently he weds his willing creation. Ironically, it is his growing love for Sofia that causes Reavis not only to reject a $25,000,000 Federal offer for the barony, but to finally admit the fraud. He later serves a six-year jail sentence.

Price had ample occasion to dramatize in this expansive atypical Western. Yet, he did not win plaudits for his first full-blooded lead role, but was called to task for a lack of control and inspiration. "His performance is somewhat diluted by monotomy..." (New York *Herald-Tribune)* "...(he is) given to studied posing and declamation." *(The New York Times)* "Price seems too much aware of himself..." *(Variety)*

CURTAIN CALL AT CACTUS CREEK *(Universal, 1950) 86 min.*

Producer, Robert Arthur; director, Charles Lamont; story, Stanley Robers, Howard Dimsdale; screenplay, Dimsdale; art director, Bernard Herzbrun, John F. DeCuir; camera, Russell Metty; editor, Frank Gross.

Donald O'Connor (Edward Timmons); Gale Storm (Julie Martin); Walter Brennan (Rimrock); Vincent Price (Tracy Holland); Eve Arden (Lily Martin); Chick Chandler (Ralph); Joe Sawyer (Jake); Harry Shannon (Clay); Rex Lease (Yellowstone); I. Stanford Jolley (Pecos).

Pleasant color lowjinks as an itinerant acting troupe parades about the Old West offering untempered skits on the curse of drink. The hearty group consists of hammy Shakespearean performer Tracy Holland (Vincent Price), stage-struck stagehand Edward Timmons (Donald O'Connor), and the mother and daughter team of Lily Martin (Eve Arden) and Julie Martin (Gale Storm).

Beyond the smooth musical interludes of four tunes from another era, there are the winning efforts of milquetoast Edward to survive both Tracy's harangues and the wisecracks of over-ripe Lily, and his accidentally successful efforts to capture folksy bank robber Rimrock (Walter Brennan).

As the washed-up actor, Price had ample chance to overact (with great glee) and to steal all available scenes.

HIS KIND OF WOMAN *(RKO, 1951) 120 min.*

Producers, Howard Hughes, Robert Sparks; director, John Farrow; story-screenplay, Frank Fenton; art director, Albert S. D'Agostino; music director, C. Bakaleinikoff; songs, Sam Coslow, Harold Adamson, and Jimmy McHugh; camera, Harry J. Wild; editor, Eda Warren.

Robert Mitchum (Dan Milner); Jane Russell (Lenore Brent); Vincent Price (Mark Cardigan); Tim Holt (Bill Lusk); Charles McGraw (Thompson); Marjorie Reynolds (Helen Cardigan); Leslye Banning (Jennie Stone); Jim Backus (Myron Winton); Raymond Burr (Nick Ferraro); John Mylong (Martin Krafft); Carleton G. Young (Hobson); Erno Verebes (Estaban); Dan White (Tex Kearns); Richard Berggren (Milton Stone); Stacy Harris (Harry); Robert Cornthwaite (Hernandez); Jim Burke (Barkeep); Paul Frees (Corle); Joe Granby (Arnold); Daniel De Laurentis (Mexican Boy); John Sheehan (Husband); Sally Yarnell (Wife); Anthony Caruso (Tony); Robert Rose (Corle's Servant); Tol Avery (The Fat One); Paul Fierro, Mickey Simpson (Hoodlums); Ed Rand, Jerry James (Cops); Joel Fluellen (Sam); Len Hendry (Customer); Joey Ray,

Barry Brooks (Card Players); Stuart Holmes, Jim Davies (Men); Marie San Young (Chinese Watiress); Mary Brewer, Jerri Jordan, Joy Windsor, Mamie Van Doren, Barbara Freking (Girls); Marietta Elliott (Redhead); William Justin (Gyppo); Bill Nelson (Captain Salazarr); Bud Wolf (Seaman); Ralph Gomez (Mexican Foreman); Mike Lally (Henchman); Saul Gorss (Viscount); Gerry Ganzer (Countess).

On a promise of payment of fifty-thousand-dollars, professional gambler Dan Milner (Robert Mitchum) treks to Mexico to await instructions on how he is to earn it. On the way he meets sultry singer Lenore Brent (Jane Russell), who later confesses to having a mild romance with egocentric movie star Mark Cardigan (Vincent Price). At the remote South-of-the-border resort lodge, Mitchum belatedly discovers he has been hired to drop out of sight (and be killed) so deported racketeer Nick Ferraro (Raymond Burr) can utilize his identity and return to the States.

Bogus rich girl Russell sings "Five Little Miles from San Berdoo," "Kiss and Run," and "You'll Know," proving that her appeal is not entirely geographical (she does wear a spectacular black bathing suit). Sleepy-eyed Mitchum is appropriately tough during the sadistic yacht sequences when he is at the mercy of oily Burr and his henchmen. However, it is Price as the narcissistic matinee idol who goes hog-wild in this film. Whether escaping the clutches of his possessive wife (Marjorie Reynolds), sighing over a screening of his latest costumed film, or proving his astuteness as an amateur hunter, he rates a near one hundred on the baloney chart. Most outrageous of all is his leadership of the last-minute rescue squad to save Mitchum from a dire end. Even the Mexican police compatriots are bewildered at Price's oversized behavior.

ADVENTURES OF CAPTAIN FABIAN (Republic, 1951) 100 min.

Producer, William Marshall; associate producer, Robert Dorfman; director, Marshall; based on the novel *Fabulous Ann Madlock* by Robert Shannon; screenplay, Errol Flynn; music, Rene Cloerec; assistant director, Marc Maurette; sets, Eugene Lourie, Max Douy; costumes, Arlington Valles; sound, Roger Cosson; camera, Marcel Grignon; editor, Henri Taverna.

Errol Flynn (Captain Michael Fabian); Micheline Presle (Lea Marriotte); Vincent Price (George Brissac); Agnes Moorehead (Aunt Jesebel); Victor Francen (Henri Brissac); Jim Gerald (Constable Gilpin); Helena Manson (Madam Pirott); Howard Vernon (Emil); Roger Blin (Phillipe); Valentine Camax (Housekeeper); Georges Flateau (Judge Jean Brissac); Zanie Campan (Cynthia Winthrop); Reggie Nalder (Constant); Charles Fawcett (Defense Attorney); Aubrey Bower (Mate).

There is hardly a good word to be said about this dull celluloid exercise supposedly adapted for the screen by star Error Flynn. The claptrap drama reveals many parallels to Edna Ferber's novel *Saratoga Trunk* but neglects to borrow any of its entertainment values. This "floundering fiasco" *(The New York Times)* was filmed in France.

Creole servant girl Lea Mariotte (Micheline Presle) is framed on a murder charge by snobbish New Orleans citizenry. Roving sea captain Michael Fabian (Flynn), who has a score to settle with the same wealthy landowners, rescues her, but he refuses to fall prey to her wiles. Accompanied by her pipe-smoking octoroon campanion (Agnes Moorehead), she sets out to seek revenge on those "responsible" for her present plight. Part of her ambitious scheme calls for her to wed weak-willed George Brissac (Vincent Price) and goad him into murdering his dominating uncle (Victor Francen). Eventually her vindictive actions inspire a donnybrook that rocks the southern city. However, she escapes the fracas and returns to the now-willing arms of Flynn.

THE LAS VEGAS STORY *(RKO, 1952) 88 min.*

Producer, Robert Sparks; director, Robert Stevenson; screenplay, Earl Felton, Harry Essex; art director, Albert S. D'Agostino, Field Gray; music director, C. Bakaleinikoff; songs, Hoagy Carmichael, Orrin Tucker; camera, Harry J. Wild; editor, George Shrader.

Jane Russell (Linda Rollins); Victor Mature (Dave Andrews); Vincent Price (Lloyd Rollins); Hoagy Carmichael (Happy); Brad Dexter (Thomas Hubler); Gordon Oliver (Drucker); Jay C. Flippen

(Harris); Will Wright (Fogarty); Bill Welsh (Martin); Ray Montgomery (Desk Clerk); Colleen Miller (Mary); Robert Wilke (Clayton); Syd Saylor (Matty); George Hoagland, Roger Creed, Jimmy Long, Bert Stevens, Norman Stevens, Ben Harris, Ted Jordan, Philip Ahlm, Mary Bayless, Diana Mumby, Marg Darby, Barbara Freking, Barbara Thatcher, Beverly Thomas, Jean Corbett, Hazel Shaw, Sue Casey, Evelyn Lovequist, Betty Arlen, Jeane Cochran, Carole Morton (Bits); Clarence Muse (Pullman Porter); Oliver Hartwell (Redcap); Wallis Clark (Witwer); Dorothy Abbott, Joan Mallory, Jane Easton (Waitresses); Mavis Russell (Blonde); Midge Ware (Chief Money Changer); John Merrick (Gus); Roy Darmour, Pat Collins, Sam Finn, Joe Gilbert, Brooks Benedict (Stickmen Dealers); Carolyn Block, Betty Onge, Helen Blizard, Mona Knox (Change Girls); Robert Milton (Sheriff); Steve Flagg (Deputy); Harry Brooks, Al Murphy, Dick Ryan (Bartenders); Ralph Alley, Mitchell Rhein, Forrest Lederer, Charles Cross, Carl Sklover (Dealers); Virginia Lynden, Connie Castle, Suzanne Ames, Anabelle Applegate, Joyce Niven, Shirley Tegge, Anne Dore, Chili Williams, Sylvia Lewis (Guests); Milton Kibbee (Coroner).

If *Viva Las Vegas* (1964) and *Ocean's Eleven* (1960) provide outdated views of the Nevada gambling capital, *The Las Vegas Story* is downright historical in its glimpses of life in he glittering gambling and entertainment center. With its haphazard production values, this black-and-white feature seemed nothing more than in "impromptu" production from the Howard Hughes-RKO factory designed merely to promote Jane Russell's fabulous chassis.

As their California-bound train nears Las Vegas, Lloyd Rollins (Vincent Price) persuades his shapely wife (Russell) to stop off for a look at the city. She unwillingly agrees, fearful of reigniting her torrid local past. A few years back she had been a singer at the Last Chance Club in downtown Las Vegas and had engaged in a sizzling romance with U.S. Air Force member Dave Andrews, (Victor Mature). Not unsurprisingly, while Rollins plunges heavily into gambling, his wife reencounters the muscular Andrews, now a lieutenant on the local sheriff's staff. Events soon tumble over themselves: Rollins loses the $10,000 credit allowed him by the Fabulous Hotel, Thomas Hubler (Brad Dexter) arrives on the scene claiming to represent the company insuring Linda's pawned $150,000 necklace, and Clayton (Robert Wilke), owner of the Last Chance is murdered. In a finale that borders on the ludicrous, Hubler, not Rollins, proves to be the real crook-murderer. he kidnaps Linda and flees in a station wagon across the desert, and Andrews pursues via helicopter. Naturally he and Linda end up arm in arm. What of Rollins? He is cleared of one crime charge, but is now arrested for an eastern embezzlement foray.

For those uncaptivated by Russell's chintzy cleavage-oriented costumes, she sings "I Get Along Without You Very Well" and "My Resistance Is Low," while honky-tonk pianist Hoagy Carmichael groans out his own novelty tune, "The Monkey Song."

PICTURA *(Pictura Films, 1952) 80 min.* *

Producers, Leonid Kipness, Herman Starr; directors, E. A. Dupont, Luciano Emmer, Robert Hessens, Alain Resnais; screenplay, George Davis, Gaston Diehl, Frederick Kohner, Richard Nickson; music, Roman Viad; music director, Jack Shaindlin; editors, Chester Schaeffer, Reine Dorian, Robert S. Robinson, Mark Sorkin.

Andres Segovita (Francisco Goya); Vincent Price, Harry Marble, Gregory Peck, Lilli Palmer, Martein Gabel, Henry Fonda (Narrators).

"A brave and respectable endeavor to transmit via the motion-picture screen something of the special experience of looking at and absorbing works of art...." (Bosley Crowther *(The New York Times)* (

Within the six-part presentation, the filmmakers have attempted to provide the viewer with an aesthetic appreciation to the art works of: Hieronymus Bosch, Vittore Carpaccio, Francisco Goya, Henri de Toulouse-Lautrec, Paul Gauguin, Grant Wood. The picture is framed within the device of narrator Price lecturing to a college art-appreciation class, with Price also providing the off-camera narrative to the survey of Bosch's creative contributions. Unfortunately, this compilation feature never rises above a static visualization of art masterpieces.

The Resnais-directed segment on Gauguin was actually lensed in 1950 with Jean Servais speaking the off-camera narrative to the accompaniment of background music by Darius Milhaud.

*Lensed in sepia.

HOUSE OF WAX *(Warner Brothers, 1953) C-88 min.*

Producer, Byran Foy; director, Andre de Toth; based on the play by Charles Belden; screenplay, Crane Wilbur; art director, Stanley Fleischer; camera, Bert Glennon; editor, Rudi Fehr.

Vincent Price (Professor Henry Jarrod); Roy Roberts (Matthew Burke); Paul Cavanagh (Sidney Wallace); Carolyn Jones (Cathy Gray); Phyllis Kirk (Sue Allen); Paul Picerni (Scott Andrews); Angela Clarke (Mrs. Andrews); Frank Lovejoy (Lieutenant Tom Brennan); Dabbs Greer (Sergeant Jim Shane); Charles Bronson (Igor); Ned Young (Leon Averill); Reggie Rymal (Barker); Philip Tonge (Bruce Alison); Darwin Greenfield, Jack Kenney (Lodgers); Ruth Warren (Scrubwoman); Riza Royce (Ma Flangan); Richard Benjamin, Jack Mower (Detectives); Grandon Rhodes (Surgeon); Frank Ferguson (Medical Examiner); Eddie Parks (Morgue Attendant); Oliver Blake (Pompous Man); Leo Curley (Portly Man); Mary Lou Holloway (Millie); Joanne Brown (Girl Friend); Lyle Latell (Waiter); Terry Mitchell, Ruth Whitney, Trude Wylwr (Women); Merry Townsend (Ticket Taker).

The prime excuse for remaking the horrific classic *The Mystery of the Wax Museum* (1933), which had starred Lionel Atwill, was to exploit the novelty of stereoscopic color 3-D and Warner Phonic sound. The results were less than creatively gratifying. According to Denis Gifford in *A Pictorial History of the Horror Film* (1973), "...the added dimension diminished the horror. Stereo separated the actors from the backgrounds but polished them into shimmery waxworks that worked in a rounded reality that was curiously unreal. The shocks came not from tangible horror but from a small ball, ping-ponged out of the screen directly at your nose." Commercially the Polaroid-glasses film was a great success, garnering over $4.3 million for the studio.

For all the ballyhoo, the lumbering plot actually provided few instances of real scares. When brilliant wax sculptor Professor Henry Jarrod (Vincent Price) is badly scarred physically and mentally in a fire, the turn-of-the-century artist sets out on a murderous spree, using the victims as the basis of new wax figures his New York shock museum. Police detective Lieutenant Tom Brennan (Frank Lovejoy) is assigned to investigate the series of

190

unexplained murders and comes to heroine Sue Allen's (Phyllis Kirk) rescue in the nick of time, saving her from a deadly waxy bath.

House of Wax returned Price to the genre he had long ago abandoned, but this time with a strong dash of redeeming Grand Guignol flavoring. Price was in "splendidly clammy form" (*Time* magazine), aided by the splendid make-up work of Gordon Bau, as he stalked the foggy streets for his latest victim. Many viewers wished that the plot had not revealed Price's repulsively mutilated face so early in the picture, since it destroyed a good deal of the tale's basic suspense.

DANGEROUS MISSION *(RKO, 1954) C-75 min.*

Producer, Irwin Allen; director, Louis King; story, Horace McCoy, James Edmiston; screenplay, McCoy, W. R. Burnett, Charles Bennett; art directors, Albert C. D'Agostino, Walter Keller; assistant director, James W. Lane; music, Roy Webb; camera, William Snyder; editor, Gene Palmer.

Victor Mature (Matt Hallett); Piper Laurie (Louise Graham); William Bendix (Joe Parker); Vincent Price (Paul Adams); Betty St. John (Mary Tiller); Steve Darrell (Katoonai); Marlo Dwyer (Mrs. Elster); Walter Reed (Dobson); Dennis Weaver (Pruitt); Harry Cheshire (Elster); George Sherwood (Mr. Jones); Maureen Stephenson (Mrs. Jones); Fritz Apking (Hawthorne); Ken Dibbs (Johnny Yonkers); Bert Moorehouse (Piano Player); Frank Griffin (Tedd); Virginia Linden (Mrs. Brown); Chet Marshall (Bellhop); Helen Brown (Miss Thorndyke); Trevor Bardette (Kicking Bear); Ann Dore (Woman); Roy Engel (Hume); Chester Jones (Porter); Richard Newton (Young Man Boone); Bill White, Jr. (Hotel Clerk); Charles Cane (Barrett); Jack Chefe (Headwaiter); Steve Rowland (ParkingLot Attendant); Russ Thorson (Radio Man); Robert Carraher (Praskins); Jim Potter (Ranger); Wymer Gard (Cobb); Mike Lally (Fletcher); Ralph Volkie, Sam Shack, Craig Moreland (Firefighters).

The gimmick of 3-D color photography and the natural grandeur of Glacier National Park are the two sole highlights of this "miserably dull and mixed-up fable." *(The New York Times)* The use of such time-honored cliff-hanging routines as broken live power lines, forest fires, and crumbling ice ledges cannot camouflage this seedy entry.

Louise (Piper Laurie) has witnessed a gangland murder in New York City and seeks refuge from the pursuing mobsters by taking a job at the remote Glacier National Park tourist hotel. Two mysterious men appear at the resort and Laurie is unsure whether Adams (Vincent Price) or Matt (Victor Mature) is the finger man hired to kill her. A sub-plot has burly Park Ranger Parker (William Bendix) trying to put pressure on Indian maiden Mary (Betty St. John) for information on her father who is wanted on a murder charge. At the same time Mary is involved romantically with Adams.

It did not require much perception on viewers' part to determine that Matt was the district attorney's man and that Adams was obviously the sinister underworld agent.

CASANOVA'S BIG NIGHT *(Paramount, 1954)* C-86 min.

Producer, Paul Jones; director, Norman Z. McLeod; story, Hal Kanter, Edmund Hartmann; screenplay, Aubrey Wisberg; art directors, Hal Pereira, Albert Nozaki; song, Jay Livingston and Ray Evans; choreography, Josephine Earl; camera, Lionel Lindon; editor, Ellsworth Hoagland.

Bob Hope (Pippo Popolino); Joan Fontaine (Francesca Bruni); Audrey Dalton (Elena DiGambetta); Basil Rathbone (Lucio); Arnold Moss (Doge of Venice); John Carradine (Foressi); John Hoyt (Maggiorin); Hope Emerson (Duchess of Genoa); Robert Hutton (Raphaele); Lon Chaney (Emo); Raymond Burr (Bragadin); Frieda Inescort (Signora DiGambetta); Primo Carnera (Corfa); Frank Puglia (Carabaccio); Paul Cavanagh (Signor DiGambetto); Romo Vincent (Giovanni); Henry Brandon (Captain Rugeelo); Natalie Schafer (Signora Foressi); Lucien Littlefield, Douglas Fowley (Prisoners); Nestor Paiva (Gnocchi); Barbara Freking (Maria); Joan Shawlee (Beatrice D'Brizzi); Oliver Blake (Amadeo); Torben Meyer (Attendant); Anthony Warde (Gondolier); John Alderson, Richard Karlan (Outside Guards); Fritz Feld (Little Man); Paul "Tiny"

Newlan (Regniatti); Skelton Knaggs (Tappani); Mike Rose (Jailer); Eric Alden (Maggiorin's Ruffian); Keith Richards (Servant); Gino Corrado (Ambassador); Bess Flowers (Marquesa); Dick Sands, Charles Hicks (Assistant Headsmen); Danny Dowling (Cloth Merchant); Trippe Elan (Small Boy); and: (unbilled) Vincent Price (Casanova).

A handsomely mounted costumed burlesque that misfired. "This is an attempt at broad comedy that misses as often as it clicks." *(Variety)* It proved to be comedian Bob Hope's last costume picture to date. With jokes such as "I can only work two canals a day," it is little wonder the public preferred watching television to movie going such as this.

In eighteenth-century Italy, cowardly tailor's apprentice Pippo Poppolino (Hope) finds himself ensconced in a new guise. Famous philanderer Casanova (Vincent Price in an unbilled guest role) must make a fast exit from the hotbed of amorous adventures and trades his clothes and "name" for Pippo's horse. Widowed grocery merchant Francesca (Joan Fontaine) is the lady fair who accompanies addled Pippo on his mission to Venice to discover for the duchess (Hope Emerson) whether her son:s financee (Audrey Dalton) is sincere or a fortune hunter. Pippo lands in the canal, in jail, and in deep trouble.

THE MAD MAGICIAN *(Columbia, 1954)* C-72 min.

Producer, Bryan Foy; director, John Brahm; screenplay, Crane Wilbur; art director, Frank Sylos; assistant director, Hal Herman; music, Emil Newman, Arthur Lange; camera, Bert Glennon; editor, Grant Whytock.

Vincent Price (Gallico); Mary Murphy (Karen Lee); Eva Gabor (Claire); John Emery (Rinaldi); Donald Randolph (Ross Ormond); Lenita Lane (Alice Prentice); Patrick O'Neal (Bruce Allen); Jay Novello (Mr. Prentiss).

Because of its obvious and derivative nature, this production has never achieved much of a horror-fan following. The 3-D movie craze was then on the wane (this was Columbia's last effort in the field) and the gimmicky track shots to scare the Polaroid-glassed moviegoers were out of date. (i.e. streams of water and some playing cards tossed at the audience).

In the 1880s (Hollywood always seemed to insist that these studies in gore be set safely in the past), illusionist Gallico (Vincent Price) thrives on creating magical tricks, satisfied to have other more famous practioners use his latest feats for their success. But when his greedy employer (Donald Randolph) tries to cheat him of a moment of glory, and he loses his pretty blonde wife (Eva Gabor) to magico Rinaldi (John Emery), Gallico goes berserk. Ormond is reduced to ashes in a crematorium, and the fate of Claire and Rinaldi—the latter meets a buzz-saw death—is no less gruesome, for revengeful Gallico has a fertile mind and a rash of infernal death machines. Others caught up in this web are Mary Murphy as Price's performing assistant, Patrick O'Neal as her police-lieutenant finance, and for eccentric appeal, Lenita Lane as a female novelist-detective and Jay Novello as her pop-eyed husband.

Considering the bent of this obvious shock yarn, Price "...gives a realistic interpretation...." *(Variety)* His velvet-toned voice and his imperial bearing did much to lesson the shallowness of his insane characterization.

SONS OF SINBAD* *(RKO, 1955)* C-88 min.

Producer, Robert Sparks; director, Ted Tetzlaff; screenplay, Aubrey Wisberg, Jack Pollenfen; art directors, Albert S. D'Agostino, Walter E. Keller; set decorator, Darrell Silvera; music director, C. Bakaleinikoff; camera, William Snyder; editors, Roland Gross, Frederick Knudtson.

Dale Robertson (Sinbad); Sally Forrest (Amcer); Lili St. Cyr (Nerissa); Vincent Price (Omar Khayhan); Mari Blanchard (Kristina); Leon Askin (Khalif); Jay Novello (Jiddah); Raymond Greenleaf (Simon); Nejla Ates (Dancer in Market); Kalantan (Dancer in Desert); Ian MacDonald (Murad); Donald Randolph (Councillor); Larry Blake (Samit); Edwina Hazard (Lota); Fred Aldrich (Torturer); John Merton, George Sherwood (Guards); Marilyn Bonney (Veronica); Janet Comerford (Latisse); Alyce Cronin (Helena); Mary Ann Edwards (Rosine); Dawn Oney (Alicia); Marvleen

*Also known as *Nights in a Harem.*

194

Prentice (Zaza); Joan Pastin (Camilla); Judy Ulian (Dalya); Suzanne Alexander, Randy Allen, Jane Easton, Jeanne Evans, Helene Hayden (Harem Girls); James Griffith (Arab Guide); Wayne Berk (Condra); Joan Jordan (Ghenia); Bob Wilke (Musa); Tom Monroe, Peter Ortiz (Cutthroat); Virginia Bates, Katherine Cassidy, Honey King, Sally Misik (Trumpeters); Kim Novak, Gerri Patterson, Nancy Moore, Bette Arlen, Joann Arnold, Anne Carroll, Claire De Witt, Marjorie Holliday, Judy Jorell, Nancy Dunn, Carolea Cole (Raiders); Max Wagner (Merchant, Maretplace); Nancy Westbrook (Wench); Gus Schilling (Jaffir); Michael Mark (Caravan Merchant); Bob Hopkins (Slave Auctioneer); Paul Frees (Mahmud).

After the contrived censorship hullaballo raised over the alleged improprieties to be savored in *Son of Sinbad,* viewing the film is a distinct disappointment. The undulating exoticism of diaphanously clad Sally Forrest, Lili St. Cyr (a former striptease artist turned cinema artist and here playing the caliph's favorite wife) and Nejla Ates would seem to obviate the obvious tedium of the story.

In the title role, Dale Robertson capers about boyishly, striving to be the hero who saves all of medieval Bagdad from the Tartars by obtaining the secret of the Great Fire and by rousing the fabled Forty Thieves to assist him. Poet Omar Khayhan (Vincent Price) tags along as Robertson's bumbling comrade in arms. There are endless jokes about the suspect quality of Omar's improvisational poetry. Price's buffoon characterization was in great contrast to the romantic interpretation supplied by Cornel Wilde in *Omar Khayhan* (1957).

THE VAGABOND KING *(Paramount, 1956)* *C-88 min.*

Producer, Pat Duggan; director, Michael Curtiz; based on the musical play by Rudolf Friml, William H. Post, Brian Hooker, from the play *If I Were King* by Justin Huntly McCarthy; screenplay, Ken Englund, Noel Langley; assistant director, William McGarry; music, Victor Young; choreography, Hanya Holm; additional songs, Friml and Johnny Burke; orchestrators, Leo Shuken, Gus Levene, Albert Sendrey; camera, Robert Burke; editor, Arthur Schmidt.

Kathryn Grayson (Catherine De Vaucelles); Oreste (Francois Villon); Rita Moreno (Huguette); Sir Cedric Hardwicke (Tristan); Walter Hampden (King Louis XI); Leslie Nielsen (Thibault); William Prince (Rene); Jack Lord (Ferrebone); Billy Vine (Jacques); Harry McNaughton (Colin); Florence Sundstrom (Laughing Margot); Lucie Lancaster (Margaret); Raymond Bramley (The Scar); Gregory Morton (General Antoine De Chabannes); Richard Tone (Quicksilver); Ralph Sumpter (Bishop of Paris and Turin); G. Thomas Duggan (Burgundy); Gavin Gordon (Majordomo); Joel Ashley (Duke of Normandy); Ralph Clanton (Duke of Anjou); Gordon Mills (Duke of Bourbon); Vincent Price (Narrator), and Richard Shannon, Larry Pennell, Frances Newman, Nancy Bajer, Rita Maria Tanno, David Nillo, Albie Gaye, Laur Raynair, Dolores Starr, Slim Gaut.

VistaVision wide-screen color photography was the most vibrant aspect of this wooden screen musical that helped to close yet another chapter in the Hollywood operetta cycle. Its plot was loosely based on Justin Huntly McCarthy's romantic drama *If I Were King* (1901), which had been twice before filmed, in 1920 with William Farnum and in 1938 with Ronald Colman. The tune version of the original show, with book and lyrics by Brian Hooker and W. H. Post and melodies by Rudolf Friml had enjoyed a 511-performance Broadway engagement in 1925 with repeated revivals thereafter. Stage star Dennis King repeated his interpretation in the 1930 Paramount film musical edition, joined on-camera by silver-throated Jeanette MacDonald and bouncy Lillian Roth.

The 1950s celluloid adaptation was saddled with Maltese opera tenor Oreste Kirkop who, in his screen debut as swashbuckling poet Francois Villon, proved he had an excellent voice but no stage presence. As his lofty vis-a-vis, ex-MGM soprano Kathryn Grayson demonstrated a visual loveliness unmatched by her unsteady handling of such well-known songs as "Only A Rose." Rita Moreno, who would win an Academy Award for *West Side Story* (1961), came alive only in her dancing to "Vive La You." The new songs concocted by Friml and Johnny Burke were not up to par.

Price's velvet-toned voice was used for the narration.

SERENADE *(Warner Brothers, 1956) C-121 min.*

Producer, Henry Blanke; director, Anthony Mann; based on the novel by James M. Cain; screenplay, Ivan Goff, Ben Roberts, John

VINCENT PRICE UNMASKED

Twist; art director, Edward Carrere; songs, Nicholas Brodszky and Sammy Cahn; costumes, Howard Shoup; operatik advisers, Walter Ducloux, Giacomo Spadoni; assistant directors, Charles Hansen, Dick Moder; camera, J. Peverell Marley; editor, William Ziegler.

Mario Lanza (Damon Vincenti); Joan Fontaine (Kendall Hale); Sarita Montiel (Juana Montes); Vincent Price (Charles Winthrop); Harry Bellaver (Monte); Vince Edwards (Marco Roselli); Silvio Minciotti (Lardelli); Frank Puglia (Manuel); Edward Platt (Carter); Frank Yaconelli (Giuseppe); Mario Siletti (Sanroma); Maria Serrano (Rosa); Eduardo Noriega (Felipe); Jean Fenn (Soprano); Joseph Vitale (Baritone); Victor Romita (Bass); Norma Zimmer (Mimi in *La Boheme*); Licia Albanese (Desdemona in *Otello*); Francis Barnes (Iago in *Otello*); Lilian Molieri (Tosca in *Tosca*); Laura Mason (Fedora in *Fedora*); Richard Cable (Shepherd Boy in *L'Arlesienne*); Richard Lert (Conductor); Jose Govea (Paco); Antonio Triano (Man in the Bull); Nick Mora (Luigi the Waiter); Joe DeAngelo, William Fox, Jack Santora (Busboys); Mickey Golden (Cabdriver); Elizabeth Flourney (Elevator Operator); Creighton Hale (Assistant Stage Manager); Martha Acker (American Woman); Joe Torvay (Mariachi Leader); Don Turner (Bus Driver); Johnstone White (Hughes the Butler); Ralph Volkie (Cop).

It required nearly two decades for Warner Bros. to translate James M. Cain's 1937 novel to the screen without running afoul of censorial institutions. Studio boss Jack L. Warner had the foresight to hire MGM's floundering prima-donna tenor, Mario Lanza, for the lead role. In addition he used a sturdy supporting cast, gracious Cinemascope color photography, and a host of operatic arias to promote the feature into a successful venture.

Portly California vineyard worker Damon Vincente (Lanza) is spotted by arts patroness Kendall Hale (Joan Fontaine—in the book the character was a man) who propels him into an operatic career. But the rich nymph, who enjoys finding and making celebrities, soon tires of stentorian-voiced Damon. She traipses off to Europe with a promising sculptor, he being the successor to a promising middleweight fighter. Damon has become so smitten with glacial Fontaine that he muffs his *Otello* performance at the Metropolitan Opera. Unable to continue with his career, he beats a speedy exit for Mexico (with on-location filming at San Miguel de Allende) where he contracts a rare virus and acquires a new girl friend (Sarita Montiel), the daughter of a once-famous bullfighter.

The remainder of the film turns into a three-way contest, with Jauna and Kendall fighting for the right to Lanza, and the confused singer desperate to reestablish his operatic career.

Among the sychophants and instructors surrounding Lanza on his rise-fall-rise to fame are Joseph Calleia as his voice teacher, Harry Bellaver as his manager, and Vincent Price as Charles Winthrop, the erudite, ascorbic impresario. Price oozes skin-deep chilliness as the worldly-wise figure who refers to Damon as Peck's bad boy of the opera. In evaluating Price's cynical entrepreneur, the *New Yorker* magazine reported, "Mr. Price delivers the jokes. They are no good."

Included in Lanza's repertoire of more than fifteen tunes are a version of "Ave Maria," "Lamenti di Frederico" from *L'Arlesienne,* the tenor aria from Act One of *Rosenkavalier,* a duet (with Licia Albanese) from *Otello,* and two unmemorable new songs, "My Destiny" and "Serenade."

WHILE THE CITY SLEEPS *(RKO, 1956) 100 min.*

Producer, Bert Friedlob; director, Fritz Lang; based on the novel *The Bloody Spur* by Charles Einstein; screenplay, Casey Robinson; art director, Carroll Clark; set decorator, Jack Mills; music, Herschel Burke Gilbert; assistant director, Ronnie Rondell; costumes, Norma; sound editor, Verna Fields; camera, Ernest Laszlo; editor, Gene Fowler, Jr.

Dana Andrews (Edward Mobley); Rhonda Fleming (Dorothy Kyne); Sally Forrest (Nancy Liggett); Thomas Mitchell (Griffith); Vincent Price (Walter Kyne, Jr.); Howard Duff (Lieutenant Kaufman); Ida Lupino (Mildred); George Sanders (Mark Loving); James Craig (Harry Kritzer); John Barrymore, Jr. (Robert Manners); Vladimir Sokoloff (George Palsky); Robert Warwick (Amos Kyne); Ralph Peters (Meade); Larry Blake (Police Sergeant); Edward Hinton (O'Leary); Mae Marsh (Mrs. Manners); Sandy White (Judith Fenton); Celia Lovsky (Miss Dodd); Pitt Herbert (bartender); Ralph Peters (Meade); Andrew Lupino (Bit).

The film's premise was slicly simple: the leading editors (Thomas Mitchell, George Sanders, James Craig) of the New York *Sentinel* are assigned to track down the culprit responsible for a series of brutal sex murders. Their reward would be a hefty staff promotion. Granted the story line fudged by revealing the crazed killer (John Barrymore, Jr.) too early in the game, but Fritz Lang's mundane direction of a sturdy group of professional actors was a shame. As Paul M. Jensen in *The Cinema of Fritz Lang* (1969) viewed the picture, "...(it) is not disastrously bad or incompetent, but it is so profoundly ordinary as to be worth even less notice than a disaster."

Vincent Price .. cast as the dissipated Walter Kyne who inherits his father's multi-media empire, but determines that a lesser being shall manage the corporations. A subplot.....Kyne's unscrupulous wife (Rhonda Fleming) playing around with Kritzer. One of the picture's potentially better scenes, seemingly tossed away by director Lang,....domineering Kyne enjoying a sublimely symbolic moment. As he sits wondering which one of the candidates will become chief of the media division, he places three peanuts on a table, then he scoops the nuts into his hand and bobs them into his mouth. The British *Monthly Film Bulletin* reported, "Vincent Price snarls engagingly."

THE TEN COMMANDMENTS *(Paramount, 1956) C-219 min.*

Producer, Cecil B. De Mille; associate producer, Henry Wilcoxon; director, De Mille; based on *Prince of Egypt* by Dorothy Clarke Wilson; *Pillar of Fire* by Reverend H. J. Ingraham; *On Eagle's Wings* by Reverend A. E. Southon; screenplay, Aeneas MacKenzie, Jesse L. Lasky, Jr., Jack Gariss, Fredcic M. Frank; art directors, Hal Pereira, Walter Tyler, Albert Nozaki; music, Elmer Bernstein; cameras, Loyal Griggs, J. Peverell Marley, John Warren, Wallace Kelley; editor, Anne Bauchens.

Charlton Heston (Moses); Yul Brynner (Rameses); Anne Baxter (Nefretiri); Edward G. Robinson (Dathan); Yvonne De Carlo (Sephora); Debra Paget (Lilia); John Derek (Joshua); Martha Scott (Yochabel); Nina Foch (Bithiah); Sir Cedric Hardwicke (Sethi); Judith Anderson (Memnet); Vincent Price (Baka); John Carradine (Aaron); Eduard Franz (Jethro); Olive Deering (Miriam); Donald Curtis (Mered); Douglas Dumbrille (Jannes); Lawrence Dobkin

(Hur Ben Caleb); Frank DeKova (Abiram); H. B. Warner (Am-
minadab); Henry Wilcoxon (Pentaur); Julia Faye (Elisheba); Lisa
Mitchell, Noelle Williams, Joanne Merlin, Pat Richard, Joyce
Vanderveen, Diane Hall (Jethro's Daughters); Abbas El Boug-
hdadly (Rameses' Charioteer); Fraser Heston (Infant Moses); John
Miljan (Blind One); Tommy Duran (Gerhsom); Francis J.
McDonald (Simon); Eugene Mazzola (Rameses' Son); Joan Wood-
bury (Korah's Wife); Woody Strode (King of Ethiopia); Esther
Brown (Princess Tharbis); Ian Keith (Rameses I); Clint Walker
(Sardinian Captain); Michael Connors (Amalekite Herder); Mi-
chael Ansara (Taskmaster); Robert Vaughn (Hebrew Spearman);
Walter Woolf King (Herald); Frankie Darro (Slave).

When Cecil B. De Mille announced a remake of his 1923 *The Ten
Commandments*, moviegoers wondered what treats the road-show
production would encompass. The final film proved to be visually
and audibly impressive (VistaVision, Technicolor, sterephonic
sound), as well as celebrity-filled but dramatically puerile. As
Gordon Gow in *Hollywood in the Fifties* (1971) recalled the new
edition, "...(it) was historionic and star-crammed, multitudinous
with extras, orgiastic in an old-hat operatic romp around the calf of
gold, but technically maladroit in its parting of the Red Sea: this
would hardly have convinced an experienced *cinephile,* even without the new-found clarity which shoqed up its contrivance deri-
sively." Not even Paramount was prepared for the enormous public
endorsement of this war-horse Biblical epic, which has already
garnered over $43 million in distributors' domestic grosses.

In the course of the 219-minute drama, Egyptian architect Baka
(Vincent Price) smites a Hebrew slave. Incipient leader Moses
(Charlton Heston) is so aroused by this act that he strangles Baka,
setting into motion the Jews' eventual departure from ancient
Egypt and the brutal control of Pharaoh Rameses (Yul Brynner).
With such a star-studded cast, Price's vignette occupied just one
brief segment of the lengthy chronicle. His villainy, while effective,
was overshadowed by the more resolute acting of Edward G.
Robinson, the latter cast as Dathan, the treacherous Jewish over-
lord.

THE STORY OF MANKIND *(Warner Broth-ers, 1957) C-100 min.*

Producer, Irwin Allen; associate producer, George E. Swink;
director, Allen; based on the book by Hendrik van Loon; screen-

play, Allen, Charles Bennett; art director, Art Loel; music, Paul Sawtell; assistant director, Joseph Don Page; costumes, Marjorie Best; camera, Nick Musuraca; editor, Gene Palmer.

Ronald Colman (Spirit of Man); Hedy Lamarr (Joan of Arc); Groucho Marx (Peter Minuit); Harpo Marx (Isacc Newton); Chico Marx (Monk); Virginia Mayo (Cleopatra); Vincent Price (Devil); Peter Lorre (Nero); Charles Coburn (Hippocrates); Cedric Hardwicke (High Judge); Cesar Romero (Spanish Envoy); John Carradine (Khufu); Dennis Hopper (Napoleon); Marie Wilson (Marie Antoinette); Helmut Dantine (Anthony); Edward Everett Horton (Sir Walter Raleigh); Reginald Gardiner (Shakespeare); Marie Windsor (Josephine); Cathy O'Donnell (Early Christian Woman); Franklin Pangborn (Marquis de Varennes); Melville Cooper (Major Domo); Francis X. Bushman (Moses); Henry Daniell (Bishop of Beauvais); Jim Ameche (Alexander Graham Bell); Dani Crayne (Helen of Troy); Anthony Dexter (Columbus); Austin Green (Lincoln); Bobby Watson (Hitler); Reginald Sheffield (Caesar); and George E. Stone, David Bond, Nick Cravat, Richard Cutting, Toni Gerry, Eden Hartford, Alexander Lockwood, Melinda Marx, Bart Mattson, Don Megowan, Marvin Miller, Nancy Miller, Leonard Mudi, Burt Nelson, Tudor Owen, Ziva Rodann, Harry Ruby, William Schallert, Abraham Sofaer.

Despite an adequate budget and exceptional studio facilities, the possibilities of transforming Hendrik Willem van Loon's discursive book *The Story of Mankind* (1921) into a coherent film were slight, since the obvious impossibility of translating the entire history of man into a hundred minutes of celluloid were greater. "The result is a protracted and tedious lesson in history that is lacking in punch, sophistication and a consistent point of view." *(The New York Times)* Or, on a more basic level, the faltering key episodes and assorted stock footage filler from the Warners' vaults were merely "superficial, slapdash" *(Cue* magazine).

In Heaven, the supreme tribunal, presided over by the high judge (Sir Cedric Hardwicke) has convened to determine the fate of life on earth. The devil (Vincent Price) argues that man is essentially evil and must be destroyed, while The Spirit of Man (Ronald Colman) drags forth pertinent illustrations from history to prove that human beings are basically good. As the global confrontation draws to a conclusion, the high judge proclaims that he is reserving final decision until a future time, suggesting that the fate of mankind depends on mankind itself.

There was more than a camp element to the cameo casting of once-famous "names," with Harpo Marx as Sir Isaac Newton, Agnes Moorehead as Queen Elizabeth, Peter Lorre as Nero, and Marie Wilson as Marie Antoinette. A tired-looking Colman was exceeding wistful as the earth's defendant, while satanical Mr. Scratch (Price) was solid and stentorian. Less kind critics said of his performance, "...(he) has, as usual, the suave and sinister air of a headwaiter in a backs-to-the-wall supper club..." *(New Yorker magazine)*

THE FLY *(20th Century-Fox, 1958) C-94 min.*

Producer-director, Kurt Neumann; based on a story by George Langelaan; screenplay, James Clavell; music, Paul Sawtell; art directors, Lyle R. Wheeler, Theobold Holsopple; set decorators, Walter M. Scott, Eli Benneche; wardrobe designer, Charles Le-Maire; costumes, Adele Balkan; make-up, Ben Nye; assistant director, Jack Gertsman; sound, Eugene Grossman, Harry M. Leonard; special camera effects, L. B. Abbott; camera, Karl Struss; editor, Merrill G. White.

David Hedison (Andre); Patricia Owens (Helene); Vincent Price (Francois); Herbert Marshall (Inspector Chares); Kathleen Free-man (Emma); Betty Lou Gerson (Nurse Andersone); Charles Herbert (Phillippe) Eugene Borden (Dr. Ejoute); Torben Meyer (Gaston); Harry Carter (Orderly); Charles Tannen (Doctor); Franz Roehn (Police Doctor); Arthur Dulac (French Waiter).

Not since the atomically induced oversized ants of *Them* (1954) had a horror film so neatly captured the public's imagination. "...this is a quiet, uncluttered and even unpretentious picture, building up almost unbearable tension by simple suggestion." *(The New York Times)*

When brilliant scientist Andre (David Hedison) is found crushed to death in a huge industrial press, in his Montreal home, his hysterical wife (Patricia Owens) is induced to relate the bizarre circumstances to her brother-in-law (Vinent Price) and to Inspector Chares (Herbert Marshall). It seemed that Hedison had created an X-ray transference machine that could re-distribute the molecular constitution of solids from one spot to another. In the course of experimenting on himself, Hedison's atoms had become mixed with those of a house fly, causing him to have the head and "arm" of the fly, with the insect in turn acquiring the scientist's head and arm. One of the picture's more sadistic scenes found the near-deranged Hedison begging Helene to kill him before he committed desperate acts. As the flashback concludes, Francois and Chares spot a fly with a tiny human head and arm about to be devoured by a spider. Chares uses a rock to kill the tortured bug.

Filmed in CinemaScope and color for a low $350,000, the feature grossed an amazing three million dollars plus, despite critics berating the cast for reacting "...in a fashion commensurate with the horror and outlandishness of what occurs." (New York *Herald-Tribune)* Ivan Butler in *Horror in the Cinema* (1970) declared that "...this is probably the most ludicrous, and certainly one of the most revolting science-horror films ever perpetrated....Even the much-publicised trick camerawork, including a not very ingenious fly's-eye view of his wife, is unremarkable."

Price was ostensibly the star of this vehicle, but he was really no more than a voyeur on the strange trip set into motion by Hedison. In the anti-climatic sequence following the shock finale, it is Price who euphemistically informs Charles Herbert of his father's demise, "He was like an explorer in a wild country where no one had ever been before...." And for the "happy" wrap-up, sensible, thoughtful Price tells Owens and the boy, "I want to look after you both...."

HOUSE ON HAUNTED HILL*(Allied Artists, 1958) 75 min.*

Producer, William Castle; associate producer, Robb White; director, Castle; screenplay, White; art director, David Milton; set decorator, Morris Hoffman; assistant director, Jack R. Berne; music director, Von Dexter; theme music, Richard Kayne, Richard Loring; wardrobe, Roger J. Weinberg, Norah Sharpe; make-up, Jack Dusick; sound, Ralph Butler, Charles Schelling; camera, Carl E. Guthrie; editor, Roy Livingston.

Vincent Price (Frederick Loren); Carol Ohmart (Annabelle Loren); Richard Long (Lance Schroeder); Alan Marshal (Dr. David Trent); Carolyn Craig (Nora Manning); Elisha Cook (Watson

Pritchard); Julie Mitchum (Ruth Bridges); Loena Anderson (Mrs. Slykes); Howard Hoffman (Jonas).

Millionaire Frederick Loren (Vincent Price) rents a notoriously haunted old house, scene of seven murders, for a night so that his wife (Carol Ohmart) may hostess a party. Since the couple have no real friends, they invite five strangers to spend the evening at the eerie mansion, promising each guest a ten-thousand-dollar reward, with the money going to their heirs should they not survive. Unknown to Loren, one of the quintent is no stranger to his wife, for Mr. David Trent (Alan Marshal) is none other than her secret lover. The grotesque evening is filled with hysteria involving blood dripping from the ceiling, a wine cellar with an acid vat, a severed head in a traveling case, ghostly apparitions, and so forth. Not-so-ingenious Annabelle and Trent intend that Loren not survive the ordeal, but he has a vitriolic victory over them.

As the urbane hero and would-be victim, mayhem-bound Price was commended by the New York *Herald-Tribune* for his "very waggish style" and his *"bon-vivant* skepticism."

Imaginative producer-director William Castle bolstered the proceeds on this film by using an Emergo gimmick in some theatres where the film was being shown. During the film's climax, an irridescent skeleton, mounted on wires, would float over theater audiences. The much-touted trick bolstered the movie's grosses.

THE BIG CIRCUS *(Allied Artists, 1959)* C-108 *min.*

Producer, Irwin Allen; director, Joseph M. Newman; story, Allen; screenplay, Allen, Charles Bennett, Irving Wallace; assistant director, Bill McGarry; music director, Paul Sawtell, Bert Shefter; title song, Sammy Fain and Paul Francis Webster; art director, Albert D'Agostino; set decorator, Robert Priestly; choreography, Barbette; costumes, Paul Zastupnevich; make-up, William Tuttle; sound, Franklin Milton, Conrad Kahn; technical adviser, Jimmie Wood; sound effects, Finn Ulback, Bert Schoenfeld; optical effects, Robert R. Hoag; camera, Winton C. Hoch; editor, Adrienne Fazan.

Victor Mature (Henry Jasper Whirling); Red Buttons (Randy Sherman); Rhonda Fleming (Helen Harrison); Kathryn Grant

(Jeannie Whirling); Gilbert Roland (Zach Colino); Vincent Price (Hans Hagenfeld); Peter Lorre (Skeeter); David Nelson (Tommy Gordon); Adele Mara (Mama Colino); Howard McNear (Mr. Lomax); Charles Watts (Jonathan Nelson); Steve Allen (Himself); Hugo Zacchini (The Human Cannonball); Dick Walker (Lion Tamer); The Flying Alexanders (Aerialists); Gene Mendez (Wire Walker); The Ronnie Lewis Trio (High-Ladder Equilibrists); The Jungleland Elephants, Tex Carr and His Chimpanzees, Dick Berg's Movieland Seals (Themselves).

A far cry from Cecil B. De Mille's sumptuous *The Greatest Show on Earth* (1952), this CinemaScope-color feature did garner some encouraging notices on unexpected levels. "There are so few good movies for children nowadays that we feel duty-bound to call this one to the attention of those of our readers who have children or are interested in their welfare. The plot-frame around the circus acts is old-hat, but the acts themselves are first-class." *(Films in Review)*. *The New York Times* was less indulgent, panning the film for being "One hour and forty-nine minutes of riotous cliches" in which the acts "...performed by the animals are a little more convincing than the ones performed by the human beings!"

Bankrupt circus owner Hank Whirling (Victor Mature) obtains a bank loan to keep his five-ring show on the road, with bank security man Randy Sherman (Red Buttons) assigned to survey the big-top operations. There is sabotage from a rival circus, and a train wreck, but aerialist Zach Colino (Gilbert Roland) manages to walk the high wire over Niagara Falls, which is all press agent Helen Harrison (Rhonda Fleming) requires to boost the company into the financial big leagues.

Vincent Price as Hans Hagenfeld the ringmaster in this has-been star cameo-studded mess, which was no better than the similarly dank *The Big Show* (1961) filmed in Europe. This film was the second joint on-camera appearance of Price and Peter Lorre, the latter cast as the sad circus clown Skeeter. David Nelson, formerly of the "Ozzie and Harriet" radio and television show unfortunately was hardly believable as the deranged aerialist who is out to sabotage Whirling's outfit.

THE BAT *(Allied Artists, 1959) 78 min.*

Producer, C. J. Tevlin; director, Crane Wilbur; based on the play by Mary Roberts Rinehart and Avery Hopwood as adapted from the novel *The Circular Staircase* by Rinehart; screenplay, Wilbur; art director, David Milton; set decorator, Rudy Butler; wardrobe, Roger J. Weinberg, Norah Sharpe; make-up, Kiva Hoffman; music, Louis Forbes; assistant director, Clifford Broughton; camera, Joseph Biroc; editor, William Austin.

Vincent Price (Dr. Malcolm Wells); Agnes Moorehead (Cornelia Van Gorder); Gavin Gordon (Lieutenant Anderson); John Sutton (Warner); Lenita Lane (Lizzie Allen); Elaine Edwards (Dale Bailey); Darla Hood (Judy Hollender); John Bryant (Mark Fleming); Harvey Stephens (Curt Fleming); Mike Steele (Jack Bailey); Riza Royce (Mrs. Patterson); Robert B. Williams (Detective).

Mary Roberts Rinehart's 1908 suspense novel, *The Circular Staircase,* was adapted into the successful Broadway play *The Bat* in 1920. Six years later it became a popular silent film starring Emily Fitzroy, Louise Fazenda, and Jack Pickford. In addition, the 1930 movie, *The Bat Whispers* featuring Chester Morris and Una Merkel, was a reworking of this perennial piece.

Mystery writer Cornelia Van Gorder (Agnes Moorehead) rents "The Oaks," a gloomy summer house, from the local bank president, who has embezzled a huge sum of money and hidden it in the mansion. Small-town physician Dr. Malcolm Wells (Vincent Price), having shot the banker, arrives at "The Oaks," bent on gaining possession of the million dollars. Before the caper is concluded, Wells and others are suspected of being the hooded killer "The Bat" who claws his victims' jugular veins.

Variety carped of the results, "What is missing is definition, both of character and incident. The film unspools in nondescript touches, leaving the viewer to care only little about the victims and, for that matter, about the identity of The Bat himself." As for Price's acting chores, the same trade paper reported, "As in nearly every other film he's made in the past two years, Vincent Price casts enough furtive glances to register as the ghoul when, indeed, he isn't....He plays his role with his usual skill and polish."

RETURN OF THE FLY *(20th Century-Fox, 1959) 80 min.*

Producer, Bernard Glasser; director, Edward L. Bernds; based on the story *The Fly* by George Langelaan; screenplay, Bernds; art directors, Lyle R. Wheeler, John Mansbridge; set decorators,

Walter M. Scott, Joseph Kish; make-up, Hal Lierley; assistant director, Byron Roberts; music, Paul Sawtell; camera, Brydon Baker; editor, Richard C. Meyer.

Vincent Price (Francois Delambre); Brett Halsey (Philippe Delambre); David Frankham (Alan Hinds); John Sutton (Inspector Chares); Dan Seymour (Max Berthold); Danielle De Metz (Cecile Bonnard); Florence Strom (Nun); Janine Grandel (Mme. Bonnard); Richard Flato (Sergeant Dubois); Pat O'Hara (Detective Evans); Barry Bernard (Lieutenant Maclish); Jack Daly (Granville); Michael Mark (Gaston); Francisco Villalobas (Priest); Joan Cotton (Nurse).

With the solid grosses of *The Fly* it was inevitable that 20th Century-Fox would rehash the original property in a sequel. The results were not as commercially or artistically as edifying. In fact *Variety* branded it .. "Inept Sequel."

Scientist Philippe Delambre (Brett Halsey), despite the warnings of his uncle (Vincent Price) continues the atom-transference experiments of his late father. Philippe reassembles the disintegration equipment only to have his assistant (David Frankham) — in the employ of a foreign power — shove his employer into the machine, and a new man-fly emerges, bent on revenge. Fortunately this time Francois is able to manage a retransference, allowing his nephew to become a human being once again.

Price was lauded for lending "...an air of authority to a sketchy film." (New York *Herald-Tribune*)

Fox would turn out yet another black-and-white sequel in 1965, *The Curse of The Fly,* made in Britain and starring Brian Donlevy.

HOUSE OF USHER *(American International, 1960) C-79 min.*

Presenters, James H. Nicholson, Samuel Z. Arkoff; executive producer, Nicholson; producer-director, Roger Corman; based on the story *The Fall of the House of Usher* by Edgar Allan Poe; screenplay, Richard Matheson; music, Les Baxter; assistant director, Jack Bohrer; make-up, Fred Philipps; production designer, Daniel Haller; paintings, Burt Schoenberg; wardrobe, Marjorie Corso; sound, Phil Mitchell; process camera, Larry Butler; special effectq Pat Dinga; camera, Floyd Crosby; editor, Anthony Carras.

VINCENT PRICE UNMASKED

Vincent Price (Roderick Usher); Mark Damon (Philip Winthrop); Myrna Fahey (Madeline Usher); Harry Ellerbe (Bristol); Bill Borzage, Mike Jordan, Nadajan, Ruth Oklander, George Paul, David Andar, Eleanor Le Faber, Geraldine Paulette, Phil Sylvestre, John Zimeas (Ghosts).

Although the French in 1927 and the British in 1950 had filmed versions of Edgar Allan Poe's sterling story, *The Fall of the House of Usher* (1939), American moviemakers failed to realize its potential until this late date of 1960. Nevertheless, the wait was worthwhile. Prolific, low-budget producer-director Roger Corman handled the proceedings with great imagination, his only failure a lack of sufficient roles to give the elongated tale adequate variety. "It is a film that should attract mature tastes as well as those who come to the cinema for sheer thrills." *) Variety)*

Poe purists may have been annoyed at the liberties taken with the story structure, but the bulk of filmgoers were delighted with the "improvements." In nineteenth-century New England, Madeline Usher's (Myrna Fahey) fiance (Mark Damon) arrives unannounced at the foreboding Usher mansion. Her brother (Vincent Price) informs him she is confined to bed and explains the family curse of madness. During one of Madeline's subsequent cataleptic fits, Price buries her alive, determined to prevent future generations of mad Ushers. She later escapes the confines, but is caught along with her brother as the old house bursts into flame and crumbles into decay...."And the deep and dank tarn closes suddenly and silently over the fragments of The House of Usher."

Thanks to Corman's symbolic directing, Floyd Crosby's lush camera work, and novelist Richard Matheson's shrewd scripting, the Poe-American International Pictures series got off to a fine start. A hearty ingredient of the success was Price's masterly adaption to the format. "Price is in fine fettle as Usher, his hair whitened, his delivery formal, stylistic, fastidiously close to yhe spirit of Poe's prose." (New York *Herald-Tribune)*

THE TINGLER *(Columbia, 1959) 80 min.*

Producer-director, William Castle; screenplay, Robb White; art director, Phil Bennett; set decorator, Milton Stumph; assistant director, Herb Wallerstein; sound, John Livadary, Harry Mills; music, Von Dexter; camera, Wildrid M. Cline; editor, Chester W. Schaeffer.

Vincent Price (Dr. William Chapin); Judith Evelyn (Mrs. Higgins); Darryl Hickman (David Morris); Patricia Cutts (Isabel Chapin); Philip Coolidge (Ollie Higgins); Pamela Lincoln (Lucy Stevens).

With this film cagey showman William Castle produced-directed another winner, this time exploiting his product with a new gimmic called Percepto. This effect required theater owners to wire assorted audience seats with vibrating and/or shock motors that on certain cues causes the patron a definite tingling sensation. Another trick used by Castle in *The Tingler* had the film stopped during each showing, the house lights coming up, and a filmgoer who has allegedly fainted carried from the theater. Meanwhile, on the sound-track Vincent Price speaks calming words of explanation to the audience.

Pathologist Dr. William Chapin (Price) discovers that unless human fear is released by efficacious loud screaming, it can create a parasitic organism that will crack the spinal column. Deaf mute Mrs. Higgins (Judith Evelyn), who operates a silent movie house, dies of fright, and the lobsterlike monster escapes from her back. Tied into the main plot is the attempt of Isabel Chapin (Patricia Cutts) to eliminate her spouse (Price). For contrasting effect, scenes of the silent film *Tol'able David* (1921) were shown, and color was used for the sequences of blood tumbling into a tub and sink.

Price was in appropriately good form for this entry, giving a vaudeville-type conviction to his performance, no mean feat when one considers the flimsiness of the script and the apparent paucity of direction.

THE PIT AND THE PENDULUM *(American International, 1961) C-85 min.*

Executive producers, James H. Nicholson, Samual Z. Arkoff; producer-director, Roger Corman; based on the story by Edgar Allan Poe; screenplay, Richard Matheson; art director, Daniel Haller; set decorator, Harry Reif; music, Les Baxter; assistant directors, Jack Bohier, Lou Place; wardrobe, Marjorie Corso; sound, Roy Meadows; special effects, Pat Dinga; camera effects, Larry Butler, Don Glouner; camera, Floyd Crosby; editor, Anthony Carras.

Vincent Price (Nicholas Medina); John Kerr (Francis Barnard); Barbara Steele (Elizabeth Barnard Medina); Luana Anders (Catherine Medina); Anthony Carbone (Dr. Charles Leon); Patrick Westwood (Maximillian); Lynne Bernay (Maria); Larry Turner (Nicholas as a Child); Mary Menzies (Isabella); Charles Victor (Bartolome).

In his movie-genre survey *Horror!* (1966) author Drake Douglas rightly raves over the second Edgar Allan Poe-American International-Vincent Price-Roger Corman cinema production. "The film is brilliantly made. The settings of the castle and, in particular, the torture chambers and dungeons are like a surrealist's nightmare. Poe's constant air of brooding horror hovers over every scene. The story content, though considerably different from Poe's original tale, is in every respect true to the Poe spirit, and (Richard) Matheson reveals considerable knowledge of the workings of Poe's mind by including in his story the Poe themes of premature burial, insanity and revenge....In no other film of horror has technicolor been put to such excellent advantage."

Elizabeth Barnard Medina (Barbara Steele) has allegedly died of fright when accidentally imprisoned in the torture-chamber dungeon of her husband's (Price) foreboding Spanish castle. The fact that he is the descendant of a nefarious grand inquisitor lends additional suspicion to his wife's mysterious demise. Her brother (John Kerr) journeys to the uninviting edifice to learn more facts of the strange case. In reality, Elizabeth and her lover (Anthony Carbone) are plotting to drive the unstable Nicholas mad and obtain his fortune. Fortunately for the brother, Nicholas' sister (Luana Anders) is on hand to rescue the hero from the dastardly happenings and Elizabeth receives her proper comeuppance.

Less enthusiastic reviewers of this picture objected to the labored archaic dialogue (which Price handled better than the others) and in particular to the florid acting of Price who emerged as "a sort of sissified Bela Lugosi." (*Time* magazine)

MASTER OF THE WORLD *(American International, 1961) C-104 min.*

Executive producer, Samuel Z. Arkoff; producer, James H. Nicholson; director, William Witney; based on the novels *Master of the World* and *Robur, the Conqueror* by Jules Verne; screenplay, Richard Matheson; music director, Les Baxter; title song, Baxter and Lenny Addelson; orchestrator, Albert Harris; art director, Daniel Haller; set decorator, Harry Reif; special props-effects, Pat Dinga; make-up, Fred Philipps; wardrobe, Marjorie Corso; assistant director, Robert Agnew; sound, Karl Zint, Bill Warmarth, Vinnie Vernon, Jerry Alexander; spevial effects, Tim Barr, Wah Chang, Gene Warren; camera effects, Ray Mercer; aerial camera, Kay Norton; camera, Gil Warrenton; editor, Anthony Carras.

Vincent Price (Robur); Charles Bronson (Strock); Henry Hull (Prudent); Mary Webster (Dorothy); David Frankham (Philip); Richard Harrison (Alistair); Vito Scotti (Topage); Wally Campo (Turner); Steve Masino (Weaver); Ken Terrell (Shanks); Peter Besbas (Wilson).

After the ultra-successful *Around the World in 80 Days* (1956), any work of novelist Jules Verne was considered marketable screen material. This entry was rated "A properly naive and lively little subteen special." (*Time* magazine) *The New York Times* advised, "Adults dragged in to watch this release will find it devoid of artistic pretensions, but a lot more sufferable than they would suppose."

In 1848, Captain Robur (Vincent Price) in his elaborate futuristic airship, the *Albatross,* rescues Government agent Strock (Charles Bronson) and his companions when their air balloon is disabled over Pennsylvania. It develops Robur is bent on creating world peace by destroying all instruments of war, with his own manufactured bombs as his prime weapon. Before Strock and his associates escape Robur's clutches, he plants a bomb that upon explosion sinks Robur and his fantastic flying ship.

Price's papier-mache warship may have lacked essential credibility but his performance as the benevolently deranged humanist rated approval. "The villain, too, is the good old-fashioned kind, in the surprisingly restrained hands of Vincent Price." (*The New York Times*)

NAKED TERROR *(Joseph Brenner, 1961)* C-74 *min.*

Narrator: Vincent Price

Two years before the shock pseudo-documentary *Mondo Cane* (1963) drew in huge global revenues, this study of the African Zulu tribe appeared, with its specious highlighting of the gorier aspects of native customs, such as indoctrinating young girls in the dance of the deadly pythons. Vincent Price supplied the narration.

NEFERTITI, QUEEN OF THE NILE *(S.F., 1961) C-106 min.*

Producer, Ottavio Poggi; director, Fernando Cerchio; story, Emerico Papp, Poggi; screenplay, John Byrne, Poggi, Cerchio; music, Carlo Rustinchelli; camera, Massimo Dallamano; editor, Renato Cinquini.

Jeanne Crain (Tanit-Nefertiti); Vincent Price (Benakon); Edmund Purdom (Thomas); Amadeo Nazzari (Amenophis IV); Liana Orfei (Merith); and Carol D'Antelo, Celia Matania, Albert Farnese, Piero Palermini, Guilio Marchetti, Umberto Raho, Luigi Marturano, Romano Giomini.

In 2,000 B.C. Egypt, Tanit (Jeanne Crain) plans to elope with apprentice sculptor Tumos (Edmund Purdom), but her plans are discovered and she is brought to the temple, where she learns that she is the daughter of Benakon (Vincent Price) the Great Priest who is the power behind the throne. Benakon demands that she wed Amenophis IV (Amadeo Nazzari), the Pharoah's demented son, and a friend of Tumos. In a subsequent religious revolt, Tanit, now Queen Nefertiti, is left to rule the land, comforted by the love of Tumos.

Price seemed bored with the pedestrian happenings in this low-class cloak-and-sandal entry dubbed into English.

RAGE OF THE BUCCANEERS *(The Black Buccaneer) (Gordon, Il Pirato Nero) (Colorama, 1962) C-88 min.*

Producer, Ottavio Poggi; director, Mario Costa; screenplay, Poggi, John Bryne; art director, Ernest Kromberg, Amadeo Mel-

Ione; music, Carlo Rustichelli; fencing masters, Andrea and Franco Fantasia; sound, Raffaele Del Monte, Fiorgengo Magli; camera, Carlo Bellero; editor, Renato Cinquini.

Ricardo Montalban (Gordon); Vincent Price (Romero); Giulia Rubini (Manuela); Liana Orfei (Luana); Mario Feliciani (Tortuga); and Giselle Sofia, Giustino Durano, Jose Jaspe, Edoardo Toniolo.

Former slaver Gordon (Ricardo Montalban) wages a campaign against the slave traders. Discovering San Salvador is the traders' new home base, he arrives there disguised as a wealthy plantation owner and learns that the governor's secretary (Vincent Price) is actually in league with his old enemy Tortuga (Mario Feliciani).

This was a more traditional handling of the pirate motif than had recently been the cinematic custom, with usually villainous Price adding dash as the power-hungry conniver who also lusts for the governor's daughter (Giulia Rubini). Nonetheless, the English-dubbed sound track of the Italian-made feature was a deficit.

TALES OF TERROR *(American International, 1962) C-120 min.*

Executive producers, James H. Nicholson, Samuel Z. Arkoff; producer-director, Roger Corman; based on stories by Edgar Allan Poe; screenplay, Richard Matheson; art director, Daniel Haller; assistant director, Jack Bohrer; wardrobe, Marjorie Corso; camera, Floyd Crosby; editor, Anthony Carras.

Episode—*Morella:*
Vincent Price (Locke); Maggie Pierce (Lenora); Leona Gage (Morella).
Episode—*The Black Cat:*
Peter Lorre (Montresor); Vincent Price (Fortunato); Joyce Jameson (Annabel).
Episode—*The Facts in the Case of M. Valdemar:*
Vincent Price (M. Valdemar); Basil Rathbone (Mr. Carmichael); Debra Paget (Helene); David Frankham (Dr. Elliot James).

The anthology of sensationalized Edgar Allan Poe stories benefitted from the economy of Roger Corman's direction and an expanded production budget. The New York *Herald-Tribune* alerted readers, "Aficionados of the weird, the strange, or what Poe called the 'grotesque' and 'arabesque' can troop, I think with good heart, to see *Tales of Terror*."

Morella: Since the death of his wife during childbirth twenty-six years before, alcoholic recluse Locke (Vincent Price) remains in his gloomy mansion guarding her mummified body. The dead woman's spirit takes possession of their daughter (Maggie Pierce), leading to the trio's destruction.

The Black Cat: Combined with elements of Poe's *The Cask of Amontillado* this episode focused on foul-tempered drunk Montresor (Peter Lorre), who prefers liquor to his wife (Joyce Jameson). When he discovers her enjoying the advances of egotistical wine taster Fortunato (Price), he lures the couple into the cellar and walls them up alive, not realizing he has also encased a telltale, howling black cat in the tomb.

The Facts in the Case of M. Valdemar: Mesmerist Mr. Carmichael (Basil Rathbone) forestalls M. Valdemar's (Price) merciful death by maintaining him in a trance. Although Valdemar is in constant physical agony, Carmichael will not break the trance unless the former's comely wife (Debra Paget) weds him.

Because of the tri-part structure, the characterizations were far tauter than usual, with Price in sharp competition to keep the limelight from Lorre and Rathbone. *Variety* complimented, "Vincent Price leers, is mad, is tender — and even laughs straight."

Tales of Terror did not make the box-office impact of previous AIP-Poe entries. Sometimes on reissue, the feature was condensed to a random selection of two of the three given episodes.

CONVICTS 4 *(Allied Artists, 1962) 105 min.*

Producer, A. Ronald Lubin; director, Millard Kaufman; based on the book *Reprieve* by John Resko; screenplay, Kaufman; art director, Howard Richmond; set decorator, Joseph Kish; assistant director, Clark Paylow; wardrobe, Roger J. Weinberg; make-up, William B. Turner; sound, Ralph E. Butler; camera, Joseph Birco; editor, George White.

Ben Gazzara (John Resko); Stuart Whitman (Principal Keeper); Ray Walston (Iggy); Sammy Davis, Jr. (Wino); Vincent Price (Carl

Carmer); Rod Steiger (Tiptoes); Broderick Crawford (Warden); Dodie Stevens (Resko's Sister); Jack Kruschen (Resko's Father); Naomi Stevens (Resko's Mother); Carmen Phillips (Resko's Wife); Susan Silo (Resko's Daughter); Timothy Carey (Nick); Roland La Starza (Duke); Tom Gilson (Lefty); Arthur Malet (Storekeeper); Lee Krieger (Stanley); Myron Healey (Gunther); Josip Elic (Barber); Jack Albertson (Art Teacher); Robert H. Harris (Commissioner); Burt Lange (Gallery Man); Andy Albin (Con); John Kellogg, Adam Williams, Robert Christopher, Warren Kemmerling, Kreg Martin, John Close, Billy Varga (Guards); John Dennis (Cell-Block Guard); Reggie Nalder (Greer).

Because "the emphasis falls upon the dreadful waste of human lives in prison, the moldering of raw materials that might have been shaped and refined into something better." (*Saturday Review* magazine) this prison tale rose above the usual cliches of the genre.

This low-keyed feature was based on the real-life account of convicted murderer John Resko (Ben Gazzara) who, during his eighteen years of prison rehabilitation, developed into a noteworthy painter and was eventually paroled in 1949. Vincent Price, one of the few non-Method acting leads here, portrayed author-critic Carl Carmer, who helped to obtain Resko's release.

CONFESSIONS OF AN OPIUM EATER
(Allied Artists, 1962) 85 min.

Producer, Albert Zugsmith; associate producer, Robert Hill; director, Zugsmith; based on the novel by Thomas De Quincey; screenplay, Robert Hill; music, Albert Glasser; art director, Eugene Lourie; set decorator, Joseph Kish; wardrobe, Roger J. Weinberg, Norah Sharpe; make-up, William P. Turner; assistant director, Lindsley Parsons, Jr.; sound, Charles Schelling, Ralph E. Butler; camera, Joseph Biroc; editors, Roy V. Livingston, Robert S. Eisen.

Vincent Price (Gil De Quincey); Linda Ho (Ruby Low); Richard Loo (George Wah); June Kim (Lotus); Philip Ahn (Ching Foon); Yvonne Moray (Child); Caroline Kido (Lo Tsen); Terence De Marney (Scrawny Man); Gerald Jann (Fat Chinese); Vivianne Manku (Catatonic Girl); Miel Saan (Look Gow); John Mamo (Auctioneer); Victor Sen Yung (Wing Young); Ralph Ahn (Wah

Chan); Arthur Wong (Kwai Tong); Alice Li (Ping Toy); Geri Hoo, Joanne Miya, Keiko (Dancing Girls).

Thomas De Quincey's sensational account, first published in 1821, received a tattered, exploitation presentation.

Adventurer Gil De Quincey (Vincent Price) arrives in 1900s San Francisco to aid his newspaper editor associate (Richard Loo) in quelling a Tong war and putting a stop to the slave trade. Before long he becomes romantically attached to Ruby Low (Linda Ho), but the fated lovers drown in a drain under the city's street during a Tong struggle.

Price's exaggerated performance and his nonheroic demeanor were hardly an intrinsic asset to this warped low-budget offering.

TOWER OF LONDON *(United Artists, 1962)* 79 *min.*

Producer, Gene Corman; director, Roger Corman; story, Leo V. Gordon, Amos Powell; screenplay, Gordon, Powell, Jeams B. Gordon; assistant director, Jack Bohrer; art director, Daniel Haller; music, Michael Anderson; camera, Arch R. Dalzell; editor, Ronald Sinclair.

Vincent Price (Richard of Gloucester); Michael Pate (Sir Ratcliffe); Joan Freeman (Lady Margaret); Robert Brown (Sir Justin); Justice Watson (Edward IV); Sara Selby (Queen Elizabeth); Richard McCauly (Clarence); Eugene Martin (Prince Edward); Donald Losby (Prince Richard); Sandra Knight (Mistress Shore); Richard Hale (Tyrus); Bruce Gordon (Earl of Buckingham); Joan Camden (Anne).

This flabby remake of the 1939 feature of the same title bore little entertainment resemblance to the earlier effort. It was neither good history nor a sufficiently scary shock film. In this edition, Vincent Price graduated to portraying Richard III (1452-1485). As the Duke of Gloucester, who was nicknamed "Crouchback," Price glided through the role of the would-be monarch who murderously removes all ready competition from the British throne. This unevenly acted feature had scant American release. As for Price, the British *Monthly Film Bulletin* ruled, "...(he) makes a very creditable stab at Richard Crookback — visually splendid, though the vocal intonations occasionally lapse into parody."

THE RAVEN *(American International, 1963)* C-86 min.

Executive producers, James H. Nicholson, Samuel Z. Arkoff; producer-director, Roger Corman; based on the poem by Edgar Allan Poe; screenplay, Richard Matheson; music, Les Baxter; music coordinator, Al Simms; art director, Daniel Haller; set decorator, Harry Reif; costumes, Marjorie Corso; make-up, Ted Coodley; assistant director, Jack Bohrer; sound, John Bury, Gene Corso; camera, Floyd Crosby; editor, Ronald Sinclair.

Vincent Price (Dr. Erasmus Craven); Peter Lorre (Dr. Bedlo); Boris Karloff (Dr. Scarabus); Hazel Court (Lenore Craven); Olive Sturgess (Estelle Craven); Jack Nicholson (Rexford Bedlo); Connie Wallace (Maid servant); William Baskin (Grimes); Aaron Saxon (Gort).

"A sappy little parody of a horror picture cutely calculated to make the children scream with terror while their parents scream with glee." (*Time* magazine)

One night sixteenth-century magician Dr. Erasmus Craven (Vincent Price) is visited by a plump talking raven (Peter Lorre) who has been turned into the oversized black bird for daring to challenge master sorcerer Dr. Scarabus (Boris Karloff). When Carven learns his supposedly dead wife (Hazel Court) is established at Scarabus' plush castle, he and the raven hasten there to challenge his eminence.

The new version bore very little relationship to Edgar Allan Poe's eighteen six-line stanza poem (1845) or to the 1935 Universal contemporized feature that boasted a cast of both Karloff and Bela Lugosi.

In retrospect, this film has gained some prominence. Ivan Butler writing in *Horror in the Cinema* (1970) concludes, "It is amusingly done, ... which is refreshingly unusual in a *genre* only too easy to mimic feebly, and Vincent Price manages to laugh at himself without guying himself."

DIARY OF A MADMAN *(United Artists, 1963)* C-96 min.

Producer, Robert E. Kent; director, Reginald Le Borg; based on stories by Guy de Maupassant; screenplay, Kent; music, Richard

La Salle; art director, Daniel Haller; set decorator, Victor Gangelin; costumes, Marjorie Corso; assistant director, Al Westen; sound, Ralph Butler; special effects, Norman Breedlove; camera, Ellis W. Carter; editor, Grant Whytock.

Vincent Price (Simon Cordier); Nancy Kovack (Odette Duclasse); Chris Warfield (Paul Duclasse); Elaine Devry (Jeanne D'Arville); Stephen Roberts (Rennedon); Lewis Martin (Priest); Ian Wolfe (Pierre); Edward Colmans (Andre D'Arville); Mary Adams (Louise); Harvey Stephens (Louis Girot); Nelson Olmstead (Dr. Borman); Joseph Ruskin ("The Horla").

After nineteenth-century French magistrate Simon Cordier (Vincent Price) fells a condemned murderer in self-defense, he finds himself possessed by the deceased man's evil spirit (the "Horla"), which causes him to perpetrate a spate of bloody murders. The moral of the tale, "Wherever evil exists in the heart of man, the Horla lives."

About this disappointing adaptation of Guy de Maupassant stories, the New York *Herald-Tribune* sighed, "Ah me, those Vincent Price Victorian-Technicolor Horror Classics are running out of gas, let alone gore, gloom and guts. ..."

BEACH PARTY *(American International, 1963) C-100 min.*

Executive producer, Samuel Z. Arkoff; producers, James H. Nicholson, Lou Rusoff; director, William Asher; screenplay, Lou Rusoff; art director, Daniel Haller; set decorator, Harry Reif; costumes, Marjorie Corso; make-up, Carlie Taylor; assistant directors, Clark Paylow, Lew Borzage; music, Les Baxter; music coordinator, Al Simms; sound, Don Rush, Roger White; camera, Kay Norton; editor, Homer Powell.

Bob Cummings (Professor Jason Sutwell); Dorothy Malone (Marianne); Frankie Avalon (Frankie); Annette Funicello (Dolores); Harvey Lembeck (Eric Von Zipper); Jody McCrea (Deadhead); John Ashley (Ken); Morey Amsterdam (Cappy); Eva Six (Ava); Dick Dale (Himself); Vincent Price (Big Daddy); The Del-Tones (Themselves); David Landfield (Ed); Dolores Wells

(Sue); Valora Noland (Rhonda); Bobby Payne (Tom); Duane Ament (Big Boy); Andy Romano, John Macchia, Jerry Brutsche, Bob Harvey (Motorcycle Rats); Linda Rogers, Alberta Nelson (Motorcycle Mice); Candy Johnson (Perpetual Motion Dancer); Roger Bacon (Tour Guide); Yvette Vickers, Sharon Garrett (Yogi Girls); Micky Dora, John Fain, Pam Colbert, Donna Russell, Mike Nader, Eddie Garner, Laura Lynn, Susan Yardley, Brian Wilson (Surfers); Lorie Summers, Meredith Macrae, Luree Nicholson, Paulette Rapp, Marlo Baers (Beach Girls); John Beach, Bill Slosky, Brent Battin, Roger Christian, Gary Usher, Bill Parker (Beach Boys).

Always on the lookout for new trends, American International kicked off a fresh cycle by using a "big"-name cast. There were some bouncy songs and the potentiality of an engaging screen team (Frankie Avalon and Annette Funicello), but, as analyzed by *The New York Times*, "The real trouble is that almost the entire cast emerges as the dullest bunch ever, with the old folks even sillier than the kids — a nice-looking lot, too. We suspect that the youngsters in the audience may find it all pretty laughable."

Professor Sutwell (Bob Cummings) is making a fresh survey of teen-age habits, and observes the antics of Frankie (Avalon), his girl friend (Funicello) and their zany surfside pals on the southern California beach. Eric Von Zipper (Harvey Lembeck) is head of the motorcycle pack that becomes embroiled in the eventual melee, with former Academy Award winner Dorothy Malone seemingly bemused as Cummings' resilient secretary. Vincent Price had a cameo assignment as "Big Daddy," the proprietor of the local teen-age set hangout.

TWICE-TOLD TALES *(United Artists, 1963)* C-119 min.

Producer, Robert E. Kent; director, Sidney Salkow; based on stories by Nathaniel Hawthorne; screenplay, Kent; music, Richard La Salle; art director, Franz Bachelin; set decorator, Charles Thompson; assistant director, Al Westen; costumes, Marjorie Corso; sound, Lambert Day; special effects, Milton Olsen; camera, Ellis W. Carter; editor, Grant Whytock.

Episode — *Dr. Heidegger's Experiment*:
Vincent Price (Alex Medbourne); Sebastian Cabot (Dr. Carl Heidegger); Mari Blanchard (Sylvia Ward).

Episode — *Rappaccini's Daughter*:
Vincent Price (Dr. Rappaccini); Brett Halsey (Giovanni Guast-conti); Abraham Safaer (Professor Pietro Baglioni); Joyce Taylor (Beatrice Rappaccini); Edith Evanson (Lisabetta).
Episode — *The House of Seven Gables*:
Vincent Price (Gerald Pyncheon); Beverly Garland (Alice Pyncheon); Richard Denning (Jonathan Maulle); Jacqueline De Wit (Hannah); Floyd Simmons (Mathew); Gene Roth (Cabdriver).

Since American International had apparently cornered the market on Edgar Allan Poe material, United Artists turned enterprisingly to the still-fertile Nathaniel Hawthorne canon, unfortunately with less felicitous results.

Dr. Heidegger's Experiment: On his seventy-ninth birthday, Dr. Carl Heidegger (Sebastian Cabot) and Alex Medbourne (Vincent Price sip amazing preservative fluits and magically regain their lost youth, as well as bring Heidegger's long-dead bride-to-be (Mari Blanchard) back to life. Heidegger then learns Medbourne had been her lover and had poisoned the comely lass when she planned to wed the doctor.

Rappaccini's Daughter: Because his wife deserted him, insane scientist Dr. Rappaccini (Vincent Price) turns his daughter into a poisonous creature who brings death to anyone she touches. She and her would-be lover (Brett Halsey) die together and Rappaccini, in turn, commits suicide.

The House of Seven Gables: A much-truncated, more horrific, version of the famed novel with greedy Gerald Pyncheon (Vincent Price) returning to the ancestral Massachusetts home with his wife (Beverly Garland), bent on finding the secreted family fortune, only to be undone by his own avariciousness.

In his showcase of roles, including a chance to try the George Sanders part from the 1939 version of *The House of Seven Gables*, in which he had co-starred, Price emerged unscathed. In fact, *Variety* observed "...(he) has a chance to display the virtuosity which has made him master of the hounds of hell."

THE COMEDY OF TERRORS *(American International, 1963) C-86 min.*

Producers, James H. Nicholson, Samuel Z. Arkoff; co-producer, Anthony Carras; associate producer, Richard Matheson; director,

Jacques Tourneur; screenplay, Matheson; production designer-art director, Daniel Haller; set decorator, Harry Reif; music, Les Baxter; make-up, Carlie Taylor; costumes, Marjorie Corso; assistant director, Robert Agnew; sound, Don Rush; special effects, Pat Dinga; camera, Floyd Crosby; editor, Carras.

Vincent Price (W. Trumbull); Peter Lorre (Felix Gillie); Boris Karloff (Amos Hinchley); Basil Rathbone (John F. Black); Joe E. Brown (Cemetery Keeper); Joyce Jameson (Amaryllis Trumbull); Beverly Hills (Mrs. Phipps); Paul Barsolow (Riggs); Linda Rogers (Phipp's Maid); Luree Nicholson (Black's Servant); Buddy Mason (Mr. Phipps).

As *Variety* succinctly put it, "Poof goes the spoof" in this outrageous mock-horror romp.

Loafing William Trumbull (Vincent Price) has wed his elderly partner's (Boris Karloff) daughter (Joyce Jameson) to gain total control of their funeral business. When finances become desperate, Trumbull and his unwilling assistant (Peter Lorre) create a new market for their mortician services by murdering assorted folks in their 1890s New England town. Meanwhile, Trumbull's Shakespearean-spouting landlord (Basil Rathbone) threatens to dispossess him, and his operatic-bent wife is carrying on with tone-deaf Lorre.

The sometimes amusing catalog of incidents kidding the horror-film genre would have benefitted from more spice and wit and more controlled acting by the anything-goes stars.

THE LAST MAN ON EARTH *('ULTIMO UOMO DELLA TERRA) (American International, 1964) 86 min.*

Producer, Robert L. Lippert; director, Sidney Salkow; based on the novel *I Am Legent* by Richard Matheson; screenplay, Logan Swanson, William P. Leicester; assistant director, Carlo Grandone; art director, Giorgio Giovannini; make-up, Piero Mecacci; music, Paul Sawtell, Bert Shefter; camera, Franco Delli Colli; editor, Gene Ruggiero.

Vincent Price (Robert Morgan); Franca Bettoia (Ruth); Emma Danieli (Virginia); Giacomo Rossi-Stuart (Ben Cortman); and Umberto Rau, Christi Courtland, Tony Corevi, Hector Ribotta.

A fatal plague scours the earth, turning the few survivors into rampaging vampires. Only scientist Robert Morgan (Vincent Price) is immune to the diseases because of a jungle fever he contracted years before. Despite the hell on earth, humanitarian Price is convinced there is hope for the future, particularly when he encounters a semi-normal vampire group. However, they soon prove him foolishly idealistic.

Because of Price's marquee name, the catchy film title, and a hard-sell promotional campaign, this quickie Italian-made, dubbed feature received more display than it warranted in the American movie market. For his heroic performance here, the New York *Herald-Tribune* tagged Price "king of the hamsters" and *The New York Times* joshed, "Guess who? Vincent Price, of course, stumping around an earthly wasteland and tangling with a gang of zombies, most of whom he skewers."

In 1971 the same studio released an expansive, Hollywood-lensed remake, *The Omega Man* in which the epic-prone Charlton Heston stalked about emptied Los Angeles, determined not to fall prey to the albino mutants. For very different reasons, Heston's "immortal mortal" hero was as equally incredible as Price's earlier portrayal.

THE HAUNTED PALACE *(American International, 1964) C-85 min.*

Producer-director, Roger Corman; based on the story by Edgar Allan Poe and a story by H. P. Lovecraft; screenplay, Charles Beaumont; art director, Daniel Haller; set decorator, Harry Reif; production manager-assistant director, Jack Bohrer; music, Ronald Stein; make-up, Ted Coodley; titles, Armand Acosta; camera, Floyd Crosby; editor, Ronald Sinclair.

Vincent Price (Charles D. Ward (Curwen)); Debra Paget (Ann Ward); Lon Chaney (Simon Orne); Frank Maxwell (Dr. Marinus Willet); Leo Gordon (Edgar Weeden); Elisha Cook (Peter Smith); John Dierkes (Jacob West); Harry Ellerbe (Minister); Cathy Merchant (Hester Tillinghast); Milton Parsons (Jaber Hutchinson); Guy Wilkerson (Leach); Darlene Lucht (Young Woman Victim); Barboura Morris (Mrs. Weeden); Bruno Ve Sota (Bartender).

In 1870s New England, the great-grandson (Vincent Price) of a man burned for witchcraft arrives at the foreboding family mansion to find the local village cluttered with deformed mutants, all descendants of accursed townfolk. Ward is unwillingly compelled by the wall portrait of his murdered ancestor to embark on eerie sacrifical rites prior to a prescribed revenge spree. Just as he was about to smote his innocent wife (Debra Paget), the villagers burn his home. With the painting destroyed, Ward returns to his former self — or has he?

An intriguing handling of H. P. Lovecraft's story, *The Case of Charles Dexter Ward,* told in psychological terms appropriate to the ambience of Poe's original story through Roger Corman's deliberate cinematic ambiguity. *The New York Times,* however, was unenthused about the production, "It has the director's usual star (Vincent Price), his usual obvious shock devices (sudden cuts to close-ups emphasizing fantastic make-up) and his usual inane dialogue...."

THE MASQUE OF THE RED DEATH *(Am erican International, 1964) C-90 min.*

Producer, Roger Corman; associate producer, George Willoughby; director, Corman; based on stories by Edgar Allan Poe; screenplay, Charles Beaumont, R. Wright Campbell; production designer, Daniel Haller; art director, Robert Jones; set decorator, Colin Southcott; make-up, George Partleton; costume supervisor, Laura Nightingale; titles, James Baker; music director, David Lee; choreography, Jack Carter; assistant director, Peter Price; sound, Richard Bird; special effects, George Blackwell; camera, Nicholas Roeg; editor, Ann Chegwidden.

Vincent Price (Prince Prospero); Hazel Court (Juliana); Jane Asher (Francesca); David Weston (Gino); Patrick Magee (Alfredo); Nigel Green (Ludovico); Skip Martin (Hop Toad); John Westbrook (Man in Red); Gay Brown (Senora Escobar); Julian Burton (Senor Veronese); Doreen Dawn (Anna-Marie); Paul Whitsun-Jones (Scarlatti); Jean Lodge (Scarlatti's Wife); Verina Greenlaw (Esmeralda); Brian Hewlett (Lampredi); Harvey Hall (Clistor); Robert Brown (Guard).

Because a plague is victimizing the Italian countryside of the twelfth century, devil-worshiping Prince Prospero (Vincent Price) gathers his corrupt friends within his castle to wait out the devastating malady. He indulges in sadistic pleasures to amuse his jaded mind, relying for inspiration on the philosophy of diabolism. Virginal peasant girl Francesca (Jane Asher), who had come to the fortress to beg for her father's life, is forced by the capricious Prince to be a spectator to the horror of his dying menagerie. Later the red-cloaked figure of Death (John Westbrook) appears at Prospero's grand masquerade ball. Prospero greets him as an emissary of Satan but soon learns that Death has no master and that, "Each man makes his own heaven and his own hell." Finally, Francesca is rescued by her beloved (David Weston). Meanwhile, the shades of Death gather in the countryside to discuss the effect of their passing. Thereafter the messengers of "Death" move off together.

The first of Roger Corman's British-made Edgar Allan Poe pictures enjoyed gorgeous photography (capturing the symbolic hues of crimson), almost-sensible period dialogue, and a coherency of concept. A mild surprise was provided when a real countenance was revealed (instead of a mummified face, skull, etc.) beneath the Man in Red's masque. Viewers and censors alike were alternately mesmerized and/or repelled by the excursions into the bizarre, decadent rituals of tortures more often suggested than shown. Two of the film's grislier scenes were when the dwarf (Skip Martin) revenges himself on a cruel guest by engineering the man's immolation during the ball, and when Prospero's mistress (Hazel Court) offers herself to Satan, meeting a horrible end at the touch of a slashing blade and the talons of a screeching falcon.

Price was at his benign best as the evil practitioner who glides from one torment chamber to another, only to eventually succumb to his brush with the Man in Red. The British *Monthly Film Bulletin* approved, "...Vincent Price, initiating horrible tortures with a characteristic air of sadistic glee, also conveys a genuine philosophical curiosity as to the unknown territories into which his guest may lead him."

THE TOMB OF LIGEIA *(American International, 1965) 80 min.*

Executive producers, James H. Nicholson, Samuel Z. Arkoff; producer-director, Roger Corman; based on the story by Edgar Allan Poe; screenplay, Robert Towne; assistant director, David Tringham; music, Kenneth V. Jones; camera, Arthur Grant; editor, Alfred Cox.

Vincent Price (Vernon Fell); Elizabeth Shepherd (Lady Ligeia/Lady Rowena); John Westbrook (Christopher Gough); Oliver Johnston (Kenrick); Derek Francis (Lord Trevaniss); Richard Vernon (Dr. Vuran); Ronald Adam (Parson); Frank Thornton (Peperel); Denis Gilmore (Livery Boy).

Mesmerized, drug-addicted widower Vernon Fell (Vincent Price) resides in the ruins of an English abbey, near the grave of his wife (Elizabeth Shepherd), who was buried years before under strange circumstances. His second wife (also played by Shepherd) is haunted by mysterious happenings and is nearly lured to her destruction by a malevolent black cat.

In its psychedelic mixture of symbolic metamorphoses, necrophilia, sado-masochism, and hypnotism, the color feature was either absurdly off base or artistically intense, all depending on one's viewpoint. *Newsweek* magazine allowed, "...(it) may not be the best of his (Corman's) series of Edgar Allan Poe divertimentos, but it is the most far-out, and, in the last half hour or so, his most concentrated piece of black magic." In retrospect, it proved a fitting finale to Corman's direct participation in the genre, for thereafter he went on to focus on other cinematic themes.

WAR GODS OF THE DEEP (CITY IN THE SEA) *(American International, 1965)* C-83 min.

Executive producer, George Willoughby; producer, Daniel Haller; director, Jacques Tourneur; based on the poem by Edgar Allan Poe; screenplay, Charles Bennett, Louis M. Heyward; additional dialogue, David Whittaker; music, Stanley Black; underwater camera-director, John Lamb; special effects, Frank George, Lee Boure; camera, Stephen Dade; editor, Jordan Hales.

Vincent Price (the Captain); Tab Hunter (Ben Harris); David Tomlinson (Harold Tufuell Jones); Susan Hart (Jill Tegellis); John Le Mesurier (Reverend Jonathan Ives); Henry Oscar (Mumford); Derek Newark (Dan); Roy Patrick (Simon); Anthony Selby (George); Michael Heyland (Bill); Steven Brooke (Ted); William Hurondell (Tom); Jim Spearman (Jack); Dennis Blake (Harry); Arthur Hewlett, Walter Sparrow, John Barrett (Fishermen); Herbert (The Rooster); George Ricarde (Bart Allison); Hilda Campbell, Barbara Bruce (Guests).

VINCENT PRICE UNMASKED

A captain (Vincent Price) commands the submerged kingdom of Lyonesse off the British coast and controls a group of smugglers driven underground by sleuths on land. An activated volcano threatens the future of the underwater city, leading the captain to kidnap an American seismologist (Tab Hunter) as well as a young girl (Susan Hart) who resembles his long-dead wife.

The British magazine *Films and Filming* pinpointed the picture's intrinsic problem, "(Director Jacques) Tourneur describes it as an adventure film and the feeble comic element doesn't go against this; but there ought to be some sense of tension and uncertainty about straying into a strange and hostile world, even if horror and suspense aren't to be part of the recipe".

Once again, Price's characterization demanded that he be haunted by the memory of a lost wife and that he play a man who strides about his domain with authority and concern. *Variety* decided, "Price convinces by underplaying the two-sided role of tyrannical ruler with benevolent overtones."

This tepid British-made entry in the science-fiction genre lacked grandness of execution and suffered from weak heros (Hunter, David Tomlinson), and a straining heroine (Hart).

TABOOS OF THE WORLD *(American International, 1965) C-95 min.*

Producer, Guido Giambartolomei; director, Romolo Marcellini; camera, Rino Fileppini; editor, Otillo Collangeli.

Vincent Price (Narrator).

This Italian documentary feature, re-edited for the English-speaking countries, gratuitously examined primitive customs around the globe, focusing on repulsive sights and strange bits of knowledge about human customs. *Variety* observed, "Although Vincent Price speaks the narrative in his best unctuous tones, it is as often as not his flippant remarks that titillate the ear of the viewer and not what the eye is beholding."

Many critics wondered aloud as to the justification of the "staged" real-life sequences filmed in shocking color.

DR. GOLDFOOT AND THE BIKINI MACHINE *(American International, 1965) 90 min.*

Producers, James H. Nicholson, Samuel Z. Arkoff; co-producer, Anthony Carras; director, Norman Taurog; story, James Hartford; screenplay, Elwood Ullman, Robert Kaufman; art director, Daniel Haller; music, Les Baxter; song, Guy Hennric, Jerry Styner; choreography, Jack Baker; sound, Vern Kramer; special effects, Roger George; camera, Sam Leavitt; editors, Ronald Sinclair, Fred Feitshans.

Vincent Price (Dr. Goldfoot); Frankie Avalon (Craig Gamble); Dwayne Hickman (Todd Armstrong); Susan Hart (Diane); Jack Mullaney (Igor); Fred Clark (D.J. Pevney); Alberta Nelson (Reject #12); Milton Frome (Motorcycle Cop); Hal Riddle (News Vendor); Kay Elhardt (Girl in Club); Vincent L. Barnett (Janitor); Joe Floski (Cook); William Baskin (Guard); Sam and the Ape Men with Diane de Marco (Themselves); Patti Chandler, Sally Sachee, Sue Hamilton, Marianne Gaba, Issa Arnal, Pam Rodgers, Sally Frei, Jan Watson, Mary Hughes, Luree Holmes, Laura Nicholson, China Lee, Deanna Lund, Leslie Summers, Kay Michaels, Arlene Charles (Robots); Annette Funicello (Girl in the Stock); Aron Kincaid (Sports-Car Driver); Deborah Walley (Louise); Harvey Lembeck (Man Chained to a Motorcycle).

A mindless, broadside jab at the current cycle of gadgety, super-spy flicks. Warped, zany Dr. Goldfoot (Vincent Price) has invented an electronic duplicating machine that mass-produces robots, all of whom are golden bikini-clad girls geared to trap wealthy men so that their international financial resources will accrue to Goldfoot. His bumbling assistant Igor (Jack Mullaney) falters on the job, allowing aardvark robot Diane (Susan Hart) to pass inspection. She, in turn, accidentally makes passes at S.I.C. secret agent Craig Gamble (Frankie Avalon), leading to the downfall of Goldfoot's world-domination scheme.

"Occasionally," stated *The New York Times,* "it's diverting to see just how bad or unfunny a supposed laugh-package of a movie can be." The rival New York *Herald-Tribune* concluded, "The authors and director Norman Taurog make their primary mistake in attempting to spoof everything in sight, ranging from science fiction to horror movies to (James) Bondisms, and making the attempt with sledge-hammer finesse. But no one can accuse them of inconsistency; nothing rises above the fourth-grade level."

In a performance "played past the hilt" (New York *Herald-Tribune*) Price's cultured, mad scientist had a good deal of on-camera competition from bald-headed Fred Clark. The latter veteran, as Avalon's exasperated bureau chief, provided sharp moments of biting sarcasm. As a bonus to loyal American International followers, there were cameo appearances by Annette Funicello (trapped in a wood stock), Aron Kincaid (a jazzy sports-car driver), and Harvey Lembeck (a hood chained to a motorcycle).

DR. GOLDFOOT AND THE GIRL BOMBS
(American International, 1966) C-86 min.

Producers, Louis M. Heyward, Fulvio Luciano; director, Mario Bava; story, James Hartford; screenplay, Heyward, Robert Kaufman; music, Les Baxter; song, Guy Hemric and Jerry Styner.

Vincent Price (Dr. Goldfoot); Fabian Forte (Bill Dexter); Franco Franchi (Franco); Ciccio Ingrassia (Ciccio); Laura Antonelli (Rosanna); Movana Tahi (Goldfoot's Assistant).

The finale to the madcap *Dr. Goldfoot and the Bikini Machine* had provided a good entre for succeeding celluloid editions, but this sloppy Italian-produced sequel stopped the series cold.

Supported by Red China, infamous Dr. Goldfoot (Vincent Price) plans to instigate total war between America and Russia. He plots to eliminate the majority of top NATO generals, so that with the resultant lack of international-security control, he can pummel Moscow with bombs, hoping the vindictive Russians will assume the U.S. to be responsible. Goldfoot equips his robot girls with proximity fuses implanted in their navels, geared to explode during lovemaking with the NATO officers. However, American Strategic Intelligence officer Bill Dexter (Fabian Forte) and two Italian doormen (Franco Franchi, Ciccio Ingrassia) join forces to subdue power-mad Goldfoot. The latter ends up as a Siberian prison-camp commandant.

Variety criticized, "Vincent Price, however, only slices the ham a bit thicker as the villainous title character and makes one doubt that this could be the same actor who once played Albert to Helen Hayes' Victoria."

HOUSE OF 1000 DOLLS (HAUS DER TAUSEND FREUDEN) *(American International, 1967)* C-78 min.

Executive producer, Louis M. Heyward; producer, Harry Alan Towers; director, Jeremy Summers; screenplay, Peter Welbeck; assistant director, Juan Estebrich; art director, Santiago Ontanon; music, Charles Camilleri; sound, Felix Alvaron; camera, Manuel Merino; editor, Allan Morrison.

Vincent Price (Felix Manderville); Martha Hyer (Rebecca); George Nader (Stephen Armstrong); Ann Smyrner (Marie); Wolfgang Kieling (Inspector Emil); Sancho Gracia (Fernando); Marie Rohm (Diane); Louis Rivera (Paul); Jose Jaspe (Ahmed); Juan Olaguivel (Salim); Herbert Fuchs (Abdul); Yelena Samarina (Madame Viera); Diane Bond (Liza); and Andrea Lascelle, Ursula Janis, Monique Aime, Marisol Anon, Jill Echos, Lola Munoz (Dolls).

American businessman Stephen Armstrong (George Nader) and Tangier citizen Fernando (Sancho Gracia) join forces to trace the whereabouts of Armstrong's missing wife (Ann Smyrner) and Fernando's vanished fiancee (Maria Rohm). It develops that they have been smuggled by white slavers operating from the notorious House of Dolls brothel run by illusionist Felix Manderville (Vincent Price) and his crafty partner Rebecca (Martha Hyer).

About this abysmal international co-production (dubbed into English), the British *Monthly Film Bulletin* bemoaned, "...a confusion of kidnapping, fights, flogging and a little timid strip-tease prove too much for all of Price's efforts to treat the whole thing as a joke." In addition, the technical values throughout the film were of the lowest order.

THE JACKALS *(20th Century-Fox, 1967)* C-93 min.

Producer-director, Robert D. Webb; story, W. R. Burnett; screenplay, Lamar Trotti, Austin Medord.

Cast: Vincent Price, Dana Ivarson, Robert Gunner, Bob Courtnet, Bill Brewer, Johnny Whitney.

In 1883 South Africa, five fugitive bank robbers flock to the Transvaa l, hoping to get rich quick by stealing the gold stakes of an old prospector (Vincent Price) and his granddaughter (Dana Ivarson).

This loose remake of *Yellow Sky* (1948), which had starred Anne Baxter, James Barton, and Gregory Peck, found Price and Ivarson assuming the roles once played by Barton and Baxter. The African-made feature was quickly shunted to television distribution.

THE CONQUEROR WORM (WITCHFINDER GENERAL) *(American International, 1968) C-87 min.*

Executive producer, Tony Tenser; producer, Arnold L. Miller; co-producer, Louis M. Heyward; associate producer, Philip Waddilove; director, Michael Reeves; based on the novel *Witchfinder General* by Ronald Bassett and a poem by Edgar Allan Poe; screenplay, Reeves, Tom Baker; additional scenes, Heyward; music director, Paul Ferris; art director, Jim Morahan; set decorator, Andrew Low; assistant director, Ian Goddard; sound, Paul Le Mare; special effects, Roger Dicken; camera, Johnny Coquillon; editor, Howard Lanning.

Vincent Price (Matthew Hopkins); Ian Ogilvy (Richard Marshall); Hilary Dwyer (Sara); Rupert Davies (John Lowes); Robert Russell (John Stearne); Patrick Wymark (Oliver Cromwell); Wilfrid Brambell (Master Coach); Michael Beint (Captain Gordon); Nicky Henson (Trooper Swallow); John Trenaman (Trooper Harcourt); William Maxwell (Trooper Gifford); Tony Selby (Salter); Beaufoy Milton (Priest); John Kidd, Peter Haigh (Magistrates); Hira Talfrey, Ann Tirard (Old Women); Peter Thomas (Farrier); Edward Palmer (Shepherd); David Webb (Jailer); Godfrey James (Webb); Paul Dawkins (Farmer); Jack Lynn, Martin Terry (Innkeepers); Lee Peters (Infantry Sergeant); David Lyell (Foot Soldier); Toby Lennon (Old Man); Maggie Kimberley (Elizabeth Clark); Bernard Kay (Fisherman); Gillian Aldham (Young Woman in Cell); Paul Ferris (Young Husband); Alf Joint (Sentry); Morris Jar (Paul); Dennis Thorne, Michael Segal (Villagers); Maggie Nolan, Sally Douglas, Donna Reading, Tasma Brereton, Sandy Seager (Wenches in Inn).

The murky setting of this film is mid-seventeenth-century England following the bloody Cromwellian Civil War. Professional East Anglican witch hunter Matthew Hopkins (Vincent Price) and his henchman (Robert Russell) carry out a dastardly crusade to extract confessions from the peasantry, delighting in their new-found careers as righteous but materialistic disfigurers and dismemberers. One of the pleasanter spoils of the campaign is Sara (Hilary Dwyer), the niece of an accused village priest (Rupert Davies). She is raped by Stearne, which leads her fiance and later husband (Ian Ogilvy) to pursue her assailants. With the help of soldier comrades, he kills Hopkins and Stearne.

Filmed on location in England in muted color, this is perhaps the most gratuitously visually sadistic of all of Price's motion pictures to date, filled with extremely vivid scenes of floggings, hangings, beatings, drownings, burnings at the stake, hatchet chopping, nail piercing, *ad nauseum*. The popcorn trade revelled in the simulated gore. Regarding the grand finale in which Price is hacked and wacked to a slow death, Ivan Butler in *Horror in the Cinema* (1970) explains, "The real horror of Matthew Hopkins is that he died in his bed. Had he met the end given him here one could comfortably feel that at least he had received his due."

Price seemed to be having a very good time, "...wearing his usual ghostly pallor and speaking with forked tongue..." *(The New York Daily News)*

MORE DEAD THAN ALIVE *(United Artists, 1969) C-101 min.*

Executive producer, Aubrey Schenck; producer, Hal Klein; director, Robert Sparr; screenplay, George Schenck; art director, J. Arthur Loel; set decorator, Bill Kuehl; make-up, Gary Liddiard; assistant director, Morris R. Abrams; sound, Everett Hughes; special effects, Ralph Webb; camera, Jack Marquette; editor, John Schreyer.

Clint Walker (Killer Cain); Vincent Price (Raffalo); Anne Francis (Monica Alton); Paul Hampton (Billy Eager); Mike Henry (Luke Santee); Craig Littler (Rafe Karms); Beverly Powers (Sheree); Clarke Gordon (Linus Carson); William Woodson (Warden).

231

Middle-aged "Killer" Cain (Clint Walker) intends going straight after spending eighteen years in prison for having killed a marshal. However, his gunslinger reputation trails him about the Old West. He eventually signs on with scheming Dan Ruffalo's (Vincent Price) traveling sideshow, occurring the wrath of Billy Eager (Paul Hampton), the former star of the show. Ruffalo is later killed by the berserk Eager. Meanwhile, Cain has again left in his search for a spot to live peacefully, and reencounters attractive artist Monica Alton (Anne Francis). They wed and settle down to raise cattle, only to have everything go amuck when a young lawyer (Craig Littler) appears on the scene and suddenly guns down Cain. Bereft Monica is told by Littler, "He killed my father. Eighteen years in prison doesn't make up for all the killing he did."

The New York Times branded the film a "...dogged but dinky little western with the perfect title." *Variety* observed of Price's flamboyant role, "There may be spectator reluctance at first in accepting Vincent Price as an uncouth showman who speaks ungrammatically but the veteran horror star overcomes this."

THE OBLONG BOX *(American International, 1969) C-91 min.*

Executive producer, Louis M. Heyward; producer-director, Gordon Hessler; based on the story by Edgar Allan Poe; screenplay, Lawrence Huntingdon; additional dialogue, Christopher Wicking; art director, George Provis; assistant director, Derek Whitehurst; music, Harry Robinson; sound, Bob Jones; camera, John Coquillon; editor, Max Benedict.

Vincent Price (Julian Markham); Christopher Lee (Dr. Neuhartt); Alastair Williamson (Sir Edward Markham); Hilary Dwyer (Elizabeth Markham); Peter Arne (Samuel Trench); Harry Baird (N'Galo); Carl Rigg (Mark Norton); Maxwell Shaw (Tom Hackett); Michael Balfour (Ruddock); Godfrey James (Weller); Ropert Davies (Joshua Kemp); Sally Geeson (Sally Baxter); Ivor Dean (Hawthorne); and Uta Levka, James Mellor, Danny Daniels, John Barrie, Hira Talfrey, John Wentworth, Betty Woolfe, Martin Terry, Anne Clune, Jackie Noble, Ann Barrass, Jan Rossini, Zeph Gladstone, Tara Fernando, Tony Thawton, Anthony Bailey, Richard Cornish, Colin Jeavons, Andreas Melandrinos, Hedgar Wallace, Martin Wyldeck, the Oh! Ogunde Dancers.

Sir Edward Markham (Alastair Williamson) is tortured and mutilated by African natives for a crime actually committed by his dour brother (Vincent Price). The deranged nobleman returns to nineteenth-century England where the proud Julian keeps him chained within a distant room of the family house. Sir Edward later devises a plan to be buried alive so that he may escape his brother's supervision. However, in the process, he finds himself transported to the nearby home of Dr. Neuhartt (Christopher Lee). Once Sir Edward is revived, he dons a crimson mask and embarks on a vicious scheme to revenge himself on those who have failed him. Julian stalks his brother through the woods and eventually kills him, but not before his hand is bit by the demented victim. A few days later, Julian's wife (Hilary Dwyer) discovers that her lordly husband is infected by the mutation process.

This was the eleventh American International picture to derive from an Edgar Allan Poe piece, and the tenth in the series to star Price. *The New York Times* jibed that this offering demonstrated "...that horror can be made to be quaint, laughable and unconvincing." At fault were a convoluted script that lacked a clear-cut plot line, the apocryphal appearance of an African witch doctor (complete with blowgun) in England, and a mixture of story motivations ranging from voodoo to racism to spiritualism. Pairing sonorous-toned Price with England's horror-film king, Lee, was not the spectacular event anticipated. As to Price's emoting, *Variety* noted, "Price, as usual, overacts, but it is an art here to fit the mood, and, as usual, Price is good in his part."

THE TROUBLE WITH GIRLS (THE CHAU-TAUQUA) *(MGM, 1969) C-104 min.*

Producer, Lester Welch; associate producer, Wilson McCarthy; director, Peter Tewksbury; based on the novel *The Chautauqua* by Day Keene, Dwight Babcock, and a story by Mauri Grashin; screenplay, Arnold Peyser, Lois Peyser; assistant director, John Clark Bowman; art director, George W. Davis, Edward Carfagno; music, Billy Strange; choreography, Jonathan Lucas; sound, Franklin Milton; camera, Jacques Marquette; editor, George W. Brooks.

Elvis Presley (Walter Hale); Marilyn Mason (Charlene); Nicole Jaffe (Betty); Sheree North (Nita Bix); Edward Andrews (Johnny);

John Carradine (Mr. Drewcott); Anissa Jones (Carol); Vincent Price (Mr. Morality); Joyce Van Patten (Maude); Pepe Brown (Willy); Dabney Coleman (Harrison Wilby); Bill Zuckert (Major Gilchrist); Pitt Herbert (Mr. Perper); Anthony Teague (Clarence); Ned Flory (Constable); Robert Nichols (Smith); Helene Winston (Olga Prchlik); Kevin O'Neal (Yale); Chuck Briles (Amherst); Patsy Garrett (Mrs. Gilchrist); Linda Sue Risk (Lily-Jeanne); Charles P. Thompson (Cabbie); Leonard Rumery, William M. Paris, Kathleen Rainey (Farmhands); Hal James Pederson (Soda Jerk); Mike Wagner (Chowderhead); Brett Parker (Iceman); Frank Walker (Rutgers); John Rubinstein (Princeton); Duke Snider (Crankers); Pacific Palisades High School Madrigals (Choral Group).

In the 1920s, Walter Hale (Elvis Presley) is the company manager of a touring Chautauqua troupe, currently playing the town of Radford. When hard-luck citizen Nita Bix (Sheree North) kills her pharmacist employer-lover (Dabney Coleman) in self-defense, Presley's group find themselves implicated in the homicide. Vincent Price is Mr. Morality the wandering lecturer who talks on the classics. Coming at the tail end of Presley's screen popularity, this feature had double-bill saturation play dates in mostly rural areas. It was quickly forgotten by all, especially its beleaguered releasing company. Price received a few good notices here, "...(he) makes an odd and quite appealing guest appearance..." (British *Monthly Film Bulletin)*

SPIRITS OF THE DEAD (HISTOIRES EXTRAORDINAIRES) *(American International, 1969) C-117 min.*

Episode — *Metzengerstein*: Director, Roger Vadim; based on the story by Edgar Allan Poe; screenplay, Vadim, Pascal Cousin; art director, Jean Forester; set decorator, Jean Andre; costumes, Jacques Fonteray; assistant directors, Jean-Michel Lacor, Michel Clement, Serge Vallin; music, Jean Prodromides; camera, Claude Renoir; editor, Helene Plemiannikov.

For American release: narrator; Vincent Price; song, Ray Charles.

VINCENT PRICE UNMASKED

Jane Fonda (Countess Frederica); Carla Marlier (Claude); James Robertson Justice (Countess' Advisor); Philippe Lemaire (Philippe); Andreas Voutsinas, Annie Duperrey (Guests); Peter Fonda (Baron Wilhelm); Francoise Prevost (Friend of Countess); Serge Marquand (Hugues); Audoin de Bardot (Page); Douking (du Lissier).

Episode — *William Wilson*: Director, Louis Malle; based on the story by Edgar Allan Poe; screenplay, Malle; dialogue, Daniel Boulanger; music, Diego Masson; art directors-costumes, Ghislain Uhry, Carla Leva; assistant director, Vana Caruso; camera, Tonino Delli Colli; editors, Franco Arcalli, Suzanne Garon.

Brigitte Bardot (Giuseppina); Alain Delon (Wilson); Katia Christina (Young Girl); Umberto D'Orsi (Hans); Daniele Vargas (the Professor); Renzo Palmer (the Priest).

Episode — *Never Bet the Devil Your Head or Toby Dammit*: Director, Federico Fellini; based on the story by Edgar Allan Poe; screenplay, Fellini, Bernardino Zapponi; art director-costumes, Piero Tosi; assistant director, Eschilo Tarquini; music, Nino Rota; special effects, Joseph Nathanson; camera, Giuseppe Rotunno; editor, Ruggero Mastroianni.

Terence Stamp (Toby Dammit); Salvo Randone (Priest); Fabrizio Angeli, Ernesto Colli (Directors); Marina Yaru (Child); Anna Tonietti (Television Commentator); Aleardo Ward, Paul Cooper (Interviewers); and Antonia Pietrosi, Rick Boyd, Polidor.

Histoires Extraordinaires (Tre Passi Nel Delirio), a three-part French-Italian co-production of 1968, had six minutes shorn from its 123-minute original running time when it received U.S. release in late 1969. Added for the American market were murky new color prints, wooden dubbed voices, a Ray Charles song ("Ruby"), and a Clement Biddlewood narration spoken by Vincent Price, which opens and closes the picture. According to the *Independent Film Journal,* the latter element "...reads like the overreaching literary efforts of an adolescent."

Metzengerstein: Countess Frederica (Jane Fonda) a dissolute lady who thrives on decadence hankers for young Baron Wilhelm (Peter Fonda), a member of a rival branch of the family. He rejects her, and in anger she sets fires to his stables. The lord perishes, but his favorite white stallion survives only to lead the disconsolate noblewoman to a fiery end.

William Wilson: In a confessional, Austrian officer William Wilson (Alain Delon) informs the priest that he has just killed a man. He relates that for several years this person, his exact double, has always appeared to stop Delon from committing a venomous act. During a card game, Delon is flogging a beautiful woman (Brigitte Bardot) when the alter ego intervenes but is stabbed for his efforts. When the priest fails to appease Delon, the latter throws himself from the church tower and dies.

Never Bet the Devil Your Head or Toby Dammit: In Rome a star in the first "Catholic Western," a drunken British movie star (Terence Stamp) has two visionary encounters with a little blonde girl (Marina Yaru). On the second occasion, he is driving in his newly acquired Maserati sports car, when he is induced by the girl's beckoning to attempt to jump his automobile across a partially destroyed bridge. He fails and is decapitated by a wire stretched across the road. The waiting girl smirks, picks up the head, and walks off.

The component elements of this feature were generally panned by the critics and ignored by the public. The Los Angeles *Times* weighed it as an "...omnibus film (one of) those easy-to-finance international co-productions that lure big names into mindless projects...the only real accomplishment of this shoddy trilogy is to make Roger Corman's Poe pictures look awfully good in comparison."

SCREAM AND SCREAM AGAIN *(American International, 1970) 95 min.*

Executive producer, Louis M. Heyward; producers, Max J. Rosenberg, Milton Subotsky; director, Gordon Hessler; based on the novel *The Disoriented Man* by Peter Saxon; screenplay, Christopher Wicking; art director, Don Mingaye; music, David Whittaker; songs, Dominic King and Tim Hayes, D. King; camera, John Coquillon; editor, Peter Elliot.

Vincent Price (Dr. Browning); Christopher Lee (Fremont); Peter Cushing (Major Heinrich); Alfred Marks (Superintendant Bellaver); Anthony Newlands (Ludwig); Peter Sallis (Schweitz); David Lodge (Detective Inspector Strickland); Uta Levka (Jane); Christopher Matthews (David Sorel); Judy Bloom (Helen Bradford); Clifford Earl (Detective Sergeant Jimmy Joyce); Kenneth Benda (Professor Kingsmill); Michael Gothard (Keith); Marshall Jones

(Konratz); Julian Holloway (Griffin); Edgar D. Davies (Rogers); Yutte Stensgaard (Erika); Lincoln Webb (Wrestler); Nigel Lambert (Ken Sparten); Steve Preston (Fryer); Lee Hudson (Matron); Leslie Ewin (Tramp); Kay Adrian (Nurse); Rosalind Elliott (Valerie).

This disturbing concoction of science fiction, horror, and murder mystery was crudely assembled to take advantage of the marquee power of Vincent Price, Christopher Lee, and Peter Cushing. A good deal of the interwoven vampire theme was gratuitous, seemingly slipped into the plot to accommodate the stereotyped images of the trio.

The police, particularly David Sorel (Christopher Matthews), are suspicious that a murderer of superhuman strength should die in a vat of acid at Dr. Browning's (Price) clinic where the killer was previously a patient. Meanwhile, Konratz (Marshall Jones), an agent of a foreign power, brings pressure to force British official Fremont (Christopher Lee) to stop the investigations. However, Sorel persists in his snooping and discovers that the diabolical Dr. Browning is manufacturing a new species of superhuman beings in a transplant surgery. Before long, Konratz and Browning clash over their *modus operandi,* and each is dispatched to a gory end. Fremont and the rescued Sorel depart the clinic, the latter unaware of the implications behind the scientific experimentations.

There was a good deal of decadence to Price's Dr. Browning, as demonstrated in his wild living quarters. Price handled his banal dialogue with relish, leading *Variety* to write, "Price is once again effective as the rock-generation's Boris Karloff, not a bad guy really but a misunderstood mad scientist a little ahead of his time."

CRY OF THE BANSHEE *(American International, 1970) 87 min.*

Executive producer, Louis M. Heyward; producer-director, Gordon Hessler; story, Tim Kelly; screenplay, Kelly, Christopher Wicking; assistant director, Ariel Levy; art director, George Provis; music, Les Baxter; camera, John Coquillon; editor, Ossie Hafenrichter.

Vincent Price (Lord Edward Whitman); Elisabeth Bergner (Oona); Essy Persson (Lady Patricia); Patrick Mower (Roderick);

Hugh Griffith (Mickey); Hilary Dwyer (Maureen); Sally Geeson (Sarah); Pamela Farbrother (Margaret); Marshall Jones (Father Tom); Carl Rigg (Harry Whitman); Michael Elphick (Burke); Stephen Chase (Sean); Andrew McCullock (Bully Boy); Robert Hutton (Guest); Godfrey James (Rider); Terry Martin (Brander); Richard Everett (Timothy); Quin O'Hara (Tavern Witchgirl); Jan Rossini (Tavern Wench); Peter Forest (Party Man); Joyce Mandre (Party Woman); Gertan Klauber (Landlord).

Because Lord Edward Whitman (Vincent Price), a six-teenth-century magistrate, is sadistically tracking down and torturing all followers of an old religion, he and his family are cursed by high priestess Oona (Elisabeth Bergner). She is abetted by a helping spirit who appears at Whitman's mansion in the guise of a young gentleman (Patrick Mower). At Oona's bidding he systematically destroys the lord's family. At the finish, a horrified Whitman is being driven in a coach to his destruction, with Mower as the coachman.

While *Variety* could indulgently remark, "It is a measure of Price's image that he can enjoin a banquet room full of guests, drink, dance, and be merry,' and the line comes out ominous," this British-made feature was tacky in its thin execution. It proved a mighty sad screen return for once-eminent Continental actress Bergner, and a prodigious celluloid bore for even the firmest of Price followers.

THE ABOMINABLE DR. PHIBES *(American International, 1971) C-93 min.*

Executive producers, Samuel Z. Arkoff, James H. Nicholson; producers, Louis M. Heyward, Ronald S. Dunas; director, Robert Fuest; screenplay, James Whiton, William Goldstein; music, Basil Kirchin in association with Jack Nathan; production designer, Brian Eatwell; art director, Bernard Reeves; assistant director, Frank Ernst; wardrobe, Elsa Fennell; make-up, Trevor Crole-Rees; sound, Dennis Whitlock; special effects, George Blackwell; camera, Norman Warwick; editor, Tristam Cones.

VINCENT PRICE UNMASKED

Vincent Price (Dr. Anton Phibes); Joseph Cotten (Dr. Vesalius); Hugh Griffith (Rabbi); Terry-Thomas (Dr. Longstreet); Virginia North (Vulnavia); Audrey Woods (Goldsmith); Susan Travers (Nurse Allan); Alex Scott (Dr. Hargreaves); Edward Burnham (Dr. Dunwoody); Peter Gilmore (Dr. Kitaj); Peter Jeffrey (Inspector Trout); Maurice Kaufman (Dr. Whitcombe); Norman Jones (Sergeant Schenley); John Cater (Waverly); Derek Godfrey (Crow); Sean Bury (Lem Vesalius); Walter Horsbrugh (Ross); Barbara Keogh (Mrs. Frawley); David Hutceson (Dr. Hedgepath); Caroline Munro (Victoria Phibes); Dallas Adams, Alan Zipson (Police Officials); Thomas Heathcote, Ian Marter, Julian Grant, Alister Williamson (Policemen).

This neatly handled mock-horror tale reveled in its art-deco camp ambience, and proved to be a strong audience pleaser.

Wealthy ex-vaudevillian Dr. Anton Phibes (Vincent Price), who has been grossly disfigured in a car accident, vows revenge on the nine physicians involved in the fatal operation on his wife several years before. From his grotesque mansion he plots his acts of retribution in a grandiose style, finding diversion in gazing on his spouse's preserved body, cavorting with his zombie-like assistant (Virginia North) or tapping out 1930s tunes on his oversized organ in the gaudy ballroom. For maniacal inspiration he relies on the Biblical curses of rats, locusts, bees, etc. to dispatch his intended victims. His nemesis of the moment proves to be Dr. Vesalius (Joseph Cotten), a man determined to outsmart Phibes and retrieve his kidnaped son (Sean Bury).

The New York Times complained, "The plot, buried under all the iron tinsel, isn't bad. But the tone of steamroller camp flattens the fun." Others admitted picture was an amusing "bloody camp" and that it contained a delicious spoof of the present nostalgia cycle. *Variety* opined, "...anachronistic period horror musical camp fantasy is a fair description, loaded with comedic gore of the type that packs theaters and drives child psychologists up the wall..." *The Abominable Dr. Phibes* was such a successful film venture that a sequel was hastily put into production.

Here Price's role was more visual than verbal, for his character could only speak through an electric socket implanted in his neck. Thus forced to pantomine, he proved very effective in projecting reactions through gestures and facial movements.

DR. PHIBES RISES AGAIN *(American International, 1972) C-89 min.*

Executive producer, Samuel Z. Arkoff, James H. Nicholson; producer, Louis M. Heyward; director, Robert Fuest; based on characters created by James Whiton, William Goldstein; screenplay, Fuest, Robert Blees; music, John Gale; make-up, Trevor Crole-Rees; assistant director, Jake Wright; art director, Brian Eatwell; sound, Les Hammond, Dennis Whitlock; sound editor, Peter Lennard; camera, Alex Thomson; editor, Tristan Cones.

Vincent Price (Dr. Phibes); Robert Quarry (Biederbeck); Valli Kemp (Vulnavia); Fiona Lewis (Diana); Peter Cushing (Captain); Beryl Reid (Mrs. Ambrose); Terry-Thomas (Lombardo); Hugh Griffith (Ambrose); Peter Jeffrey (Inspector Trout); John Cater (Waverly); Gerald Sim (Hackett); John Thaw (Shavers); Keith Buckley (Stuart); Lewis Flander (Baker); Milton Reid (Manservant).

A preordained blood transfusion replaces the embalming liquid that had preserved Dr. Anton Phibes (Vincent Price) since his prior adventures. He again quests after a restorer for his dead wife Victoria, now convinced that a rare ancient scroll will lead him to the source of a miraculous underground river in Egypt. It proves that antiquarian Biederbeck (Robert Quarry) has possession of the valuable paper, and the two inventive opponents race to Egypt, with the pragmatic police on their trail. Once in the desert, Phibes leisurely eliminates members of Biederbeck's expedition, finally capturing his rival's mistress (Fiona Lewis) whom he offers to exchange for the key to the subterranean elixir of life. The climax finds a double-crossed Biederbeck dissolving from old age, while victorious Phibes and his coffin-laden barge chart down the dark unknown waters seeking their destination to the musical background of "Over the Rainbow."

"It's refreshing to find a sequel that's better than its prototype." (British *Monthly Film Bulletin*) It was an inspired act on the part of the producers to team Price with English director Robert Fuest (of TV's "The Avengers" fame) and with actor Quarry of *Count Yorga* movie popularity. The art-deco trappings, the nostalgic jazzy music (from the Phibes Clockwork Band), the witty touches in disposing of Price's victims, provided continued zest for the deliberately awful script. Not to be overlooked were the comic policemen (Peter Jeffrey, John Cater).

THEATER OF BLOOD *(United Artists, 1973)* C-102 min.

Executive producer, Gustave Berne, Sam Jaffe; producer, John Kohn, Stanley Mann; director, Douglas Hickox; screenplay, Anthony Greville-Bell; assistant director, Dominic Fulford; production designer, Michael Seymour; set director, Ann Mollo; music, Michael J. Lewis; choreography, Tutte Lemkow; sound, Simon Kaye; stunt arranger, Terry York; special effects, John Stears; camera, Wolfgang Suschitzky; editor, Malcolm Cook.

Vincent Price (Edward Lionheart); Diana Rigg (Edwina Lionheart); Ian Hendry (Peregrine Devlin); Harry Andrews (Trevor Dickman); Coral Browne (Miss Chloe Moon); Robert Coote (Oliver Larding); Jack Hawkins (Solomon Psaltery); Michael Hordern (George Maxwell); Arthur Lowe (Horace Sprout); Robert Morley (Meredith Merridrew); Dennis Price (Hector Snipe); Diana Dors (Mrs. Psaltery); Joan Hickson (Mrs. Sprout); Renee Asherson (Mrs. Maxwell); Madeline Smith (Rosemary); Milo O'Shea (Inspector Boot); Eric Sykes (Sergeant Dogge); Tutte Lemkow, Jack Maguire, Joyce Graham, John Gilpin, Eric Francis, Sally Gilmore, Stanley Bates, Declan Mulholland (Meths Drinkers); Brigid Eric Bates (Agnes); Bunny Reed, Peter Thornton (Policemen); Tony Calvin (Police Photographer).

When drama critics George Maxwell (Michael Hordern) and Hector Snipe (Dennis Price) are found murdered, the London police are forced to conclude that perhaps allegedly dead Shakespearean actor Edward Lionheart (Vincent Price) is still alive and avenging himself on his peers, who deeply offended him by giving their annual London Theatre Critics' Circle Award to another actor. Lionheart cunningly conceives his rash of murders to correspond to the Shakespearean dramas in which he once performed so ably."

"If you know the Shakespearean plots, you'll get some fun trying to guess how scripter Anthony Greville-Bell has adapted them for each murder." (*Films in Review*) Many noted the similarities between *Theater of Blood* and *The Abominable Dr. Phibes*, but the former is a far more heady affair, less campy, less visually gory, and less eerily unsatisfactory. In fact, the British *Monthly Film Bulletin* opined, "To cast Vincent Price as a mad Shakespearean actor is to allow him for once to display his deliciously Gothic theatrical style to proper advantage, and Price rises to the challenge superbly, hissing his way through the full gamut of Shakespearean characterization and frequently rewriting roles to fit his purpose...His Richard III (shades of *Tower of London* (1939, 1962)) pastiche is one of the finest moments of his screen career, with Lionheart stalking in full royal garb between the labelled vats of a wine cellar and declaiming 'Now is the winter of our discontent...' before luring an inebriated critic into a tub of his favourite wine..."

For the first time in years Price was surrounded by a most sterling cast of colorful professionals, ranging from Robert Morley's obese gastronomist to Coral Browne's trenchant play reviewer, and of course, Diana "The Avengers" Rigg as the shapely, athletic daughter of the film's sympathetic *hero*(Price). That one eventually comes to believe in Price's deranged revenge scheme is a fine compliment to the Gothic film star, his comely consort, Rigg, and the staggering array of memorable victims.

MADHOUSE *(American International, 1974)* C-89 min.

Executive producer, Samuel Z. Arkoff; producers, Max J. Rosenberg, Milton Subotsky; associate producer, John Dark; based on the novel *Devilday* by Angus Hall; adaptor, Ken Levison; screenplay, Greg Morrison; art director, Tony Curtis; assistant director, Allan James; music, Douglas Gamley; song, Gordon Clyde; make-up, George Blackler; wardrobe, Dulcie Midwinter; sound, Danny Daniel, Gerry Humphreys; special effects, Kerss and Spencer; camera, Ray Parslow; editor, Clive Smith.

Vincent Price (Paul Toombes); Peter Cushing (Herbert Flay); Robert Quarry (Oliver Quayle); Adrienne Corri (Faye); Natasha Pyne (Julia); Michael Parkinson (TV Interviewer); Linda Hayden (Elizabeth); Barry Dennen (Blount); Ellis Dayle (Alfred); Catherine Willmer (Louise); John Garrie (Harper); Ian Thompson (Bradshaw); Jenny Lee Wright (Carol); Julie Corsthwaite (Ellen); Peter Halliday (Psychiatrist).

This inaptly titled feature represents the solidification of the turning stage in Vincent Price's horror-film career. As *Variety* perceived, "Price is now at a point in his long career where his familiar flamboyance is used to evoke audience sympathy as much as fear.

Within the blatantly contrived story, Price portrays actor Paul Toombes who rose to cinema fame as the celluloid personification of Dr. Death, a cinema monster who used disguises and elaborate schemes in his sadistic slayings. When, some years later, Price's movie star goes to England to headline a *Dr. Death* video series, a whole new batch of homicides occur, all executed in the trademark Dr. Death style. Is Price, whose onscreen character once suffered a nervous breakdown, the heinous victim?

Because of the picture's behind-the-scenes structure, there is provision for assorted film clips from Price's AIP vintage Gothic entires. Thus, in a mild way, *Madhouse* becomes a sort of *Sunset Boulevard* affair for the star. Since Price performs with general dignity, sympathy, and a relative restraint, his characterization emerges with dimension and sincerity.

England's on-camera menace Peter Cushing (as the vengeful script writer) and AIP's own *Count Yorga*, Robert Quarry (as the sinister, cruel, TV-show producer) are efficient but not classically memorable in their assignments here. Adrienne Corri is the pathetic ex-movie beauty reduced to a cringing existence in Cushing's dank basement.

Yes, it is Price singing the Gordon Clyde song over the closing credits of *Madhouse*.

PERCY'S PROGRESS *(MGM, 1975)* C-

Producer, Betty E. Box; director, Ralph Thomas; screenplay, Sid Colin, Ian La Frenais; assistant director, Simon Relph; art director, Albert Witherick; costumes, Emma Porteous; sound, Paul Le Mare; camera, Toni Imi; editor, Roy Watts.

With: Leigh Lawson, Vincent Price, Elke Sommer, Denholm Elliott, Harry H. Corbett, Milo O'Shea, Barry Humphries, Julie Ege, T. P. McKenna, Ronald Fraser, Madeline Smith, George Coulouris, Bernard Lee, James Booth, Judy Geeson, Alan Lake.

A continuation of *Percy* (MGM, 1971) in which producer Betty E. Box and director Ralph Thomas cinematically traced the repercussions to Edwin Anthony (Hywel Bennett) who undergoes the world's first penis transplant.

THE COBBLER AND THE THIEF

Producer, Brian Lewis; director, Richard Williams; based on the book *Nasruddin* by Indries Shah; screenplay, Williams.

Voices of: Vincent Price (Grand Vizier of Persia); Joan Sims (the Witch); and Kenneth Williams, Anthony Quayle, Joss Ackland, Thick Wilson.

A feature-length, color, animated film presently being produced in London.

Vincent Price on American Radio and Television
Compiled by Alvin H. Marill

*Major Radio Performances**

NBC	6.18.36	Standard Brands Hour with Rudy Vallee in scene from *There's Always Juliet* with Cornelia Otis Skinner
NBC	6.13.37	RCA Magic Key in scene from *Victoria Regina* with Helen Hayes, George Macready
NBC	10.31.37	RCA Magic Key in scene from *The Lady Has a Heart* with Elissa Landi
NBC	4.14.38	Standard Brands Hour with Rudy Vallee in scene from *Ever After* with Edith Barrett
NBC	2.39-4.39	Valiant Lady as serial regular Paul Morrison
NBC	2.26.39	Great Plays ep** *The Doll's House*
NBC	3.12.39	Chase and Sanborn Hour in scene from *Victoria Regina* with Helen Hayes, Don Ameche
CBS	6.22.41	Helen Hayes Theater ep *Victoria and Albert* with Helen Hayes
NBC	1.15.42	Heirs of Liberty
NBC	2.3.42, 2.17.42, 3.3.42, 3.17.42, 5.5.42, 5.19.42	Philip Morris Show: Johnny Presents
NBC	2.42.-7.43	Helpmate as serial regular Walter Owens
CBS	5.10.42	Columbia Workshop reading of *Flight to Arras*
NBC	6.28.42	Interamerican University of the Air reading of free-verse poem
CBS	9.27.42	Radio Reader's Digest ep *The Fight of the Chetniks*
CBS	11.29.42	Radio Reader's Digest ep *The Love Story of Mark Twain*
CBS	11.23.43	Suspense ep *The Strange Death of Charles Umberton*
CBS	3.13.44	Lux Radio Theater ep *The Letter* with Bette Davis, Herbert Marshall

* *Guest spots on ABC unavailable from network.*

** *Episode.*

CBS	6.1.44	Suspense ep *Fugue in C Minor* with Ida Lupino
NBC	1.29.45	Cavalcade of America ep *A face for Lennie*
CBS	2.5.45	Lux Radio Theater ep *Laura* with Gene Tierney, Danna Andrews, Otto Kruger
CBS	7.16.45	Screen Guild Players ep *Flesh and Fantasy* with Edward G. Robinson, Dame May Whitty
CBS	7.17.45	Columbia Presents Corwin ep *Undecided Molecule*
CBS	10.9.45	Theater of Romance ep *Angel Street* with Anne Baxter, Sir Cedric Hardwicke
CBS	2.3.46	Hollywood Star Time ep *Shock* with Lynn Bari
CBS	4.1.46	Screen Guild Players ep *On Borrowed Time* with Lionel Barrymore, Agnes Moorehead, Ted Donaldson
CBS	4.7.46	Hollywood Star Time ep *Hangover Square* with Linda Darnell
CBS	4.11.46	Suspense ep *The Name of the Beast*
CBS	4.21.46	Hollywood Star Time ep *The Song of Bernadette* with Vanessa Brown
CBS	5.19.46	Hollywood Star Time ep *The Lodger* with Cathy Lewis
CBS	7.27.46	Hollywood Star Time ep *Hot Spot* with Brian Donlevy
CBS	9.12.46	Suspense ep *Hunting Trip* with Lloyd Nolan
CBS	10.7.46	LUX RADIO Theater ep *Dragonwyck* with Gene Tierney
NBC	11.21.46, 1.16.47, 3.20.47, 5.1.47, 6.19.47	Sealtest Village Store (guest)
CBS	11.23.46	This Is Hollywood ep *A Scandal in Paris* with Akim Tamiroff
CBS	1.20.47	Screen Guild Players ep *Dragonwyck* with Teresa Wright
CBS	2.8.47	Hollywood Star Time ep *The Letter* with Ann Todd
CBS	2.17.47	Lux Radio Theater ep *Devotion* with Jane Wyman, Virginia Bruce
CBS	5.17.47	This Is Hollywood ep *Stairway to Heaven* with David Niven, Kim Hunter
CBS	7.9.47-9.24.47	The Saint as series regular Simon Templar

CBS	7.17.47	Suspense ep *Beyond Good and Evil*
CBS	9.27.47	Lux Radio Theater ep *The Web* with Ella Raines, Edmond O'Brien
CBS	6.18.48	Screen Guild Players ep *Up in Central Park* with Deanna Durbin, Dick Haymes
CBS	9.13.48	Lux Radio Theater ep *Another Part of the Forest* with Walter Huston, Ann Blyth
CBS	2.4.49	Ford Theater ep *No Time for Love* with Claudette Colbert, Glenn Ford
NBC	2.6.49	Jack Benny Show (guest)
CBS	2.25.49	Philip Morris Playhouse ep *Leona's Room*
CBS	5.6.49	Phillip Morris Playhouse ep *Murder Needs an Artist*
NBC	7.3.49	July 4th Special: *Author of Liberty* (guest)
NBC	7.19.49	Dean Martin & Jerry Lewis Show (guest)
NBC	1.3.50	Art Linkletter's People Are Funny (guest)
CBS	1.31.50	Escape ep *Present Tense*
NBC	3.13.50	American Red Cross Parade of Stars (guest)
CBS	3.17.50	Escape ep *3 Skeleton Keys*
NBC	4.13.50	Screen Guild Theater ep *Heaven Can Wait* with June Allyson, Dick Powell
NBC	6.11.50-9.10.50	The Saint as series regular Simon Templar
CBS	6.30.50	Escape ep *Bloodbath*
NBC	10.5.50	Screen Guild Theater ep *Champagne for Caesar* with Ronald Colman, Audrey Totter, Barbara Britton
NBC	10.22.50-5.20.51	The Saint as series regular Simon Templar
NBC	1.5.51	Duffy's Tavern (guest)
NBC	6.22.52	Best Plays ep *Angel Street*
NBC	10.15.55-1.10.56	Your Radio Theater (substitute host for Herbert Marshall)
CBS	4.21.57	CBS Radio Workshop ep *The Son of Man*
CBS-NBC	9.15.57	Civil Defense Special: *The Story of Civil Defense* (host)
CBS	11.10.57	Suspense ep *The Pit and the Pendulum*
NBC	4.29.57	Conversation: On the Art of Collecting (guest)
CBS	6.1.58	Suspense ep *Rave Notice*
CBS	7.19.58	Suspense ep *Occurrence at Owl Creek Bridge*

Major Television Performances*

CBS	10.4.49-11.29.49	Pantomine Quiz (game-show guest)
NBC	12.25.49	A Christmas Carol (narrator)
CBS	1.8.50-3.26.50	Pantomine Quiz (game-show guest)
NBC	4.1.50	The Saturday Night Revue with Jack Carter (guest)
CBS	7.3.50-7.10.50	Pantomine Quiz (game-show guest)
NBC	10.14.50	The Saturday Night Revue with Jack Carter (guest)
NBC	1.2.51-3.26.52	Pantomine Quiz (game-show guest)
NBC	2.17.51	The Saturday Night Revue with Jack Carter (guest)
CBS	6.25.51	Lux Video Theater ep *The Promise*
NBC	1.28.51	Lights Out ep *The Third Door*
CBS	2.11.52	Lux Video Theater ep *The Game of Chess*
NBC	3.6.52	Chesterfield Presents ep *Count Von Lustig*
ABC	3.12.52	Pulitzer Prize Playhouse ep *Monsieur Beaucaire* with Anna Lee
CBS	3.21.52	Schlitz Playhouse ep *The Human Touch* with Diana Lynn
ABC	4.10.52	Green Playhouse ep *Dream Man* with Andrea King
NBC	5.26.52	Robert Montgomery Presents ep *The Ringmaster* with Paul Lukas, Anna Lee
ABC	7.13.53	ABC Summer Theater ep *Dream Job* with Joan Leslie
CBS	8.21.53	Schlitz Playhouse ep *Sheila*
CBS	11.5.53	Schlitz Playhouse ep *Ballet for a Stranger*
NBC	8.4.54	The Betty White Show (guest)
NBC	8.10.54	Truth or Consequence (guest)
NBC	9.23.54	Lux Video Theater ep *The Heiress* with Marilyn Erskine
NBC	1.11.55	The Buick-Berle Show (guest)
NBC	4.7.55	The Sheilah Graham Show (guest)
CBS	9.2.55	Climax ep *Night Execution*
ABC	11.7.55	TV Reader's Digest ep *The Brainwashing of John Hayes*
CBS	1.15.56	G.E. Theater ep *The Ballad of Mender McClure*

* Guest Spots on ABC unavailable from network.

250

NBC	2.3.56	Science Fiction Theater ep *Operation Flypaper*
NBC	2.14.56	The Martha Raye Show (guest)
ABC	3.2.56	Crossroads ep*The Rebel*
CBS	4.5.56	Climax ep *A Spin into Darkness*
NBC	4.23.56	NBC Matinee Theater ep *Whom Death Has Joined Together*
CBS	5.6.56-6.17.56	The $64,000 Challenge (game-show guest) with Billy Pearson
NBC	5.30.56	Tonight (guest)
NBC	6.24.56	The Steve Allen Show (guest)
NBC	7.12.56	Lux Video Theater ep *Sting in the Tail*
CBS	7.13.56	Pantomine Quiz (game-show guest)
NBC	7.22.56	The Alcoa Hour ep *Sister* with Gladys Cooper, Cathleen Nesbitt
NBC	9.7.56	Science Fiction Theater ep *One Thousand Eyes*
NBC	9.19.56	It Could Be You (game-show guest)
CBS	9.23.56-10.28.56	The $64,000 Challenge (game-show guest) with Edward G. Robinson
CBS	10.4.56	Playhouse 90 ep *Forbidden Area* with Charlton Heston
NBC	10.26.56	The Walter Winchell Show (guest)
NBC	11.3.56	The George Gobel Show (Guest)
ABC	11.30.56	Crossroads ep *God's Healing* with Frieda Inescort
NBC	12.16.56	Washington Square with Ray Bolger (guest)
CBS	1.10.57	Shower of Stars (guest)
CBS	4.12.57	Schlitz Playhouse ep *The Blue Hotel*
CBS	4.21.57	Odyssey (as actor, art collector)
CBS	4.25.57	Climax ep *Avalanche at Devil's Pass*
NBC	5.15.57	It Could Be You (game-show guest)
NBC	5.15.57	The Tennessee Ernie Ford Show (guest)
CBS	9.29.57	Revolution of the Eye (art expert)
CBS	10.18.57	Schlitz Playhouse ep *High Barrier* with Carolyn Jones, Jeff Richards
CBS	10.20.57	Alfred Hitchcock Presents ep *The Perfect Crime*
CBS	11.5.57	Playhouse 90 ep *The Clouded Image*
NBC	12.12.57	The Jane Wyman Theater ep *The Perfect Alibi*

CBS	12.26.57	Playhouse 90 ep *The Lone Woman*
NBC	2.1.58	People are Funny (guest)
CBS	3.9.58	G.E. Theater ep *Angel in the Air*
CBS	4.25.58	Schlitz Playhouse ep *The Kind Mr. Smith*
NBC	5.6.58	It Could Be You (game-show guest)
NBC	5.9.58	NBC Matinee Theater ep *Angel Street* with Judith Evelyn, Leo G. Carroll
NBC	8.22.58, 11.7.58, 3.5.59, 4.17.59, 7.21.59, 9.2.59, 12.4.59, 2.18.60, 6.23.60, 12.12.60 The Jack Paar Show (guest)	
CBS	10.17.58	Person to Person (subject)
CBS	12.27.58	Have Gun, Will Travel ep *The Moor's Revenge* with Richard Boone, Patricia Morrison, Morey Amsterdam
NBC	12.31.58	Kraft Music Hall With Milton Berle (guest)
NBC	4.23.59	Masquerade Party (game-show guest)
CBS	7.22.59	Keep Talking (master of ceremonies)
NBC	10.27.59	Ford Startime: Art Linkletter's Secret World of Kids (guest)
ABC	2.8.60	Adventures in Paradise ep *The Color of Venom*
NBC	6.23.60	Truth or Consequences (guest)
NBC	8.14.60	The Chevy Mystery Show ep *Runaround*
NBC	9.4.60, 9.11.60, 9.18.60, 9.25.60, The Chevy Mystery Show (host)	
NBC	11.2.60	Here's Hollywood (guest)
CBS	11.30.60	Family Classics ep *The Three Musketeers*
CBS	12.14.60	U.S. Steel Hour ep *Shame the Devil* with Betsy Palmer
NBC	11.27.61	Truth or Consequences (game-show guest)
NBC	1,5,62	Your First Impression (game-show guest)
NBC	4.13.62	The Tonight Show (guest)
NBC	8.27.62	The Today Show (guest)
NBC	11.30.62	The Tonight Show (guest)
CBS	1,14,63	Stump the Stars (game-show guest)
NBC	5.24.63	Play Your Hunch (game-show guest)
NBC	10.12.63	Exploring ep *Gulliver in Lilliput* (narrator)
CBS	2.4.64, 4.14.64, 2.9.65, 1.25.66, 4.25.67, 11.14.67, 9.4.68, 1.6.70, 3.10.70 The Red Skelton Hour (guest)	
CBS	4.19.64	Celebrity Game (game-show guest)
CBS	4.22.64, 1.13.65, 12.15.65, 4.6.66 Danny Kaye Show (guest)	
NBC	3.29.65	The Tonight Show (guest)

NBC	4.2.65	The Jack Benny Show (guest)
NBC	5.19.65	Truth or Consequences (game-show guest)
NBC	7.6.65	Moment of Fear ep *The Secret Darkness*
NBC	10.8.65	The Man From U.N.C.L.E. ep *The Foxes and Hounds Affair*
CBS	1.31.66	Hollywood Talent Scouts (guest)
ABC	- - .66	F Troop ep
ABC	10.19.66, 10.20.66	Batman ep *An Egg Grows in Gotham*
CBS	11.9.66	Clown Alley with Red Skelton (guest)
NBC	5.15-19.67,	5.29.67-6.2.67, 6.5-6.9.67, 6.26-6.30.67, 9.11-9.15.67 Hollywood Squares (game-show guest)
NBC	5.24.67	The Tonight Show (guest)
CBS	6.3.67	Eye on Art: The St. Louis Scene (narrator)
NBC	8.21-8.25.67	You Don't Say (game-show guest)
NBC	8.7.67	The Tonight Show (guest)
ABC	11.2.67, 11.9.67	Batman ep
CBS	1.11.68	Ed Sullivan Show in scene from *Darling of the Day* with Patricia Routledge
NBC	4.22-26.68,	5.13-5.17.68, 6.24-6.28.68, 7.8-7.12.68, 8.19-8.23.68, 10.23-10.27.68, 11.11-11.15.68 Hollywood Squares (game-show guest)
NBC	4.29-5.3.68	You Don't Say (game-show guest)
NBC	7.5.68, 7.26.68, 9.16.68	Hollywood Squares (nighttime version) (game-show guest)
NBC	7.17.68	The Tonight Show (guest)
NBC	11.25.68, 12.30.68	Rowan & Martin's Laugh-In (guest)
NBC	1.13-1.17.69,	3.24-3.28.69, 4.7.-4.11.69, 5.5-5.9.69, 8.11-8.15.69, 9.29-10.3.69, 10.13-10.17.69 Hollywood Squares (game-show guest)
NBC	1.30.69	Daniel Boone ep *Copperhead Izzy*
NBC	6.18.69	Personality (interview)
CBS	9.18.69	The Merv Griffin Show (guest)
NBC	10.6-10.10.69	Name Droppers (game-show guest)
CBS	10.17.69	The Good Guys ep
NBC	1.19-1.23.70,	1.26-1.30.70, 2.2-2.6.70, 2.9-2.13.70, 5.25-5.29.70, 6.1-6.5.70, 6.22-6.26.70, 7.20-7.24.70, 9.14-9.18.70, 9.21-9.25.70 Hollywood Squares (game-show guest)

NBC 2.3-2.5.70   Life with Linkletter (guest)

NBC 2.11.70   The Tonight Show (guest)

NBC 8.21.70, 9.21.70, 10.30.70, 12.4.70 Dinah's Place with Dinah Shore (guest)

NBC 10.26.70, 11.30.70 Rowan & Martin's Laugh-In (guest)

CBS 11.9.70   Here's Lucy (guest)

ABC 11.6.70   Love, American Style (skit)

ABC 12.1.70   Mod Squad ep *A Time for Hyacinthe*

NBC 2.8.71   Red Skelton Show (guest)

NBC 1.25-1.29.71, 3.29-4.2.71, 4.26-4.30.71, 6.14-6.18.71, 7.5-7.9.71, 7.26-7.30.71, 9.13-9.17.71, 10.11-10.15.71, 10.25-10.29.71, 11.15-11.19.71 Hollywood Squares (guest)

CBS 3.19.71, 7.15.71, 9.24.71, 10.31.71 Merv Griffin Show (guest)

NBC 9.22.71   Rod Sterling's Night Gallery ep *Class of 99* with Brandon De Wilde

NBC 3.30.71, 11.9.71 The Tonight Show (guest)

NBC 7.20.71, 8.24.71, 9.7.71 Make Your Own Kind of Music (guest)

ABC 12.18.71   ABC Wednesday Night ut the Movie ep *What's A Nice Girl Like You*...with Brenda Vaccaro

NBC 2.7-2.11.72, 2.28-3.3.72, 5.8-5.12.72, 5.29-6.2.72, 6.12-6.16.72, 6.26-6.30.72, 7.3-7.7.72, 7.17-7.21.72, 7.31-8.4.72, 10.30-11.3.72, 11.6-11.10.72, 11.20-11.24.72, 12.4-12.8.72 Hollywood Squares (game-show guest)

CBS 2.9.72   The Carol Burnett Show (guest)

NBC 2.13.72   The Jimmy Stewart Show ep

NBC 5.12.72, 10.19.72 The Tonight Show (guest)

CBS 5.1-5.5.72   Amateur's Guide to Love (game-show guest)

NBC 9.24.72   Rod Sterling's Night Gallery ep *Return of the Sorcerer* with Bill Bixby

CBS 11.22.72   Carol Burnett Show (guest)

NBC 1.2-1.5.73, 1.15-1.19.73, 2.26-3.2.73, 3.5-3.9.73, 9.3-9.7.73, 9.10-9.14.73, 9.17-9.21.73 Hollywood Squares (game-show guest)

NBC 9.17-9.21.73   Baffle (game-show guest)

NBC 9.23.73   Columbo ep*Lovely but Lethal*

NBC 9.27.73   The Tonight Show (guest)

NBC 10.19.73   The Dean Martin Show (guest)

VINCENT PRICE UNMASKED

NBC 11.26.73, 11.3.73 Hollywood   Squares   (nighttime   show)
            (game-show guest)
CBS   12.5.73   Sonny & Cher Show (guest)

Vincent Price in Print

I LIKE WHAT I KNOW — *A Visual Autobiography by Vincent Price. Doubleday & Co., Inc., 1959, $4.50*

Sparked by the success of his appearances on television's "the $64,000 Challenge" and on the advice of his lecture manager, W. Colston Leigh, Price wrote this freely structured account of his adventures in the world of art. "The main theme of the book, that America is now producing good artists, and that the joys of collecting are not the exclusive property of the fabulously wealthy, is sustained throughout with persuasiveness and dignity." (Kirkus Reviewing Service)

THE BOOK OF JOE: ABOUT A DOG AND HIS MAN, *by Vincent Price, illustrated by Leo Hershfield. Doubleday & Co., Inc., 1962, $3.50*

Pleased with the sales of *I Like What I Know*, Doubleday requested that Price prepare another book. For his subject, Price chose the family dog of long standing — Joe. With the canine as his main character, Price was able to fill the narrative with delightful anecdotes concerning other household pets he has owned throughout the years. One particularly interesting chapter sketched notes on animals as actors in Hollywood.

DRAWINGS OF DELACROIX, *Edited by Vincent Price. Borden Publishing Company, 1962, $4.95; $2.25 (paperback)*

This small volume was edited by Price, and its foreword written by him. As its title indicates, the book was a series of reproductions of etchings and drawings by Ferdinand Delacroix (1798-1863), admittedly a favorite artist of Price. The author's introduction detailed the reasons behind the French painter's leadership in the Romantic school in painting and focused on some of the highlights in his professional life.

THE MICHELANGELO BIBLE, *edited by Vincent Price. Philadelphia Bible Press, 1965, $30.00*

Measuring ten inches by seven inches, bound in hand-tooled leather, and filled with one hundred and twenty-one reproductions of the drawings, sculptures, and paintings of Michelangelo (1475-1564), this volume aimed to bridge the gap between religion and art for the American public. With fifty-six color plates, the book demonstrated the relationship between the works of the Italian Renaissance artist and the written word of God.

The boxing of this book was decorated with prints of the Sistine Chapel. The text was available in either a King James or a Revised Standard version.

A TREASURY OF GREAT RECIPES, *by Vincent Price and Mary Price, edited by Darlene Geis. Bernard Geis Associates, 1965, $25.00*

In terms of sales, this gourmet volume stands as the most successful of all the Price books. In the near-decade since its publication, it has sold over thirty thousand copies.

Although simple in context, the book is remarkably attractive and useful. With a padded gold-enameled binding designed by Arthur Hawkins, and illustrations by Fritz Kredel, the book makes fitting use of tantalizing color photographs of sumptuous mountains of food. All recipes were tested by an outside arbiter, Ann Seranne, and each of the almost five hundred pages was of the highest quality glare-proof antique paper.

The text, obviously, is concerned with recipes, but with a difference — recipes from the great restaurants of the world. The great restaurants of major cities of France, Italy, Holland, Scandinavia, England, Spain, Mexico, and the United States are explored. Though many of the dining spots described are famed for high prices as well as *haute cuisine,* outfits such as that at Chavez Ravine (the home of the Los Angeles Dodgers baseball team) are complimented for their recipes for hot dogs.

Included in the book was a novel idea, a calorie guide to the different foods, as well as the more traditional items such as an herb and spice chart, a table of weights and measures, and a table for cooking temperatures.

If the reader is interested in owning one Price cookbook, this would be the one. It is the standard by which all the rest are judged.

NATIONAL TREASURY OF COOKING, by Vincent and Mary Price, edited by Helen D. Ballock. Stravon Educational Press, 1967, Five volumes (paperback), each at $1.95

With a format similar to that of most standard cookbooks, the text centers on favorite recipes and dishes from all corners of the United States. Restaurants and local custmms are mentioned, where necessary, and on many occasions the Prices explain why certain culinary trends appeal and apply to different geographical regions.

Art Columns for the Chicago Tribune-New York News Syndicate, variously called

LOOKING AROUND, VINCENT'S VIEW, PRICE ON ART, etc., by Vincent Price, edited by Stephen Booke, 1967-1969

In 136 weekly columns, consisting of approximately eight hundred words each, Price offered his views of art and the world in a format well tailored to his breezy prose. With few restrictions in the way of subject matter, he explored the contents of American and European museums, gave instructions on the appreciation of art, delved into the "unknown" fine arts of architecture and design, praised and/or condemned certain practitioners, patrons, and dealers, and covered the area in a professional reportorial manner.

Because much of this time (1967-1969) was spent filming one or another of his American International "horror" pictures in England, the American reader benefited from Vincent's on-the-scenes observation of the English countryside and the British way of life.

If all 136 columns were read, an excellent knowledge of the world of art would be derived, as well as a particular awareness of Price's tastes and standards. The weekly column was well received by readers and distributed to over eighty American newspapers, reaching an audience of over fifty million readers.

Price was very involved with the project and worked very long hours researching and writing it. Editor Booke has said, "Vincent approached the column with the sensitivity of an actor, the knowledge of an art historian, and the discipline of a businessman."

THE COME INTO THE KITCHEN COOK BOOK, *by Vincent and Mary Price. Stravon Educational Press, 1969, $10.00*

Having covered most of the material in their first books, this effort by the Prices became rather a list of their favorite recipes that were basically simple to prepare.

THE VINCENT PRICE TREASURY OF AMERICAN ART, *by Vincent Price. Country Beautiful Corporation, 1972, $25.00*

Praised by critics as one of the most comprehensive, informative, and ambitious art books to be published, this was also one of the genre's most creatively designed volumes. Price's text commences in the year 1674 and continues to the present, with each selected artist discussed and represented by an accompanying reproduction.

In his survey discussion, the nineteenth century is particularly well represented, allowing Price the first chance to note the development of an art that was becoming purely American. Men such as Thomas Eakins, James McNeill Whistler, and Winslow Homer are examined at length, but again in the company of their fellow contemporary artists, some as important but lesser known to the general public.

The major segment of the book is devoted to modern American art, its development and importance. Explaining away most of the reservations the general public maintains toward the abstract or cubist or minimal art schools, he informs the reader why the art world is so entranced with modern American art.

In comparision to the volume's color plates, the black-and-white illustrations, at first glance, pale. But upon closer examination, these stark reproductions reveal themselves as fitting examples of design and themes of a particular artist, rather than unfulfilled examples of that artist's special use of color.

The Authors

JAMES ROBERT PARISH, New York-based free-lance writer, was born near Boston on April 21, 1944. He attended the University of Pennsylvania and graduated as a Phi Beta Kappa with a degree in English. A graduate of the University of Pennsylvania Law School, he is a member of the New York Bar. As president of Entertainment Copyright Research Co., Inc., he headed a major researching facility for the film and television industries. Later he was a film reviewer-interviewer for *Variety* and *Motion Picture Daily*. He has been responsible for such reference volumes as *The American Movies Reference Book: The Sound Ear* and *The Emmy Awards: A Pictorial History*. He is the co-author of *The MGM Stock Company: The Golden Era* and *The Great Spy Pictures*, and the author of such volumes as *The Fox Girls, Actors' Television Credits*, and *The RKO Gals*. With Steven Whitney he prepared *The George Raft File*.

Twenty-eight-year-old STEVEN WHITNEY is an actor-writer-director making his second appearance under the Drake Publishing banner. His credits include *The George Raft File* with Mr. Parish and two experimental plays, *Children of All* and *Audition/Performance/Review*, each of which received professional production by off-off-Broadway companies. He is currently at work on a third play, *Family*, and has recently completed a novel entitled *Singled Out*. As an actor, he has appeared in over thirty-five stage productions, as well as various prime-time television series. He has been active in daytime television serials. He has also been responsible for making six short films, as well having directed over twenty plays in professional repertory and regional theater companies. His personal interests are animals, art, basketball, criminology, and of course, haunting movie theaters.

Vincent Price Unmasked
Acknowledgements

Manuscript Verifier: Edward M. Connor
Rudy Behlmer
Richard Bojarski
Mrs. Loraine Burdick
Country Beautiful Corporation
Howard Davis
Robert Deindorfer
Morris Everett, Jr.
Olivier Eyquem
Film Fan Monthly
Filmfacts
Films and Filming
Films in Review
Charles Finley
Bernard Geis Associates
Pierre Guinle
Mrs. R.F. Hastings
David Johnson
Ken D. Jones
Judy Bonder Katz
The Leigh Bureau
Paige Lucas
Doug McClelland
David McGillivray
Albert B. Manski
Alvin H. Marill
Eva Metzger
Peter Miglierini
Norman Miller
Edith Mills
Monthly Film Bulletin
Movie Poster Service (Bob Smith)
Lambert and Kathryn Ochsenschlager
Screen Facts
Screen Thrills Illustrated
Charles Smith
Mrs. Lucy Smith
Don Stanke
Stravon Educational Press
Charles K. Stumpf
Robert Zarem

......and special thanks to Paul Myers, curator of the Theater Collection of the New York Public Library at Lincoln Center, Astor, Lenox, and Tilden Foundations, and his staff: Monty Arnold, David Bartholomew, Rod Bladel, Donald Fowle, Maxwell Silverman, Dorothy Swerdlove, Betty Wharton, and Don Madison of photographic services.

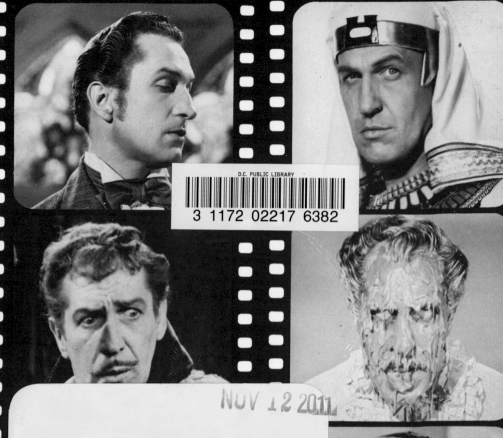